THE E

THE EROTICS
OF GRIEF

EMOTIONS AND THE CONSTRUCTION
OF PRIVILEGE IN THE MEDIEVAL
MEDITERRANEAN

MEGAN MOORE

CORNELL UNIVERSITY PRESS
Ithaca and London

Copyright © 2021 by Cornell University

All rights reserved. Except for brief quotations in a review, this book, or parts thereof, must not be reproduced in any form without permission in writing from the publisher. For information, address Cornell University Press, Sage House, 512 East State Street, Ithaca, New York 14850. Visit our website at cornellpress.cornell.edu.

First published 2021 by Cornell University Press

Library of Congress Cataloging-in-Publication Data

Names: Moore, Megan, 1977– author.
Title: The erotics of grief : emotions and the construction of privilege in the medieval Mediterranean / Megan Moore.
Description: Ithaca [New York] : Cornell University Press, 2021. | Includes bibliographical references and index.
Identifiers: LCCN 2021006162 (print) | LCCN 2021006163 (ebook) | ISBN 9781501758393 (hardcover) | ISBN 9781501758409 (epub) | ISBN 9781501758416 (pdf)
Subjects: LCSH: Literature, Medieval—History and criticism. | Literature, Medieval—Themes, motives. | Grief in literature. | Eroticism in literature. | Grief—Social aspects—Mediterranean Region—History—To 1500. | Elite (Social sciences)—Mediterranean Region—History—To 1500.
Classification: LCC PN682.G74 M66 2021 (print) | LCC PN682.G74 (ebook) | DDC 809/.02—dc23
LC record available at https://lccn.loc.gov/2021006162
LC ebook record available at https://lccn.loc.gov/2021006163

Between death and the reeling, heady motion
of the little death the distance is hardly noticeable.

—Georges Bataille, *Erotism*

Who am I, without you?

—Judith Butler, *Precarious Life*

Contents

Acknowledgments ix

Introduction: Desire and Death in Elite
Medieval Emotional Communities — 1

1. *Philomena* and the Erotics of Privilege
   in the Middle Ages — 24
2. Widows and the Romance of Grief — 59
3. Masculinity, Mourning, and
   Epic Sacrifice — 90
4. Toward a Mediterranean Erotics
   of Grief — 119

Conclusion: The Erotics of Grief
and the Stakes of Community — 156

*Appendix 1: Selected Illuminations
of Knights Being Grieved* 165

*Appendix 2: Selected Illuminations
of Lovers in Death* 167

Bibliography 169

Index 185

Acknowledgments

My interest in emotions and how they shape our realities was first nurtured in a biology class with Sara Vispoel, who made it possible for a group of high schoolers to attend the thirtieth annual Nobel Conference on Neuroscience in 1994, at which both Oliver Sacks and Antonio Damasio spoke of their (then) recent research on the relation between perception and the biological construction of reality. Sara's exceptional work to create such an opportunity not only inspired my continued interest in the neurobiology of emotions but also made me skeptical of received notions delineating certain reactions as inherently biological and others as exclusively cultural.

Conversations with, critical questions posed by, and feedback from Christine Chism, Deborah McGrady, Anna Watz, Simon Gaunt, Peggy McCracken, Ingela Nilsson, Stavroula Constantinou, Anthony Kaldellis, Ryan Milov-Córdoba, Marla Segol, Christopher Davis, David Rollo, Romain Brèthes, and David Konstan have challenged my thinking in this project. My continued discussions of medieval affect with Emma Lipton, Johanna Kramer, Anne Stanton, and Rabia Gregory have proven invaluable. Invitations to present parts of this work by Stephanie Trigg, Claire Gilbert, Lynn Ramey, Adam Goldwyn, Aglae Pizzone, and Dimitrios Krallis have provided space for me to test and refine many of the ideas presented here.

Stimulating conversations during meetings of the Mediterranean Seminar, a wonderful gathering of thoughtful, generous scholars, proved invaluable to this project. The seminar dedicated to "Emotions, Passions, and Feelings," which was organized by Marianne Kupin-Lisbinat and Thomas Devaney, at which I workshopped the fourth chapter, was integral to shaping this book. I am so grateful to Sharon Kinoshita and Brian Catlos, the founders of the seminar, for the many ways their work continues to shape our field of inquiry as well as enhance the collegiality of and connections between our work, and to Sharon in particular for her feedback.

I offer my thanks to the libraries and institutions whose support changed the trajectory of this book, above all to the staff of the manuscript reading room at the Bibliothèque Nationale for their time and energy in helping me find and identify pertinent manuscripts; I am grateful to the Bibliothèque Municipale in Lyon, the British Library, the Bodleian Library, the Bayerische Staatsbibliothek, the Getty Museum, the Pierpont-Morgan Museum, and the Newberry Library. Likewise, the attentiveness and support of the students, faculty, and staff during my brief residency at the Center for the History of Emotion in Melbourne helped me refine the kinds of questions I wanted to address in the project in its nascent stages. I thank the Australian Research Council for facilitating my stay and especially Stephanie Trigg for her feedback on emotions and performance.

I am grateful to the University of Missouri Research Board for sponsoring the researching and writing of this project, and to many of my colleagues for their feedback over several years. Without the enthusiasm and support of Flore Zéphir this project would not have been possible, and I am so grateful to Daniel Sipe for the many conversations we have had about the relation between emotion and human experience. I also thank my colleagues Kristy Bowers, Lee Manion, Phong Nguyen, and John Evelev for ideas and suggestions as I have begun to think forward from this project, as well as Myles Freborg and Veronica Mohesky for their help in conducting research.

Thanks also to Jessie Aucoin, Emilia Yasamin, Amy Newbrough, Andrew Donnelley, Erica Titus, and Christine Livingston for offering readings of the erotics of death in modern culture. Special thanks to my mother, Wendy Chappelear, who as a psychologist piqued my interest in the brain's responses to feelings, and to David Palit, whose discussions of emotions always resolutely returned to stoicism and the suppression of emotion as a sign of refinement; to Marie Lerchner, whose spirit and constant care made my writing that much easier; and to Alicia Platte, whose smiles filled our home with joy while I wrote. Lastly, I am grateful to Toby Oshiro for his wonderful, critical ear and his love for words, what they can do, and the richness they can convey.

THE EROTICS OF GRIEF

Introduction
Desire and Death in Elite Medieval Emotional Communities

> Their hands were so cold they were touching only in intention, an illusion, in order for this to be fulfilled, for the sole reason that it should be fulfilled, none other, it was no longer possible. And yet, with their hands frozen in this funereal pose, Anne Desbaresdes stopped moaning.
>
> —Marguerite Duras, *Moderato cantabile*

Ribald, raunchy, and rooted in the desires of the body, the fabliaux offer some of the most remarkable and least restrained problematizations of death, grief, and sexuality in medieval culture. The memorably vulgar thirteenth-century *Cele qui se fist foutre sur la fosse de son mari*, for example, imagines widows' grief as barely masking untrammeled, uncontrollable desire. The story begins with a widow who refuses to vacate her husband's grave after his interment; her steadfast grief is initially lauded by the narrator as an exemplary performance of spousal duty:

Si a mout bien son preu prové,
Ce semble, a toz vers son seignor,
Ainz fame ne feist tel dolor, . . .
Et poins de tordre et cheveus trere (118–19)

Thus, she proved her worth
to her lord well, it seems,
and no woman has ever shown such grief, . . .
and wringing of her hands and pulling of her hair[1]

---

1. In this book, translations are mine, unless otherwise noted. Citations from *De celle qui se fist foutre sur la fosse de son mari* in *Recueil général et complet des fabliaux des XIIIe et XIVe siècles*, ed. Anatole de Montaiglon (Paris: Librairie des Bibliophiles, 1872).

INTRODUCTION

The narrator cites the widow's grief as a model performance of both spousal devotion and femininity, and a cursory reading seems to tie her performance of emotion to the performance of her gender. But the fabliaux are often deceptively simple, and here the widow's grief does other kinds of work. It also performs her husband's prowess: the fabliau's end-rhyme offers an audible alignment of *dolor* and *seignor* ("grief" and "lord") that links women's grief to the construction of masculinity, tying emotion to the performance of both gender and status.

When the lady refuses to leave her husband's grave, her cries eventually attract an errant lord and his squire, who ride up and interrogate her while she sobs, in a scene reminiscent of many episodes within romances both medieval and modern. The squire immediately rebukes his lord for pitying her grief, betting instead in vulgar language that "si dolente comme el se fait, / la foutrai" (even as sorrowful as she seems, / I will fuck her there). The squire's wager that the lady's performance is not what it "seems" resonates with widespread concerns about the relation between truth and appearance, and, as I discuss further in this book, with concerns about the veracity of emotions in patristic texts, sermons, trial records, and fictional texts. The misogynistic question asked in fabliaux—"Are women's emotions reliable?"—may be transformed to be read as a question about whether *any* emotions represent a truthful testament to an internal psychological landscape, revealing concerns about how emotions intersect with veracity and intent as they are deployed to negotiate relationships between people.

Not only does this fabliau stage a critical disjuncture between emotional sign and signifier; it also imagines that the signs themselves are ephemeral in ways that undermine their significance. Indeed, the punch line here is that the squire vaunts his sexual prowess, claiming in explicit and vulgar terms that he killed his last lover by making love to her so well:

> Je avoie mis tout mon cuer
> En une dame que j'avoie.
> Et assez plus de moi l'amoie,
> Qui ert bele, cortoise et sage;
> Ocise l'ai par mon outrage.
> —Ocise l'as? Coment, pechierre?
> —En foutant, voir, ma dame chiere,
> Ne je ne voudroie plus vivre.
> —Gentilz bon, vien ça, si délivre
> Cest siècle de moi, si me tue

> I had placed all of my heart
> in a woman that I had

and I even loved her more than myself,
and she was beautiful, courteous, and wise;
I killed her by my wantonness.
—You killed her? How, sinner?
—By fucking, truly, my dear lady,
and I no longer even want to live.
—Dear good man, come here, and so deliver me
from this century, and kill me thusly.

When the widow is aroused by the squire's claims and acquiesces to his proposition, she becomes a sign of women's general unreliability. Here, the lady's unproblematized elision of death and desire resonates with widespread concerns about the sexuality of medieval widows, and in particular it recalls patristic concerns that widows' loud laments were meant to attract nearby men.[2] However, what interests me in this episode is not the veracity of its emotions, or its misogynistic view of women's reliability, but rather its curious twinning of death and desire, of grief and love, in order to weave a complicated and multivalent picture of how emotional performances describe the contours of communities of privilege.

In this book, I explore how privilege is shaped by what I am identifying as an erotics of grief, and I explore what that can tell us about the interplay between gender, emotion, and power. Specifically, I focus on how twelfth- and thirteenth-century narratives designed for and commissioned by the medieval elite imagine the contours of their communities of privilege through *eroticized* grief. In texts as diverse as the fabliaux, travel narratives, chansons de geste, and romance, grief and sexuality are never far apart.

Ribald and outrageous, *Cele qui se fist foutre* both eroticizes and problematizes grief as imperfect; its genius plays upon the foundational fear that old lovers will be forgotten in the face of new desire. Yet it invites us to take a closer look at grief's erotics: what is it about the grieving widow that is so arousing? The widow may be beautiful in her grief, but as I argue in this book, that grief is also eroticized because of its promise to narrate and commemorate. The men's wager is as much about actually having sex with her as it is about transferring her narrative potential from one man (her dead husband) to another (a new lover). As such, *Cele qui se fist foutre* not only ties grief and sexuality to a discussion of the nature of emotions, but also to the narrative functions of grief's power to commemorate, imbuing grief

---

2. See discussions of Jerome's "Letter to Furia," Ambrose's "Concerning Widows," and John Chrysostom in Leslie Callahan, "The Widow's Tears," in *Constructions of Widowhood and Virginity in the Middle Ages*, ed. Cindy L. Carlson and Angela Jane Weisl (New York: St. Martin's, 1999), 245–63.

with not only sexual, but also narrative, power. This is our erotics of grief: a complicated weaving of death and desire, love and grief, power and loss; it is an erotics performed, policed, and explored in the nexus of medieval communities of privilege; it is an erotics that functions across and calls into being a spectrum of gender performances; it is an erotics of commemoration and sacrifice fundamental to narrating and producing patriarchy.

Defining Emotions

In the past twenty years scholars have investigated emotions in fields as disparate as anthropology, sociology, neurology, and visual studies; entire institutes dedicated to the study of emotions are conducting investigations from perspectives ranging from neurobiological to sociological and historical.[3] Nearly every field has had a critical discussion of what emotions mean, whether they are biological or cultural (or neither, or both), and how considering them relates to the primary focus of study; in the humanities, this has often been framed in terms of subjectivity and community. As this spate of recent scholarship attests, we cannot begin to discuss emotions without a common understanding of generalized emotion words such as "affect," "feeling," and "emotion," and, more particularly in this book, "desire," "erotic," "grief," "mourning," *amor,* and *dueil*—words that are not only specific to discipline, but also to time, place, culture, and language.

In my writing, I distinguish between the terms "affect" as a physiological, biochemical process in the body; "feeling" as post-cognitive; and "emotion" as the deployment of feelings in community. Ruth Leys offers a good working explanation of the differences between affect (precognitive), feeling (personal, cognitive), and emotion (social) when she summarizes that "affect is not a personal feeling. Feelings are personal and biographical, emotions are social, . . . and affects are pre-personal. . . . An affect is a non-conscious experience of intensity; it is a moment of unformed and unstructured potential. . . . Affect cannot be fully realised in language."[4] Yet, as I explain in my

---

3. A mere handful of examples include Sara Ahmed, *The Cultural Politics of Emotion*, 2nd ed. (New York: Routledge, 2014); Barbara H. Rosenwein, *Emotional Communities in the Early Middle Ages* (Ithaca, NY: Cornell University Press, 2006); William M. Reddy, *The Navigation of Feeling: A Framework for the History of Emotions* (Cambridge: Cambridge University Press, 2001); Ruth Leys, "The Turn to Affect: A Critique," *Critical Inquiry* 37, no. 3 (Spring 2011): 434–72; Jan Plamper, *Geschichte und Gefühl. Grundlagen der Emotionsgeschichte* (Munich: Siedler Verlag, 2012); Carroll E. Izard, *Human Emotions* (New York: Plenum, 1977); Rom Harré, *The Social Construction of Emotions* (Oxford: Blackwell, 1986); Nico H. Frijda, *The Emotions* (Cambridge: Cambridge University Press, 1986).

4. Shouse summarized in Leys, "Turn to Affect," 442.

readings, medieval texts—and in particular, medieval *languages*—resist such discrete differentiations, and I follow their lead in exploring how emotions are entangled with the communities in which they are expressed. In this book, and in keeping with recent scholarship by Stephanie Trigg, Barbara Rosenwein, and William Reddy, I use the term "emotion" to discuss how externalized, bodily expressions of feelings become read, exchanged, and socially contextualized as community.

While I am careful in how I use these terms, it is not my goal to reproduce a neat taxonomy of human feeling. Rather, I seek to shed light on how biological processes become socially mediated expressions of emotion that both expose and collapse this crucial difference. That is, I read the texts in this study as attesting to emotions as socially conditioned, produced within and for the communities in which individuals are socialized. In the medieval period that is the focus of this research, some languages themselves collapse this difference, tightening the relation between emotion and community. As I discuss below, whereas modern English scholarly usage may expect to differentiate between affective states, feelings, and the socialized practice of emotions, medieval terms are more capacious in ways that may be productive not only for understanding medievals and their communities, but also for challenging conversations insistent on cleaving feelings from their practices within affect studies.

Monique Scheer asserts that culturally contextualized displays of feelings are produced and received by what she calls "knowing bodies." She views emotions as "acts executed by a mindful body, as cultural practices."[5] For Scheer, our widow's grief would be an embodied performance that renders "cultural practices" visible in ways that confound distinctions between mental and physical, between private and public performance. As she explains, "the habits of the mindful body are executed outside of consciousness and rely on social scripts from historically situated fields. That is to say, a distinction between incorporated society and the parts of the body generating emotion is hard to make."[6] Here bodies producing emotions become generative, sites of social scripts that might also be construed as communal norms.

Hippocratic and Galenic medicine offered the predominant model of the body through which medieval physicians approached emotional

---

5. "Are Emotions a Kind of Practice (And Is That What Makes Them Have a History)? A Bourdieuian Approach to Understanding Emotion," *History and Theory* 51, no. 2 (May 1, 2012): 205.
6. Ibid., 207.

disturbances in their patients.[7] Galen held the body to be grounded in four essential humors (black bile, yellow bile, blood, and phlegm), and affective states were tightly linked to the ratios of the four humors. In this model, all sorts of problems stemmed from humoral imbalances, including disease, reproductive difficulties, and, especially, mood and emotional disorders.[8]

The humoral model asserted that men and women had naturally different baseline humoral ratios, thereby naturalizing a gendered approach to describing and treating emotions. If women were to be aligned with cold and wet, they were more likely to be phlegmatic and aggrieved; similarly, since the Greeks first aligned men with dry, hot temperaments, they were "naturally" more choleric. Later philosophers and theologians followed the humoral approach presupposing gender-distinctive emotional patterns in men and women—a move that essentially socializes the biology of emotions and describes community (male, hot, rational) in opposition to "other" (female, cold, emotional). As Alison Levy points out, Augustine's discussion of mourning suggests that he believed men and women should grieve differently, creating a "distinct dichotomy between male and female manners of mourning: Monica's loud and constant lamentation is countered by Augustine's stoicism and silence; presumed female hysteria is checked by male composure."[9]

The humoral model invites us to consider how gender and emotion interface in our medieval texts. As I suggest here, medieval literature troubles the hierarchical naturalization of gender and emotion propagated in medieval medical discourses; some of the most powerful, poignant moments of medieval literature are those that complicate medical discourses, which seem to fall apart and become inadequate, as when Charlemagne wails in despair over the death of his beloved Roland, tearing out his hair in a wild display of grief. Medieval literary examples eroticizing grief offer another model for

---

7. As in Leys, who remarks, "the problem here is not the idea that many bodily (and mental) processes take place subliminally, below the threshold of awareness. Who would dream of doubting that they do?" "Turn to Affect," 456.

8. For more on medieval medical theories of emotion see Olivia Weisser, "Grieved and Disordered: Gender and Emotion in Early Modern Patient Narratives," *Journal of Medieval and Early Modern Studies* 43, no. 2 (2013): 247–73; Ortrun Riha,"Emotionen in Mittelalterlicher Anthropologie, Naturkunde und Medizin," *Das Mittelalter: Perspektiven Mediävistischer Forschung* 14, no. 1 (2009): 12; Mones Abu-Asab, Hakima Amri, and Marc S. Micozzi, *Avicenna's Medicine: A New Translation of the 11th-Century Canon with Practical Applications for Integrative Health Care* (Rochester, VT: Healing Arts, 2013); Faith Wallis, *Medieval Medicine: A Reader* (Toronto: University of Toronto Press, 2010).

9. Allison Levy, "Augustine's Concessions and Other Failures: Mourning and Masculinity in Fifteenth-Century Tuscany," in *Grief and Gender, 700–1700*, ed. Jennifer C. Vaught and Lynne Dickson Bruckner (New York: Palgrave, 2003), 85.

understanding the power of emotions in community, and challenge assumptions about the relation between emotion and gender.

If some medieval humoral treatises naturalize gendering emotion, others focus on the physiological production of emotional signs. Gregory of Nyssa, following late classical medical teachings, for example, identifies the stomach as the seat of tears, which contracts upon the other organs and subsequently compresses the bile duct, pushing moisture up and out into the brain, whereupon ducts drain into the eyes and produce tears.[10] Reading Gregory, Mary Carruthers points out that this school did not see tears as indicative of any particular emotional *reality*, but only as an "agent or instrument rather than a symptom or representation—and their product must be carefully examined."[11] Like us, medievals worried about the disjuncture between truth and bodily reality, and wondered, Can tears, gasps, blushing, or fainting help us discern whether affective displays are genuine? And can feelings be controlled by a body or a mind? If feelings are not controllable, who should be held accountable when we are moved to do the unthinkable? The wager in our fabliau concedes that all we know about a woman in mourning is that she *seems* upset, and the supposition of the wager itself is couched in the unreliability of bodily signs: "si dolente comme el se *fait*" (as grief-stricken as she *makes herself seem*). These concerns remind us that feelings become emotions as they are produced *and read* in community. Feelings become emotions as they gesture successfully toward a shared understanding between people, as bodies become sites for performing community.

Performativity: Emotions as Cultural Practices

Bodily displays of feeling can be likened to performatives—they make feelings real for others, they are exterior signs that are supposed to perform an inner psychological reality. In *The Erotics of Grief*, I take emotions to be culturally contextualized performances of feelings. And the felicity of performatives, as J. L. Austin and Judith Butler separately remind us, depends on community.[12] Reading others' affective displays creates community—it puts the emitter (the feeler) in dialogue with the reader, who processes the display

---

10. Mary Carruthers, "On Affliction and Reading, Weeping and Argument: Chaucer's Lachrymose Troilus in Context," *Representations* 93, no. 1 (2006): 8.

11. Ibid., 9.

12. On the performative and its powers see Judith P. Butler, *Excitable Speech: A Politics of the Performative* (New York: Routledge, 1997); J. L. Austin, *How to Do Things with Words* (Oxford: Clarendon, 1975). See also William Reddy's "Against Constructionism: The Historical Ethnography of Emotions," *Current Anthropology* 38, no. 3 (June 1997): 327.

of feeling and translates it into a culturally specific performance of emotion. For the performance to be felicitous, both emitter and receiver must understand the same visual and physical cues to accompany the emotion in question; they must share the same physical language of emotion. For example, if in my culture we laugh at funerals, but in your culture you wail, we may perform the same emotion, but it will not be received the same way; for you, my performance would be a misperformance, it would be infelicitous. Put another way, when Medea or Procne are judged for enraged revenge, the felicity of their performances of rage is being received and judged not in a vacuum, but by the moral, legal, religious, and gendered constructs of their place and time; rage and its intersection with justice and gender read very differently in different eras, as students often note.

These emotional performances are not innate; they are learned. When the men in our fabliau bet on the instability of the lady's grief, they suspect that she is performing grief because of a cultural expectation rather than because of "true," internal psychological distress. Barbara Rosenwein explains that "no one is born knowing appropriate modes of expression, or whether to imagine emotions as internal or external, or whether to privilege or disregard an emotion. These things make up the 'feeling rules' that societies impart."[13] Every group has its own feeling rules, imparted through an emotional education designed to shape a shared set of practices. And as William Reddy has argued in *The Navigation of Feeling*, the expression and reception of emotions in community are at least partially shaped and evaluated by others. Our feelings are shaped and evaluated by society; our cultural expectations shape what emotions we choose to express; our education imparts which feelings may be expressed, by whom and when and where, and when they are to be understood as "real" or "fake." What may look like rejection in one culture could ostensibly be interpreted as affection in another; similarly, what one culture chooses to see as pride may not be so received in another cultural context.

In this study, I lean on feminist and Marxist theories of emotion to explore how the practice of emotions often privileges some kinds of community over others. I agree with feminist theorists of emotion such as Sarah Ahmed and Judith Butler that because emotions perform and are performed within community, they are inherently political. I take emotions to perform privilege, to offer not only community, but community as inclusion and exclusion: an expression of power. Our medieval texts—performed in the heart

---

13. Rosenwein, *Emotional Communities in the Early Middle Ages*, 15.

of the communities of medieval privilege—suggest that some lives are more grievable than others, and they tie mourning to privileged bodies. Though medieval texts may not be inherently political in ways that are immediately intelligible today, we can read the work of the emotional communities represented in these texts and through the reading communities produced by their luxury codices as reinforcing a culture of privilege, with political implications for the dissemination of power.

By framing emotions as producing a certain kind of cultural politics, we are thus invited to consider, What were the medieval elite taught to feel about desire and grief by these texts? What communities were created by the texts, and how do their feeling rules empower some, while disenfranchising others? In short, what is being taught to the consumers of these stories and their manuscripts by the depiction of elite emotions, especially in a paradoxical erotics of grief?

Grief as a Performance of Community

Whereas grief may be a nearly universal response to death, its affective display in rituals of mourning varies enormously by language, class, era, and religion.[14] Our modern English "grief" is decidedly different from its use in medieval texts. Whereas current English-language criticism may differentiate between mourning as a practice and grief as an emotion, medieval usage seems to resist this distinction and is more capacious than its Latin etymology would suggest. In Middle English, for example, derivatives of "grief" more often address tort claims, sickness, or anger than sorrow; it is the German-derived *mŏrning* that is more frequently deployed to encapsulate both feeling and practice. In Old French, *grief* is a less prevalent adjective qualifying a kind of weight, meaning "heavy" with sorrow, best translated through the modern French *grave*; as a noun, it is employed to evoke unhappiness.

Attention to etymology reminds us that we may not simply superimpose onto medieval texts expectations produced by a modern critical vocabulary primed to differentiate between grief and mourning as semantically separate. The most common forms for grief in Old French, for example, *dol, doler,* and *doland/t,* pick up on a Latin etymology linking emotional suffering to physical, bodily pain. But in Old French—and in contrast to modern English—*dol* also is more capacious, collapsing affect (as neurobiological process) and

---

14. See, for example, the panoply of expressions of mourning in Jean-Pol Ferbus and Dominique Garny's 1979 documentary on multicultural responses to death, *Des Morts*.

emotion (as social process), because it not only connotes feeling, but it also encapsulates the social functions of mourning, as I argue in chapters 2 and 3. For Old French storytelling linking love to death, the feeling of loss was *dolor*, a suffering capacious enough to entwine grief and mourning, a dolorous and painful puncture in the fabric of emotional life.[15]

Death entails community: the present and the missing, the living and the dead, the lover and the absent (or unattainable) beloved. From macabre plague songs to literature to tapestry to funerary processionals, medieval sources bear witness to death as a social event, one meant to comfort the dying, reaffirm the place of religion in assuring the soul's afterlife, and cement community ties among the living. Death was an activity with which all ages and social strata were familiar, and its attendant emotional codes were known to all. Dying and dead bodies were, as Carolyn Walker Bynum informs us, constitutive of life for medieval people; as Ruth Mazo Karras notes in her study of sexuality in medieval Europe, "[in] a battle between Eros and Thanatos in the Middle Ages, some argue, Thanatos wins every time."[16]

We still imagine funerary ritual and shared practices of mourning to create community and to heal grief; and though, as Thomas Laqueur points out in *The Work of the Dead*, life with the dead has been carefully contained in many cultures today, the coronavirus has made the stakes of grieving our dead painfully clear. And the coverage of COVID-19 reveals that we still privilege some deaths over others, as attention to its effects on "First World" citizens is pointedly different from the attention accorded to the destructiveness of, say, Ebola. Some lives seem more mournable than others, even today.

Not only were death and funerary rituals a social process for medieval people; they were also practiced as a spiritual journey. For Christians, the individual, earthly life was ultimately useless, rejected at death in favor of sublime, collective spiritual unity in heaven. Most medieval Christian

---

15. Though it is not representative of all medieval literature, a comparative search of the TFA database, ARTFL's Old French full-text database, reveals that *dol.** has 2,134 occurrences, while *grief.** has 252 occurrences. Likewise, in ARFTL's Provençal database, *dol.** has 525 occurrences and 0 for derivatives of *grief.**

16. "Chronicles, wills, and letters inform us that aristocratic deaths were public events, attended by relatives, friends, courtiers, even children and servants. Not only was dying part of life; the dead, especially dead bodies, were part of life as well," writes Bynum in "Death and Resurrection in the Middle Ages: Some Modern Implications," *Proceedings of the American Philosophical Society* 142, no. 4 (December 1, 1998): 591. Ruth Mazo Karras concurs, writing that "medieval people saw sick and dying bodies every day, and if they temporarily forgot the ubiquity of death, they were reminded on church walls and in sermons," in *Sexuality in Medieval Europe: Doing unto Others* (New York: Routledge, 2005), 152.

theology taught the ascension of the soul upon death and focused on the afterlife; in the *Confessions*, Augustine rebukes his own grief for his mother's passing as an imperfect recognition of the Christian eternal. Although the nature of grief's place in theological practice is not the subject of this book, I take that same theology as fundamental to the beliefs of the Christian nobility, and I recognize a parallel interest in immortality, practiced in secular texts through commemoration and memorial.

Though it is clear that Christian iconography eroticizes the death of Christ, in *The Erotics of Grief*, my focus is not specifically in the emotional community of *Christianity* (what I characterize here as a religious identity), but rather on the emotional community of the *elite* (a culture of diverse religious practices in the medieval world, but united, I claim, by the rarest of privileges in a highly stratified society). While the spiritual context for the emotional communities of noble love explored here is clearly Christian, it is the social expression and regulation of emotion that I pursue here. That is, while acknowledging the importance of a specifically Christian milieu undergirding most medieval western cultures of privilege, this book invites additional scholarly exploration of how religious communities relate to an erotics of grief. Further work on the physicality of eroticized grief in mystical devotion to Jesus, in the art surrounding the Crucifixion, or in the practices of other religions would be both enriching and fascinating, and it would offer an important complement to this research.

Although I acknowledge the importance of Christianity in informing models of love in the texts in this study, then, I also acknowledge the multiplicity of religious identities in the medieval world by situating this work in a study of how status—rather than religion—informs the erotics of grief. In this way, my work complements William Reddy's recent consideration of the intersection between religious and cultural practices of medieval emotion in locales as diverse as Bengal Orissa or Heian Japan.[17] However, whereas Reddy is careful to delineate the differences between desire in these disparate medieval communities, I seek intersection and connectivity by situating my thinking in the connections forged by class parity among the Mediterranean elite: I seek to understand how a common emotional culture permitted elite nobles to figure community within linguistic, geographic, and political difference, where shared emotional practices facilitated the imagining and negotiation of shared communities of power.

---

17. William M. Reddy, *The Making of Romantic Love: Longing and Sexuality in Europe, South Asia, and Japan, 900–1200 CE* (Chicago: University of Chicago Press, 2012).

More specifically, I refer to a disparate group of individuals whose access to and practices of power were more similar to each other as members of the ruling class than they were to those of the peoples they ruled and the organizations through which they worshiped. As a Mediterraneanist, I recognize competition and commonalities among the families who ruled the medieval Mediterranean and whose presence is imagined in the literature commissioned by, produced for, and narrated to them in the texts I consider in *The Erotics of Grief*. My argument for examining the emotional practices of the medieval "1 percent" through a comparative, Mediterraneanist lens is threefold: (1) the texts, tombs, and artifacts that have survived depict and produce communities of privilege; (2) Mediterranean intermarriage solidified medieval networks of privilege; and (3) Mediterranean texts produce their own language of elitism by creating and propagating mournable subjects.

The majority of the extant manuscript evidence transmitted to us from the medieval period is a testament to privilege, as these objects themselves constitute an archive of inequalities based not only on socioeconomic status, gender, and racial inequities but also on disparate rates of literacy; it would reshape our understanding of the medieval period if we had rich literary archives known to be penned by women and minorities. Instead, and in this study, we are limited to gleaning what we can from how the most privileged delineated themselves from their "others" and acknowledging the biases in our sources, which are luxury objects.

Luxury objects attest to, circulate among, and themselves create communities of privilege. As I discuss throughout this book, the manuscript history and codicological context of the objects I analyze suggest that they were luxury objects produced for and by a community who could afford not only to pay for manuscripts but also to become educated enough to read and interact with them. From the expenses of raising animals to turn into parchment; to commissioning authors, scribes, and illuminators; to the supposition that one had enough leisure time to pursue literacy, the vast majority of extant twelfth- and thirteenth-century medieval fictional texts are a testament to status. Historians of the book have long recognized manuscripts as luxury goods, and it is reasonable to theorize, as I do in chapter 4, that certain manuscripts not only required a great deal of money and time to finance, but they also created a circuit of power between givers and receivers, commissioners and readers, texts and audiences.

We have other witnesses to this kind of narrative circuitry, such as the *Tapisserie de Bayeux*, which depicts the *Roland* being sung before the battle of

Hastings. We know that texts were used and deployed to make meaning with their audience. In their deep interest in figuring the rules of elite community, I argue that the texts I study here call clearly to a certain kind of readership, one that could understand their contents and recognize themselves in their folios. Not only were the objects themselves products of and producers of luxury; they were makers of textual and reading communities structured by the economic and social realities of literacy in the medieval period, certainly one kind of privilege.

Second, though the groups imagined in the folios of these manuscripts speak different languages, worship differently, and live in a variety of places, they share some commonalities around practices of exceptional desire through which they narrate their own privilege. In this book, ancient and medieval texts written in Greek, Latin, Old French, Middle English, Occitan, Medieval Greek, and Medieval Spanish imagine that elite love is exceptional and can transgress the boundaries reserved for the other 99 percent, to use language common to us today. This is not to say that on the ground, everyday practices of sexuality, eroticism, and mourning that remain unexplored in the folios of elite literature did not run the gamut available to us today and were not widespread; rather, it is to investigate how elite objects imagine and propagate elite power through an erotics of mourning.

Though one could argue that to be elite is to be *unified* by common practices of transgressive desire, I purposefully deploy the term "emotional exceptionalism" to explore how practices of power and emotion are co-constructive in order to tease out complexity and competition within and among medieval elites across the Mediterranean. Within these texts, emotional practices are deployed in a variety of ways to articulate privilege: sometimes erotic transgression as power over other nobles (as in *Philomena* in chapter 1); sometimes as valorizing elite sacrifice (as in the heroic deaths I read in chapter 3); sometimes as emotional "othering" reflecting political competition between warring nobles (as in the emotional othering of "Eastern" eroticism that happens in travel narratives I examine in chapter 4). Yet, despite differences within these communities, in *The Erotics of Grief* I argue that literature about elites depicts power through practices of eroticism it imagines as unavailable to most medieval people, to those that this literature constructs as the unmournable subjects of medieval culture.

Third, I conceive of the relation between privilege and medieval emotional regimes through the essential question, "Who is a mournable subject?" In *Precarious Life*, Judith Butler questions why some contemporary mourning practices suggest that only some lives matter, an interrogation rife with potential for medieval studies. Here, I explore the construction of the grievable life in medieval literature, and I focus on how narratives about the elite imagine that elite lives are the only lives worth grieving. The self-referential and mutually reinforcing focus of medieval manuscripts responds to this question and generates its own kind of privilege: irrespective of the particulars of any feudal system, bureaucracy, or empire, medieval privilege imagines that only privileged lives matter, and they are the grievable subjects of these fictional literary texts. The erotics of grief reveal how emotional practices and power structures are entwined in the locus of grievable subjects; codicological and literary presences produce power as they attest that certain lives are the ones that can be commemorated.

Though we may operate under the assumption that all lives matter equally, reading closely with grievable subjects invites deeper interrogation. Like in the medieval period, some lives are depicted as more grievable than others; like in the medieval period, some now have better access to health care, transportation, basic staples of everyday life, and information (in our case, the internet); like in the medieval period, inequalities fester and are made more visible by the unequal threat of death. Even today, mourning creates "social life," and as Norbert Elias and Michel de Certeau have separately noted, ritual creates the practices of everyday life, including the practices of power.

And so, in this book I turn to focus on how emotions perform power in ways that differ from traditional scholarship on privilege as it is constructed through systems of class and capital; through access to technology; or through genealogy.[18] I use terms such as "elite" and "privilege" not as micro-historical markers of a *particular* feudal culture, but rather as a way of exploring how power and emotions intersect in a *spectrum* of Mediterranean practices. Irrespective of the particulars of local practice, in *The Erotics of Grief* I claim that grief produces its own power system, endowing some with "grievability" and others with no recognition within medieval narratives produced for the elite. The affective bonds between elite manuscripts and their readers, between rulers and their fighters, and between

---

18. On medieval power see, for example, Georges Duby and Jacques Le Goff, "Famille et parenté dans l'occident médiéval: Actes du colloque de Paris (6–8 juin 1974)" (Rome: l'École Française de Rome, 1977); Constance Brittain Bouchard, *"Those of My Blood": Constructing Noble Families in Medieval Francia* (Philadelphia: University of Pennsylvania Press, 2001); Timothy Reuter, "Nobles and Others: The Social and Cultural Expression of Power Relations in the Middle Ages," in *Nobles and Nobility in Medieval Europe: Concepts, Origins, Transformations*, ed. Anne J. Duggan (Woodbridge, UK: Boydell & Brewer, 2000), 85–98; R. Howard Bloch, *Etymologies and Genealogies: A Literary Anthropology of the French Middle Ages* (Chicago: University of Chicago Press, 1983).

ladies and the elites they mourn recognizes privilege as the mournable subject of medieval literature.

Love, Desire, and the Erotics of Grief

In considering how and why grief is eroticized in service of the elite, I am also exploring the construction of power in tandem with sexualized love. I often probe the tangled relation between love and desire, and in so doing I follow the texts, objects, and visual artifacts considered here. I contend that these artifacts imagine passion—desire—to be the natural result of worthy, elite love. Moreover, they thematize the emotion by exploring its physiological response, tying bodies that desire to forms of love. When worthy lovers fall in love, they nearly die of longing for each other; when battlefield warriors attest to their love of each other and their leaders before they die, onlookers lust after the affective display of an aggrieved emperor.

To be clear, the terminology of love is complex. Love, desire, and eroticism are not interchangeable, though they sometimes overlap. Like today, in the medieval period love could be affection, devotion, sexual desire, or friendship; likewise, desire could be a wish or longing, or it could be sexual. Like today, context is essential for understanding how the feeling of deep affection becomes a performance of love and/or desire in dialogue with another person or in a wider community context. And different, competing models of desire coexist; there is no single way to love, no single unifying model for any of these emotions. Instead, our texts bear witness to differing and culturally specific strategies for how emoting performs structures of community and hierarchies of power.

Digital humanities (DH) work can help us understand how the medieval textual communities under consideration here may have conceptualized desire and love. The Textes de Français Ancien (TFA) database, a digitized corpus of Old French texts hosted by the University of Chicago's Project for American and French Research on the Treasury of the French Language (ARTFL), provides scholars access to full-text search and collocation analysis of over two hundred texts written between roughly 1150 and 1500, with 3,014,389 discrete words. A search for *amor.** (with period and asterisk) turns up any truncations of the most common spelling of "love" in Old French, revealing 1374 hits (*amur.** has 445 occurrences), most frequently appearing in texts written between 1170 and 1230. In these texts, the rhyme schemes tend to contrast love and desire with death and grief. In the love story *Tristan and Yseut*, for example, which details the deep despair of an infelicitous love relationship between a king (Marc), and his wife (Yseut) and nephew (Tristan), who accidentally drink the love potion meant for the nuptial couple, and another, false wife (aptly named the false Yseut), the narrator deploys end rhyme to highlight and comment on their unfortunate predicament, where "entre ces quatre ot estrange amor / tut en ourent painne e dolur" (between these four there was a strange love, / everyone had pain and grief from it).[19] Other frequent appositions include *amor/honor* (love/honor) and *amor/peor* (love/fear)—all suggesting that love was a passionate upheaval, an emotion that could delineate the contours of community (by creating honor) and estrangement (by fomenting fear).

In *Upheavals of Thought*, Martha Nussbaum theorizes emotions as a relationship with an "intentional object."[20] A frequency scan of *amor* in the ARTFL TFA database reveals how love is imagined as an emotion in community through a hierarchy of "intentional objects." The database collocates several objects in the same sentence with *amor.**:

cuer (heart) (106 occurrences)
moi (me) (86 occurrences)
jor (day) (65 occurrences)
roi (king) (52 occurrences)
chevalier (knight) (37 occurrences)
amie (lover or friend, female) (47 occurrences)

Here, DH research suggests that love is often employed to instantiate an emotional community between the self (*moi*) and a beloved, intentional other (*roi/chevalier/*or *amie*). The most frequent collocated noun with an alternate spelling of love, *amur*, is *dolur*, the elocution of choice for grief (41 occurrences), inviting inquiry as to how and why the two emotions are entangled. This data about love offers a preliminary suggestion that affection expressed as love concomitantly performs community, spurring our investigation of how the erotics of grief that metonymize (a now absent, dead) love can also perform privilege.

DH work can also illuminate some of the affective valences for "desire," in keeping with my own desire to permit medieval texts to generate their own affective valences and vocabulary. Evidence from this database also suggests that desire was figured as affective rather than emotional, that to desire was to feel impulse, irrespective of target, and often in tandem with self-destructive

---

19. Félix Lecoy, ed., *Le roman de Tristan (Thomas)* (Paris: Champion, 1991), 51.
20. Martha Nussbaum, *Upheavals of Thought: The Intelligence of Emotions* (Cambridge: Cambridge University Press, 2001), 27.

tendencies. In *Tristan et Yseut*, for example, the distinction seems to hold for Yseut, who "ne set ou deliter / fors Tristran sanz delit amer. / De lui desire avoir deduit" (53) (does not know where to delight, / outside of loving Tristan carnally. / From him she desires to take her pleasure). And in the TFA database, *desir.** collocates pleasure even more clearly with death:

cuer (heart) (57 occurences)
mort (death) (35 occurences)
plaisir (pleasure) (35 occurrences)

Thus, while variations of Old French and Anglo-Normand point to an expansive vocabulary for interpersonal attachments, in many of our texts, love is more capacious, more social; "desire" and *delit* seem to connote bodily drives and wishes that are often sexual. Both, however, point to love and desire as integral to the emotional subjectivity (the "moi") of this elite textual community.

Though capacious, ARTFL's TFA database is by no means exhaustive, and it does not cover the entirety of extant medieval literature; we cannot extract definitive, universalizing claims about "what medieval literature does" with love or desire, nor is that the intent. Likewise, digital humanities work is no substitute for close, attentive reading or for scholarly analysis. However, DH work does offer insight into how desire and love were thematized through suffering; in relation to particular love objects; and within a contemporaneous textual and reading community in ways that defy definitions of love produced by readings of any singular medieval author.

While Anthony Kaldellis and Steven Jaeger have separately argued that medieval historiography reports a kind of elite stoicism, our texts and objects suggest that affective extremes shaped reading communities moved by and interested in consuming stories of exceptional passion. Jaeger, for example, has convincingly tied privilege to emotion, writing that "ennobling, virtue-giving love [is] a shared value of the nobility. True, there are fundamental differences in the regulation of life and the style of life in . . . various communities, but there are also shared forms, and love and friendship are among them. It may have been a force that leveled the forms of aristocratic life in worldly monasteries, cathedral communities, and worldly courts, rather than demarcating and distinguishing them."[21] I agree with Jaeger that the

---

21. C. Stephen Jaeger, *Ennobling Love: In Search of a Lost Sensibility* (Philadelphia: University of Pennsylvania Press, 1999), 78.

nobility imagined their love as a form of privilege, and I follow a similar methodology in imagining communities to police and be defined by their relation to emotional expression. I disagree, however, that the kinds of love that are "ennobling" are by default platonic, asexual, or free from passion. My readings of fabliaux, romances, chansons de geste, the *romans antiques*, and travel narratives in this book all suggest an eroticization of grief in a culture dedicated to valorizing its own losses, and accordingly I differ with current work that de-eroticizes love. In my analysis, I focus instead on how a spectrum of gendered love relations is grounded in desire in ways that the texts suggest produce privilege. This study, with its focus on understanding how power was constituted through an intensely sexual eroticism available to and practiced by a spectrum of gendered relations and partnerships, intersects then only obliquely with explorations of love as only ever non-libidinal, the highest expression of (men's) virtue.

Instead, in *The Erotics of Grief*, I read the interstices of privilege and passion at the limits of taboo and transgression. Passion is constitutive of noble privilege and fundamental to noble community—what the Marquis de Sade would later express as the pleasure in and duty to destroy when he writes that murder is a pleasure.[22] My readings in this book suggest that transgressive passion—the kind that mingles death and desire—is at the heart of elite identity; desire is entwined with mourning and is fundamental to the narrative of elite exceptionalism.[23]

I am calling attention in this book to "an erotics of grief," that uncomfortable confrontation between desire and death that occurs in elite medieval culture. We find examples in the oddest moments of encounter, where death and its byproduct—grieving—are eroticized in a bystander's gaze, as in the famous example where Enide is nearly assaulted by an onlooker for her erotic wailing over Erec's dead body. Her tears, her scratched face, her torn hair, and her rent garments only incite an onlooking count's lust, leading him to threaten to rape her next to her husband's unresponsive corpse. The count's lust for our sniveling, bloodied Enide begs the question: what is so desirable about grief?

---

22. Marquis de Sade, *La nouvelle Justine ou Les malheurs de la vertu*, in *Oeuvres*, ed. Michel Delon (Paris: Gallimard, 1995), 2:322.

23. Other texts, which I do not discuss in detail, also inform love's valences in the Middle Ages. Ovid's *Ars amatoria*, the *Libro de buen amor*, Aquinas's consideration of the soul's passions in I: II Q 22–48, and Christian ascetics all inform the conversation about the relation between love and desire, and between love and grief, in the Old French–speaking world, and would make welcome additions to the scholarly conversation about medieval love.

My work in this book situates the responses to this question in dialogue with Georges Bataille's *L'érotisme* (1957), in which he theorizes the construction of the erotic through readings of transgression and power in Sade and Baudelaire. Though his work does not explore medieval desire and offers an asynchronous theoretical model for the readings presented here, I claim that Bataille's erotics have strong resonance with medieval models of desire, perhaps in ways that he himself did not anticipate in his insistence on using eroticism to establish a distinctly modern subjectivity. The medieval, I argue, is integral to—and cannot be cleaved from—understanding how desire and power are co-constructive.

In *L'érotisme*, Bataille reads eroticism as an emotion at the nexus between desire and the forbidden, in taboo. He explains that "eroticism . . . is assenting to life up to the point of death . . . [and] unlike simple sexual activity, is a psychological quest independent of the natural goal of reproduction"; it is "assenting to life even in death."[24] Bataille's work in delineating eroticism as an emotion reveals a fundamentally different understanding of emotions from the one at stake in this book, where I characterize internal feelings as individual and private, and emotions as integral to the public performance of communities of power. Whereas here I focus on how the public ramifications of eroticism are fundamental for the construction and performance of power, for Bataille, eroticism—and therefore his understanding of emotion—is inherently internal and private: "My starting point is that eroticism is a solitary activity. At the least it is a matter difficult to discuss. For not only conventional reasons, eroticism is defined by secrecy. It cannot be public. I might instant some exceptions but somehow eroticism is outside ordinary life. In our experience taken as a whole it is cut off from the normal communication of emotions. There is a taboo in force."[25] Bataille's erotics rely on certain suppositions, ones my work seeks to foreground and perhaps even unravel. Here, for example, the claim that eroticism can only be private, taboo, and secret is in direct opposition to the kinds of eroticism practiced as power by some of the most terrible figures in history and in literature, such as Nero, Titus Andronicus, or any of our medieval characters. Even Sade himself makes the private transgression of taboo legible as power as he writes and documents: writing becomes a public performance of eroticism as power.

---

24. Georges Bataille, *Erotism: Death and Sensuality*, trans. Mary Dalwood (San Francisco: City Lights Books, 1962), 11.

25. Ibid., 252.

20   INTRODUCTION

In particular, Bataille's erotics are founded on certain oppositions that may not prove tenable, such as the rupture between the medieval and the modern, as I explain in chapter 1. Bataille's work also contains certain underlying assumptions about privilege that he effectively effaces through suppression; yet I claim that medieval representations such as those found in *Philomena* and *Erec et Enide* may make us better readers of the modern, by making explicit how privilege and eroticism are entwined in ways that perhaps efface the usefulness of that divide. I use Bataille's formulation of the erotic as a private feeling of desire-as-death, of desire-as-taboo as a point of departure for exploring how medieval texts can nuance and attenuate our understanding of how power, subjectivity, and narrative entwine even today, and I use Bataille not only to theorize the erotics of grief, but also to think beyond the borders of studies that inaugurate the modern (or the postmodern) in opposition to the medieval.

Texts, sculptures, and manuscript illuminations all attest to the relation between power, taboo, and desire in medieval culture. The evidence for these erotics is not only literary, but also visual and codicological. Indeed, in figure I.1 we see one of Boccaccio's tales, in which Carisendi exhumes a pregnant Catalina and longingly plants a necrophile's kiss upon her lips. Other examples of embracing the dead include miniatures found in several manuscripts detailed in appendix 2. The erotics of grief figure love in many medieval media, and they are by no means merely a literary phenomenon.

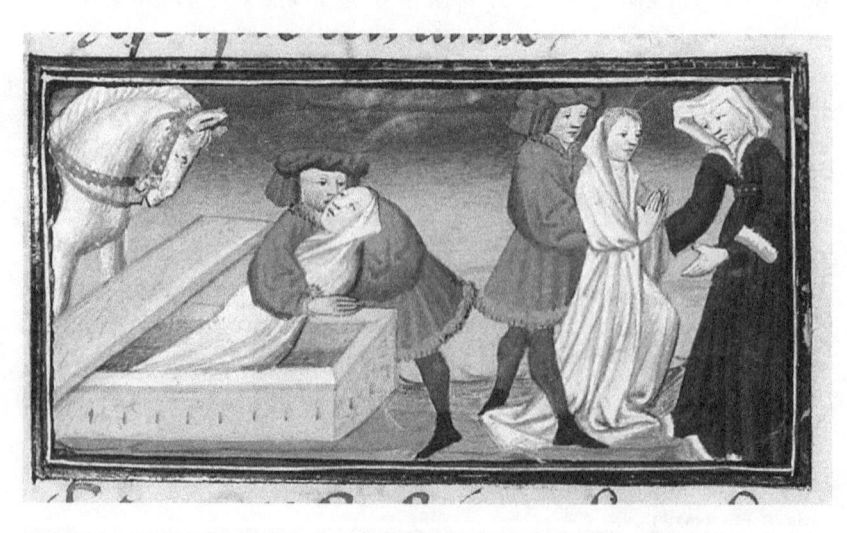

FIGURE I.1. Gentil Carisendi exhumant Catalina (BNF Fr. 239, fol. 273)

Narrating the Erotics of Grief

Grief has many functions in medieval communities, one of which is to spur narration—witnessing and commemoration are, after all, some of the functions of postmortem prayer, and one could argue that they are the primary function of texts such as *Beowulf*. Likewise, fiction imagines grief as a way of figuring commemoration: here, I argue that grief *is* narration. Wace's *Brut*, for example, recounts the story of the wet nurse whose teenage charge is crushed by a giant and whose grief imprisons her to guard the tomb (11800); the story is not only a warning about the perils of youthful beauty and monstrous old men, but also a cautionary tale in which grief serves as an invitation to narration:

> Li quens i vint l'espée traite,
> Une vielle feme a trovée,
> Ses dras desrons, escavelée;
> Dejoste le tombel gisoit,
> Mult se plaignoit et dol menoit; . . .
> Bone fame, dist Bedoer,
> Parole à moi, lai le plorer,
> Di moi qui es, et por qoi plores?
> En ceste ille porqoi demores?
> Qui gist en ceste sepulture?
> Conte moi tote t'aventure. (11655–59; 11672–77)[26]

> The count came there with drawn sword,
> and found an old lady there,
> her clothing torn and her hair all disheveled;
> she was lying on the tomb,
> and was crying and lamenting very much; . . .
> "Good lady," said Bedoer,
> "speak to me, leave off with crying,
> tell me who you are, and why you are crying.
> Why are you staying in this place?
> Who lies in this sepulcher?
> Tell me all of your story."

---

26. Robert Wace, *Le roman de Brut. Tome 2 / par Wace, poète du XIIe siècle; Publié pour la première fois d'après les manuscrits des bibliothèques de Paris, avec un commentaire et des notes par Le Roux de Lincy* (Rouen: É. Frère, 1836).

Here, the representation of the old woman's wracking sobs is not only the emotional apex of the story; it also imagines that *grief requires and produces narrative*. In the *Brut*, as in many medieval texts, grief's power is imagined to be narrative; grief is an invitation to tell a story. Like so many texts in which grief incites narrative, the *Brut* demands a story of its mourners: "Who lies in this sepulcher? Tell me all of your story."

I explore possible responses to the way grief invites documentation in chapter 1, where I read a tapestry of grief produced in *Philomena*, a medieval retelling of an Ovidian tale of rape and infanticide recounted in the *Metamorphoses*. In *Philomena*, I am most interested in how communal constraints on emotions mediate the construction of agency in tension between the powerful king and the vulnerable virgin: Whose feelings may be expressed, whose feelings matter? Who can practice desire beyond the bounds of the law?

In chapter 2, I highlight this question and the responses it solicits in an exploration of the relation between grief, gender, and narration in romance. In Chrétien de Troyes's *Erec et Enide* and his *Yvain*, for example, women who are mourning their dead lovers are considered most desirable while telling the tale of their dead lovers' glory. I am interested in understanding how love is thematized in order to articulate particular kinds of community, here the kind of identities that are grievable for and by elite communities.

While the readings of chapter 2 might seem to imagine women as grief's workers, in chapter 3 I explore how the erotics of grief structure the relationships between leaders and their men in chansons de geste. As King Arthur's and Charlemagne's eroticization of sacrifice suggests, reading from the perspective of emotion permits us to query how a spectrum of love relations work together to uphold and reinforce the codes of a medieval elite shaped by the commemoration of heroic masculinity.

In chapter 4, I explore how medieval travel texts imagine the Mediterranean as integral to figuring the relation between privilege, community, and emotional practices. Focusing not only on ancient Mediterranean texts, but also on contemporaneous romances written in Medieval Greek, Middle English, and Old French, in chapter 4 my readings highlight the erotics of grief as a kind of shared, Mediterranean language linking emotion to power.

There is something enigmatic, paradoxical, and timeless about how desire relates to death, perhaps explaining the theme's continual reappearance. In the eighteenth century, the Marquis de Sade articulated a theory of freedom through an eroticism that is now manipulated and repackaged in pulp romances, while in the twentieth, Marguerite Duras's heroine is aroused by the love-as-death she witnesses in our epigraph, taken from the scene of a lover's murder in her *Moderato cantabile*. More concretely, HBO's television series *Westworld* explores an erotics of grief in science fiction, imagining that rich humans would pay to travel to a western theme park where they could enact their every fantasy upon robots. In *Westworld*, humans express their socioeconomic privilege through desire beyond boundaries, raping and killing humanlike robots such as the innocent farm girl Dolores, who begins to remember and mourn her own violent ends. In such fictional representations, death simultaneously forecloses individual existence and figures the most basic thrust of continuation and privilege, of life.

In *The Erotics of Grief*, I am interested in understanding how emotions come to be used to figure the boundaries of living human community, ascribing livability, desirability, and mournability to some, but not others. Such is our "erotics of grief," a figuring of desire with death, a figuring of love through grief that courses through, entangles, and structures human communities.

CHAPTER 1

Philomena and the Erotics of Privilege in the Middle Ages

> Darkling I listen; and, for many a time
> I have been half in love with easeful Death
>
> —Keats, *Ode to a Nightingale*

The *Romance of the Rose*, widely regarded as the most encyclopedic treatise on medieval love, in which "l'art d'aimer est toute enclose," opens with a dreamer who is often illuminated in a sumptuous bed surrounded by birds, specifically nightingales, and devolves into a tale of violent desires. What would medieval people have seen in these nightingales, a visual addition totally absent from the text and its complex discussion of the relation between love, desire, and power? What would they have understood by the nightingale's warbles in so many other medieval texts about desire, from Marie de France's *Laüstic* to the *plaints* of the troubadours? Did they hear what Homer constructed as a hymn of sorrow in his *Odyssey*, what Shakespeare called a "mournful hymn?"[1] Or, what, even later, Keats would interpret as death's call to poetic inspiration? Did they feel gratitude at the beautiful, commemorative song, as Christine de Pizan suggests in the fourteenth century?[2] Annoyance at the

---

Portions of this chapter appeared in a preliminary form in "Romancing Death: The Erotics of Grief in the Old French *Philomena*," *Literature Compass* 13, no. 6 (2016): 400–411. Unless otherwise noted, all translations are mine.

1. Shakespeare, Sonnet 103: "Not that the summer is less pleasant now / Than when her mournful hymns did hush the night / But that wild music burthens every bough / And sweets grown common lose their dear delight."

2. Christine writes that nightingales add to the *douceur* of a heavenly encounter in the *Le livre du chemin de lonc estude* (Paris: Librairie Générale Française, 2000), 137–38.

FIGURE 1.1 Nightingale sings competitively to its death (BNF Fr. 15213, fol. 61v, Faune)

nocturnal disruption? Did they, as the miniatures from many a medieval bestiary would suggest, associate the nightingale with a fatal contest, a bird whose pleasure in singing led inevitably to its death in the throes of song, as in figure 1.1?[3]

Or would a separate shiver have gone down their spine, a frisson of fear for their own daughters' well-being as they recalled the association between the bird and the transmogrified, tongueless screams of Philomela, in the Ovidian tradition? Did the nightingale's midnight trill, lauded by lovers such as Tristan and Yseut, spur them on with twinges of the erotic?[4] Was it a song both hauntingly revolting and shamefully titillating? A song of death sung in the midnight moment of love?

So often are nightingales present in scenes of tragedy that Aara Suksi has asked, "What are these nightingales, so markedly featured, *doing?*"[5] Competing responses seem to pit love against death, as one school hears the nightingale's sweet melodies and thinks of lovers' trysts (as in the Occitan

---

3. See Bibliothèque de la Faculté de Médecine, H. 437; see also the representations of nightingales as competitive singers in other bestiaries such as Aberdeen University Library, Univ. Lib. MS 24; Koninklijke Bibliotheek, KB, KA 16, fol. 93r; BNF Lat. 6838B, fol. 26v; Bodleian Library, MS Bodley 764, fol. 78v; Kongelige Bibliotek, Gl. kgl. S. 1633 4°, fol. 42r.

4. As in BNF Fr. 2186, fol. 79r and 79v.

5. Aara Suksi, "The Poet at Colonus: Nightingales in Sophocles," *Mnemosyne*, fourth series, 54, no. 6 (December 1, 2001): 646. Emphasis mine.

tradition),[6] while the other hears a mournful lament and associates it with death and destruction (as in Marie de France). As Sarah Kay has pointed out, in Occitan poetry, it is a bird associated with lyrical productivity and creativity.[7] And, according to Bruce Holsinger, in a religious context, it is most often associated with liminality, a bird able to "negotiate the boundary between life and death."[8] Perhaps the polyphony of the nightingales' voices points away from the need to dichotomize and instead toward a complex and multilayered poetics of both death and desire.

In this chapter, I read the nightingale's polyvalency as a fruitful way to approach the thematization of desire through suffering, as the nightingale highlights the interconnectivity of two seemingly dichotomous emotions—love and grief—as a way of exploring how emotional exceptionalism constructs stories of noble power. Here, I focus on Chrétien de Troyes's twelfth-century Old French *Philomena*, a retelling of an Ovidian story of the nightingale that explains the eponymous protagonist's transmogrification and metamorphosis and that offers a mythicized etymology of the Old French word *philomèle*. *Philomena*, I argue, offers an early test case for an erotics of grief developed more extensively in later romances, and it investigates the relation between the performance of elite emotions and the construction of noble power. In this chapter, I read the valences of love and desire, grief and death that enshroud the nightingale as synecdochal of the complex emotional community of privilege within romance.

The Lovers' Lament: A Mediterranean Song of Death

Whether interpreted as desire or despair, the cry of the nightingale has a long and haunted Mediterranean history.[9] Early naturalists focused on the

---

6. As in Gilles de Viés-Maison's poem "Se per mon chant," discussed in Sarah Kay, *Parrots and Nightingales: Troubadour Quotations and the Development of European Poetry* (Philadelphia: University of Pennsylvania Press, 2013), 130. On the Occitan tradition see also Simon Gaunt, *Love and Death in Medieval French and Occitan Courtly Literature: Martyrs to Love* (Oxford: Oxford University Press, 2006).

7. Kay claims that "the lyricist's emblem is the nightingale, not the parrot," in *Parrots and Nightingales*, 1. She later explains that while the nightingale may seem tightly associated with the spontaneity of lyric, lyricists' work more closely resonates with that of the parrot, whose mimicry is a careful reconstruction of previously heard morsels, thereby differing quite extensively with the nightingale's extemporaneous mode of composition (197).

8. Bruce W. Holsinger, *Music, Body, and Desire in Medieval Culture: Hildegard of Bingen to Chaucer* (Stanford, CA: Stanford University Press, 2001), 226.

9. For more on the history of the nightingale in the literary and artistic tradition see Véronique Gély, Jean-Louis Haquette, and Anne Tomiche, eds., *Philomèle: Figures du rossignol dans la tradition littéraire et artistique* (Clermont-Ferrand: Presses Universitaires Blaise Pascal, 2006); Kay, *Parrots and Nightingales*; Elizabeth Eva Leach, *Sung Birds: Music, Nature, and Poetry in the Later Middle Ages* (Ithaca,

nightingale's diurnal rhythms as well as its noteworthy song. For Hesiod, the nightingale's melody is poetry, whereas for Sappho, the nightingale is a "lovely-voiced . . . messenger of Spring."[10] Antigone calls out to the nightingale to be her companion in an endless life of tears.[11] Later, in his *Natural History*, Pliny the Elder writes of nightingales' association with excess and death: "They vie with one another, and the spirit with which they contend is evident to all. The one that is vanquished, often dies in the contest, and will rather yield its life than its song."[12] In his eight-century *Etymologies*, Isidore of Seville accentuates the bird's etymological underpinnings as the giver of light, *luscinia*.[13] Hugh of Fouilloy builds off of Isidore in his medieval *Aviarium*, contained in the *Aberdeen Bestiary* (MS 24, fol. 52v–53r), where he draws a comparison between its lighthearted, incessant singing and the sustaining qualities of exemplary motherhood:

> It is an ever-watchful sentinel, warming its eggs in a hollow of its body, relieving the sleepless effort of the long night with the sweetness of its song. It seems to me that the main aim of the bird is to hatch its eggs and give life to its young with sweet music no less than with the warmth of its body. The poor but modest mother, her arm dragging the millstone around, that her children may not lack bread, imitates the nightingale, easing the misery of her poverty with a night-time song, and although she cannot imitate the sweetness of the bird, she matches it in her devotion to duty.[14]

Other classical authors underscore the darkest associations between the nightingale and death.[15] The most famous myth is that of *Philomela*, a tale

---

NY: Cornell University Press, 2006); Wendy Pfeffer, *The Change of Philomel: The Nightingale in Medieval Literature* (New York: Peter Lang, 1985).

10. Suksi, "Poet at Colonus," 649.

11. See Euripides, *Phoenissae* (Cambridge: Cambridge University Press, 1994), ll. 1514–15.

12. *The Natural History* (online), chap. 43, http://data.perseus.org/citations/urn:cts:latinLit:phi0978.phi001.perseus-eng1:10.43. As also depicted in BNF Fr. 1951, fol. 2v; BNF Fr. 15213, fol. 61v.

13. Book 12, 7:37, in Stephen A. Barney et al., trans., *The Etymologies of Isidore of Seville* (New York: Cambridge University Press, 2010), 266.

14. Transcription and translation from http://www.abdn.ac.uk/bestiary/ms24/f52v. As in Bodleian Library, MS Bodley 764, fol. 78v; Koninklijke Bibliotheek, KB, KA 16, fol. 93r; Aberdeen University Library MS 24 (Aberdeen Bestiary), fol. 52v; Morgan Library, M. 81, fol. 54r.

15. In his *Georgics*, for example, Virgil deploys the nightingale as both exemplary motherhood and as a metaphor for Orpheus's own sorrow: "As in the poplar-shade a nightingale / Mourns her lost young, which some relentless swain, / Spying, from the nest has torn unfledged, but she / Wails the long night, and perched upon a spray / With sad insistence pipes her dolorous strain" (book 4, 494). http://data.perseus.org/citations/urn:cts:latinLit:phi0690.phi002.perseus-eng1:4.494–4.527.

first spun in *The Odyssey*, where one of the daughters of King Pandareos "pours out the melody, mourning / Itylos . . . her own beloved / child, whom she once killed with the bronze when the madness was on her" (*Odyssey* 19.518–24). In Homer's account, mourning and longing are entwined with this bird, and the mother sings her heart out in desperation for her dead child, inviting a reading of wayward motherhood as an unforgivable transgression even in the face of extraordinary violence.[16] Subsequent ancient Greek texts associate the nightingale almost uniquely with death. In Aeschylus's *Suppliant Women*, for example, the nightingale is described as "hawk-chased," depicting femininity as persecuted prey; other iterations include passages within Aeschylus's *Agamemnon*, Sophocles's *Trachiniae*, Euripides's *Hecuba* and *Rhesus*, Aristophanes's *Frogs*, and Apollodorus's *Library*.[17] Likely one of the first complete rewritings, Sophocles's now fragmentary play *Tereus* follows out Homer's myth about the maiden to imagine Procne as transformed into a nightingale commonly read as a "powerful symbol of death."[18] In all these renderings, the nightingale is used to depict desire as coupled with death, singing the song of love through grief.

Ovid offers the best-known story of the nightingale in *Philomela*, contained in book 6 of his *Metamorphoses*. Though overtly about the metamorphosis of three wrongdoers into birds, Ovid's tale can also be read as an exploration of the nature of emotions, specifically desire. *Philomela* characterizes desire and love as entwined with grief and death, creating what I characterize in this book as an *erotics of grief*. Transgression, taboo, and violation are all at the heart of this Ovidian transformation imagining that no boundaries—social or religious, moral or legal—can contain the expressions of elite emotions, and in particular, erotic love.

Philomela is a horrific story of torture, sexual violence, infanticide, and cannibalism. It details the lust of Tereus for Philomela, his virginal sister-in-law. Tereus convinces Philomela's father to let her visit her sister, Procne, and then abducts her mid-journey, rapes her, and cuts out her tongue before

---

16. On transgressive motherhood see Peggy McCracken, "Engendering Sacrifice: Blood, Lineage, and Infanticide in Old French Literature," *Speculum* 77, no. 1 (2002): 55–75.

17. *Suppliant Women* (online), http://data.perseus.org/citations/urn:cts:greekLit:tlg0085.tlg001.perseus-eng1:58–62. See also Euripides's *Helen*, where the chorus invokes the nightingale as death, chanting, "Let me call on you, beneath leafy haunts, sitting in your place of song, you, the most sweetly singing bird, tearful nightingale, oh, come, trilling through your tawny throat, to aid me in my lament, as I sing the piteous woes of Helen and the tearful fate of Trojan women under the Achaeans' spears." http://data.perseus.org/citations/urn:cts:greekLit:tlg0006.tlg014.perseus-eng1:1107–1121.

18. Arthur S. McDevitt, "The Nightingale and the Olive," in *Antidosis, Festschrift für Walther Kraus zum 70. Geburtstag*, ed. Rudolf Hanslick et al. (Vienna: Böhlau, 1972), 231.

installing her in a forest hut. Imprisoned and mutilated, she subsequently weaves a tapestry narrating her assault and confinement, and her sister Procne comes to save her. The sisters plot revenge against Procne's husband, and they murder his son and prepare him as a cannibalistic feast for his father. The three are metamorphosed into birds, enraged and squawking for eternity. Depending on the version, it is either Procne or Philomela whose song is destined to haunt lovers for eternity as the plaintive nightingale.

Beyond its obvious questions about violence and maternity, the story is also about the nature of emotions: Are they biological drives that leave us incapable of resisting, pre-cognitive and unmediated by social norms, or are they instead constructed and expressed in the boundaries of community?—questions mediated by examining culpability. Specifically, *Philomela* explores culpability by imagining a divide between naturalized and socialized performances of emotion, and it invites readers to assess whether the horrible deeds of its protagonists can be explained as the force of nature or reason, a biological drive or a social performance.

From the outset, dark forces frame *Philomela*'s exploration of emotion, which is situated in the marriage between Procne, a royal Athenian princess, and Tereus, her Thracian suitor. It is a match that in other texts might represent a joyful resolution to political and military conflict. Instead, the Furies seize mourners' torches to light the moment of their matrimony, a baleful entwining of desire and darkness that presages doom. After several seemingly successful years of marriage that see the production of one male heir, Procne sends for her sister Philomela to visit, and Tereus sets sail to fetch her.

When he meets his sister-in-law, Tereus becomes inflamed with uncontrollable lust. Ovid uses nature to explain Tereus's desire; he not only underscores Philomela's natural beauty through comparisons with nymphs but also overtly maligns Tereus's own predisposition to lust, what he calls a "natural" feature of Thracian men. Ovid's text naturalizes an unmitigated bodily response to Thracian desire, and it imagines Thracian emotion as biological, a force of nature unmediated by human conditioning:

> Digna quidem facies: sed et hunc innata libido
> exstimulat, pronumque genus regionibus illis
> in venerem est: flagrat vitio gentisque suoque.[19] (458–60)

---

19. All Latin citations of Ovid in this chapter are from the Loeb Ovid, *Ovid III: Metamorphoses, Books I–VIII*, ed. Frank Justus Miller, 3rd ed. (Cambridge, MA: Harvard University Press, 1984). Translations are from Mandelbaum's *The Metamorphoses of Ovid*, trans. Allen Mandelbaum (San Diego: Harcourt Brace, 1995).

> It's true she's fair, but he is also spurred
> By venery, an inborn tribal urge.
> The vice inflaming him is both his own
> And that dark fire which burns in Thracian souls. (trans. Mandelbaum)

Here, Ovid imagines that, for Thracians, community does not mitigate biology: lust, love, and rape can be conflated and explained through a geocultural biology of emotions. That is, being Thracian offers a biological explanation for affective response, and it simultaneously exposes the instability of socially contextualized limits on the performance of affect. The willingness of the Thracian outsider to transgress reveals the instability and permeability of the emotional borders of Philomela's homeland. What happens when Thracians understand acceptable performances of desire one way, and other Greeks another? the text seems to wonder. The reply conflates Tereus's wayward desire with love, indissolubly blurring what in other contexts might be differentiated: a socialized performance of desire (love) and a biological response to sexual desire (lust), pointing toward an eroticism in which love is characterized through untrammeled desires, in this case violation, suffering, and transgression of taboo. Elite Thracian love is elite Thracian lust; love and desire are naturalized as one.

Chrétien de Troyes's medieval rewriting, *Philomena*, builds off of and transforms this Ovidian tradition to emphasize the relation between elite feeling rules and medieval community.[20] Specifically, and in contrast to Ovid, in the medieval text the breakdown of emotion codes points to a breakdown of the feeling rules of feudal patriarchy. Philomena's repeated protests to Tereus's advances identify normative gender and sexual codes supposed to govern lust. Philomena's protests move from highlighting her personal refusal (774) to Tereus's dishonor (781), situating her enactment of love (*aimer*) as grounded in shared emotional practices articulated through a feudal lexicon centered on the legal status of courtly identities:

---

20. Composed between 1165 and 1170, *Philomena* survives in the nineteen manuscripts of the *Ovid moralisée*. There is debate on its authorship. I follow scholarship that attributes the work to Chrétien, and I view it as consonant with his later romances. For more on the debate see Roberta L. Krueger, "*Philomena*: Brutal Transitions and Courtly Transformations in Chrétien's Old French Translation," in *A Companion to Chrétien de Troyes*, ed. Norris Lacy and Joan Tasker Grimbert (Cambridge: D. S. Brewer, 2005), 87–102; Cornelis de Boer, "Chrétien de Troyes, Auteur de *Philomena*," *Romania* 41, no. 161 (1912): 94–100; Ernst Hoepffner, "La *Philomena* de Chrétien de Troyes," *Romania* 57, no. 225–26 (1931): 13–74; Raphael Levy, "État présent des études sur l'attribution de *Philomena*," *Les Lettres Romanes* 5 (1951): 46–52; Marie-Claire Gérard-Zai, "L'auteur de *Philomena*," *Revista de istorie si teorie literara* 25 (1976): 361–68.

Je vous aim bien si com je doi
Ne je ne m'en quier ja celer,
Mes se me volez apeler
D'amour qui soit contre droiture,
Taisiez vous ent, je n'en ai cure.
—Tairai? Mes vous vous en taisiez!
Tant vous aim et tant me plaisiez
Que vueil que vous me consentez
Faire de vous mes volentez.[21] (772–80)

I like you as I ought,
and I have no intention of hiding it,
but if you want to call to me
with a love that is against custom,
be quiet, I have no desire for that.
—I should be quiet? But you should be quiet!
I love you so and you please me so much
that I want you to consent
to let me do everything I wish to you.

Here, Philomena's "si com je doi" (as I must) reveals that she expects to have her emotions contextualized and her person safeguarded by medieval proscriptions against sexual relations among kin, recognized in *droiture*.[22] She binds her emotions (*aim bien*) to her duty (*doi*), conforming both her *behavior* (act) and her *intention* (thought/emotion) to her social duty, inscribing her emotional performance within the conventions articulated in patristic doctrine, medieval sermons, and canon law destined to inform the practice of desire.[23] Philomena's speech underscores her knowledge of and dependence

---

21. Citations of *Philomena* throughout the chapter are from Emmanuèle Baumgartner, ed., *Pyrame et Thisbe—Narcisse—Philoména, trois récits du XIIe siècle* (Paris: Folio, 2000). Translations are mine, unless otherwise noted.
22. For work on medieval incest see Pierre Bonte, *Épouser au plus proche: Inceste, prohibitions et stratégies matrimoniales autour de la Méditerranée* (Paris: Éditions de l'École des Hautes Études en Sciences Sociales, 1994); Elizabeth Archibald, *Incest and the Medieval Imagination* (Oxford: Oxford University Press, 2001); David Herlihy, "Making Sense of Incest: Women and the Marriage Rule of the Early Middle Ages," in *Women, Family, and Society in Medieval Europe: Historical Essays, 1978–1991* (Providence, RI: Berghahn Books, 1995), 96–109.
23. When Philomena calls her brother-in-law *forsene* ("mad" or "senseless"), for example, because he wants to commit incest and adultery with her, she is identifying social codes for emotional performances. For an overview of the stakes of the discussion of incest in medieval canon law see C. 35 and C.32, q. 6; Q.2, c.7 in Gratian's marriage canons and Q.154 in Aquinas's *Summa Theologiae*. Gratian,

on medieval courtly conventions, feudal systems of loyalty, and theological relationships between sin and intention, as followed up by her exhortation that "Ja Diex ne place qu'entre nous / ceste desloiautez aviegne!" (may it never please God that between us / this disloyalty take place!) (781–83). Philomena's speech situates emotion within the context of the morality of the medieval Christian feudal court, agglomerating yet another ethical framework onto Ovid's classicizing moralization of Tereus's transgression. Even as they are disregarded by Tereus, in the medieval texts her emotions describe the contours of her medieval community, here imagined as functioning under the rules for noble exogamy.

Chrétien's Tereus takes pleasure in articulating the emotional, legal, and cultural boundaries of their shared courtly society even as he eschews them. He invokes a vocabulary of the self, rather than community, when he repeatedly uses moods of volition to articulate his desires for force: *vuel, consentez, volentez* are all verbs that perform his desire as power, instantiating his subjectivity through emotional performatives of domination. His emotions (*aim* and *plaisiez*) are articulated within a semantic field of *individual* power and contrast decidedly with Philomena's *socially contextualized* emotional landscape, which insists on feudal, courtly, legal, and religious regulations for noble behavior.

Whereas Philomena's feelings align with a *social* duty (insisting on the social performativity and communal nature of emotion), Tereus's define and articulate his power as an "I" at complete liberty to express his feelings regardless of their perception in society. This passage opens a discursive space for considering two competing models of identity in a noble community defined by the privilege of being able to set—and break—social codes. Desire—and its symbol in this tale, the nightingale—become a flagship case study for medieval emotions, pitting one model of reason and social context against another of precognitive, biological response, and the will of the "I." Reframing the Ovidian text within the context of feudal patriarchy, the medieval *Philomena* legend uses the erotics of grief to ask critical questions about the relation between emotions, subjectivity, and community: Can Tereus and, later, Procne, do whatever they "feel like" because of their social status? To what extent is the will of the privileged "I" modulated and regulated by

---

Gratiani Decretum: La traduction en ancien français du décret de Gratien (Helsinki: Societas Scientiarum Fennica, 1992); Thomas Aquinas, *Summa Theologiae*, ed. Petrus Caramello (Turin: Marietti, 1952). For critical analysis of Gratian's decretals about incest in Chrétien de Troyes see Kathryn Gravdal, "Chrétien de Troyes, Gratian, and the Medieval Romance of Sexual Violence," *Signs: Journal of Women in Culture and Society* 17, no. 3 (April 1, 1992): 558–85.

the "we" of medieval courtly culture? Where are the boundaries for elite medieval love, and how do they figure elite medieval power?

Love as the Language of Elite Power

The scholarship about elite love is divided over its relation to physical desire and tends to characterize love as *either* passionate, platonic, or religious. Georges Duby describes love as passion, noting that in noble marriages "*affectio* (affection) and *dilectio* (pleasure) were acceptable, but love was not."[24] Whereas Duby models noble love as passion, Stephen Jaeger, in his study *Ennobling Love*, follows the Latin etymology of *amor* to stress a *dissociation* of passionate love (*amor*) from affection (*caritas*), aligning the former with physical desire and the latter with a more chaste sentiment, what he characterizes as an "ennobling" love. In Jaeger's view, elite communities are produced through the dissociation of love from passion, through *caritas*. Yet the medieval *Philomena* and its Ovidian original attest to the story's capaciousness for complicating and layering the affective valences of love, creating space for multiple strains of love, some passionate, some parental, some platonic.

Digital humanities readings of *Philomena* reveal that some medieval texts imagine an *amor* that connoted not only platonic affection, but also passionate bonds between lovers, friends, siblings, and children. In figure 2.2, for example, "love" floats in a cloud of nouns describing familial affiliation—*seror* and *fille* are two of the most frequently used improper nouns; one level of *amor*, then, is awash in connotations of familial affection, another in forceful sexual desire.[25] The word cloud offers a visual representation that reinforces the text's own emotional and etymological polysemy, a purposeful blurring of different kinds of noble love.

---

24. Georges Duby, *Love and Marriage in the Middle Ages*, trans. Jane Dunnett (Chicago: University of Chicago Press, 1994), 32. While Duby is a historian, his work has influenced literary scholars of courtly romance, who have taken his reading of historical documents in tandem with the tenets of romance to assert that romance condoned love in adultery. (See, for example, Peggy McCracken, *The Romance of Adultery: Queenship and Sexual Transgression in Old French Literature* (Philadelphia: University of Pennsylvania Press, 1998); Douglas Kelly, *The Art of Medieval French Romance* (Madison: University of Wisconsin Press, 1992)). More recently, Keith Nickolaus has argued that our understanding of medieval courtly love has been overly influenced by the study of *fin'amors* in Provençal lyric and that "critics have failed to account in fundamental terms for the convergence of Christian and profane themes," in his *Marriage Fictions in Old French Secular Narratives, 1170–1250: A Critical Reevaluation of the Courtly Love Debate* (New York: Routledge, 2002), xvii.

25. Here, the romance's word frequency is again represented by type size; besides the proper names of the protagonists, and the familial contextualization of emotions suggested by the relational nouns like "sister" and "daughter," the emotives *amors* (love) and *duel* (grief) are some of the most frequent nouns in the text.

FIGURE 1.2 *Philomena's* vocabulary of emotion. Word frequency is represented by word size. Word cloud generated on WordItOut.com on July 29, 2020, and scrubbed for most common Old French articles (*li*, *il*, etc.) and words of emphasis (*moult*, etc.).

The innovation of Chrétien's text lies in its reworking of love's complexities within the courtly context, giving his *Philomena* the textual underpinnings of a crude romance and presaging his later work on desire in *Erec et Enide* and *Yvain*.[26] *Philomena* spends significant time developing an ethics of community based on noble love, and it offers descriptions of desire that will become hallmarks of later romance, layering the affective lens of medieval romance on top of an earlier, Ovidian fable. While scholarship on the medieval Philomena legend has focused on its relation to language and gender,[27] less work has considered

---

26. The text refers to its Ovidian source material as a "fable" (1449) and certainly shares many traits with that genre. I do not dispute its generic origins but rather wish to suggest that the tenets of this fable—in particular its treatment of death and desire, and its violent oppression of women—resonate strongly with Chrétien's later work in particular and with the conventions of romance more generally.

27. Susan Small, "The Language of *Philomena*'s Lament," in *Laments for the Lost in Medieval Literature*, ed. Jane Tolmie and M. J. Toswell (Turnhout, Belgium: Brepols, 2010), 109–27; Geoffrey Hartman, "The Voice of the Shuttle: Language from the Point of View of Literature," *Review of Metaphysics* 23, no. 2 (1969): 240–58; Krueger, "*Philomena*: Brutal Transitions"; June Hall McCash, "Philomena's Window: Issues of Intertextuality and Influence in the Works of Marie de France and Chrétien de Troyes," in *De Sens Rassis: Essays in Honor of Rupert T. Pickens*, ed. Keith Busby et al. (Amsterdam: Rodopi, 2005), 415–30; Peggy McCracken, *The Curse of Eve, the Wound of the Hero: Blood, Gender, and Medieval Literature* (Philadelphia: University of Pennsylvania Press, 2003); essays by E. Jane Burns, Elizabeth Robertson, and Nancy Jones in Elizabeth Ann Robertson and Christine

how it may inform conversations about genre (romance) and, by extension, the community of that genre (the nobility) by describing emotion. Yet working with DH tools reveals the text's commitment to reworking emotion within the ethics of a medieval, courtly context: Chrétien devotes over eighty lines to naturalizing Tereus's love by describing Philomena's unparalleled beauty and grace (124–204), and he spends significant time debating love's virtues (424–48), allegorizing Love's fight against Reason (477–94) and considering it as a sickness (648–60), all amplifications of the Ovidian tale. In the Folio edition, love is discussed in sixty-seven continuous lines of text (lines 381–448) as well as in several other abbreviated reflections, totaling about 6.5 percent of the entire text. To offer some context, love emotives stemming from *amour*[28] make up only about 2.2 percent (118 instances) of the unique words in the Uitti edition of the *Chevalier de la charrette*, a text frequently cited as prototypical of romance.[29] *Philomena* uses *amor* and *aim* over twenty-nine times in a much shorter text, and *amor*'s proportional centrality to the affective field of the text invites us to consider *Philomena*'s depiction of love within the ethics of romance as well as within the conventions of fable. This layering of genre, like the layering of love within the text, suggests an interest not only in rewriting Latinate myth for medieval audiences (*Philomena* as fable), but also in rewriting *Philomela* to depict how love structures and binds elite, medieval communities (the *matière* of romance).

If, as our digital humanities work suggests, elite love is central to *Philomena*, it is also crucially complicated by the text, which depends on both successful *and* unsuccessful performances of noble love to depict elite community. *Philomena* complicates *amor* and exposes its polyvalency in a passage that depicts love as the emotion that sways Tereus to contemplate raping his sister-in-law:

Amours vilainement le lie.
Vilainement ?—Voire, sans faille,
De vilonie se travaille,
Quant il son cuer vault atorner
A la serour sa feme amer. (214–18)

M. Rose, eds., *Representing Rape in Medieval and Early Modern Literature* (New York: Palgrave, 2001); E. Jane Burns, *Bodytalk: When Women Speak in Old French Literature* (Philadelphia: University of Pennsylvania Press, 1993); Elissa Marder, "Disarticulated Voices: Feminism and *Philomela*," *Hypatia* 7, no. 2 (1992): 148–66.

    28. Forms included are *amour, amours, amor, amors,* and verbal variations on *aimer*. Data retrieved from ARTFL, September 11, 2014, with special thanks to Glenn Roe of the ARTFL project, who identifies 5,360 unique words in the modern *Charrette* text (email to author, September 11, 2014).

    29. See Matilda Bruckner's characterization of the genre in "The Shape of Romance in Medieval France," in *The Cambridge Companion to Medieval Romance*, ed. Roberta L. Krueger (Cambridge: Cambridge University Press, 2000), 19.

> Love binds him to her villainously.
> Villainously? Truly, without fail,
> villainy is at work
> when he wants to turn his heart
> toward loving the sister of his wife.

This perplexing vision of love undergirds the discomfiting intersection of multiple kinds of villainous *amor* in our text: desire for the other (enacted as sexual violation, violating social norms), desire for the self (enacted as violent assault against one's own kin, violating incest prohibitions), and later, desire for revenge (enacted as infanticide and cannibalism, violating the boundaries of the human). Steven Jaeger has argued for an elision between noble power and *platonic* desire, but *Philomena*'s *amor* offers an important correction to his argument: here violent, sexual lust is elided directly with love, an expression of noble power as an erotics of grief, pain, and dismay—hardly dispassionate.[30]

The text's insistent, vicious conflation of many emotional categories (parental, fraternal, amicable, or sexual) in the Old French *amor* reveals it to be a multivalent and complex term deployed by Chrétien to represent an even broader sentiment than its Latin etymology and Ovidian use would suggest, especially for the emotional community invoked by and depicted in his *Philomena*. The sustained debate between Reason and Love amplified in Chrétien's version uses multilayered framings of love, including staged philosophical debates, soliloquies, and violent assault, to explore how emotion and privilege intersect at the peripheries of elite community. An allegorized Reason characterizes Tereus's desire as so wayward that it falls outside the boundaries of love:

> amours ne doit nulz ce clamer.
> —Amour?—Non voir.—Et quoi?—Outrage
> Desloiauté et forsenage,
> Quar, s'au voir cuit bien assener,
> N'est pas amour de forsener. (482–86)

---

30. In contrast to the ways I develop forceful passion as foundational to the display of noble power in *The Erotics of Grief*, Jaeger explains what he calls "ennobling love" as foundational to the public expression of nobility: "primarily a public experience . . . a way of behaving, only secondarily a way of feeling . . . a form of aristocratic self-representation. Its social function is to show forth virtue in lovers, to raise their inner worth, to increase their honor and enhance their reputation." C. Stephen Jaeger, *Ennobling Love: In Search of a Lost Sensibility* (Philadelphia: University of Pennsylvania Press, 1999), 6.

No one should call this love.
—Love?—Not truly.—Then what?—Outrage,
disloyalty and madness,
because, if you are aiming for the truth,
it is not love to go out of your mind.

Famously disregarded by the lover both here and in the later *Roman de la Rose*, this earlier, allegorized Reason argues that rage and senselessness fall outside the boundaries of what Stephanie Trigg has called acceptable "emotional scripts" with which to express love.[31] That is, Reason claims they are not acceptable scripts for the performance of love in the community developed within the text and, by extension, for Chrétien's readership. Yet here, too, Reason is discarded as *Philomena*'s Tereus imagines love as synonymous with a desire enacted through the violation of taboo and social *mores*—if the text succeeds in tracing the contours of any social norms, it does so by delineating their boundaries from an abject periphery, a kind of misperformance of noble affective community. The layering of love's valences here only further contributes to the perversions the text seems to espouse: incest, rather than sororal respect; rape, rather than willing affection; mutilation, rather than chivalric heroism; infanticide, rather than maternal devotion; cannibalism, rather than innate paternal revulsion.

From the perspective of story line, word count, and word cloud, then, the emotional tenor of *Philomena* articulates love as polyvalent, sometimes bordering on the disgust of the abject and directly related to the expression of noble power. Though some might argue that, like Philomena herself, the text condemns this love as wayward, its felt, lived status in Tereus's mind is not lessened by personal, moral, or cultural prohibitions, revealing the centrality of erotic love to the construction of elite exceptionalism. The linguistic and ontological complications proposed by *amor* within *Philomena* reveal that the invocation of love relies on a capaciousness foreign to modern readers: not only affection as we know it today, but also loyalty, pride, and even a kind of predatory lust and murderous rage. Even as it may offer a cautionary tale to its readers in banishing its actors from the human, an ultimate disenfranchisement from language and emotion, the metamorphosed nightingale figures love and power through a close alignment with the pain of death in elite culture.

---

31. Stephanie Trigg, "Introduction: Emotional Histories—beyond the Personalization of the Past and the Abstraction of Affect Theory," *Exemplaria* 26, no. 1 (2014): 3–15.

The Erotics of Grief: Desire in the Locus of Despair

Though grounded in words about love, in Chrétien's *Philomena* the first emotion word is actually *duel* (grief, mourning, sorrow, from the Latin *doleo*—to feel pain, to suffer). *Duel* occurs a mere nineteen words into the text, when the narrator focuses the listener's attention on the tale's emotive qualities by lamenting love's relation to pain. He presages the great distress of Philomena's and Procne's father:

> Ha, Diex! quel duel qu'il ne savoit
> La grant dolour et le damage
> Qui puis vint de ce marriage,
> Dont il plora puis mainte lerme
> Et morut de duel ains son terme! (4–8)

> Oh, Lord! What sorrow that he did not know
> The great suffering and the pain
> That would come from this marriage,
> About which he cried after many tears
> And died of grief before his time!

Here, grief frames the articulation of desire, and our narrator amplifies Ovid's description of Procne and Tereus's wedding night as attended by two specific goddesses of destruction: Tisiphone, the Fury who avenges murder; and one of the three Moirai, or goddesses of Fate, Atropos, who brings death by cutting the thread of life. Whereas we anticipate the celebration of the noble match to detail feasting and pleasure, instead the wedding is haunted by darkness, disturbed by the crowing of darkling night birds and the murmurs of Greek goddesses of death. *Philomena* creates a conscious coupling of grief and desire.

Violence, pain, and sexuality are indelibly linked in modern consciousness to the Marquis de Sade, whose eighteenth-century libertine philosophy of freedom imagines pleasure as the expression of power over others. Sade articulated domination, subjugation, and submission as forms of liberty in which pleasure is not constrained by social context, but rather expressed as the power of individual desire. He declares, "Je suis l'homme de la nature avant d'être celui de la société" (I am a man of nature before being one of society),[32] leading critics to characterize him as deploying nature to construct

---

32. Marquis de Sade, *Oeuvres*, ed. Michel Delon (Paris: Gallimard, 1995), 2:623.

a violent subjectivity particular to his class, to the political moment of the Revolution, and to the Enlightenment.[33] Of note to us are the implications this declaration has for the study of emotions: Sade imagines power as the ability to act on drive, on a biological formulation of emotion, unmitigated by any social boundary. His work has been characterized (perhaps most notably by Barthes and Bataille) as both revolutionary in its expression of desire as power and unique to the modern, defined against or as separate from medieval conceptions of subjectivity, sexuality, and class.[34]

Sade maintains that true liberty exists in the individual will, in pleasures neither limited by socially constrained notions of taboo nor rooted in socially defined emotional regimes; it is therefore a Sadean kind of liberty to acquiesce to torture by another, as it is pleasure to maim and assault, to follow desires unchecked. In *Justine* (1791), he articulates his philosophy as the liberty to do *anything*, to admit desiring anything, as he voices his victim Justine, who explains, "Il n'y eut rien qu'il ne me dit, rien qu'il ne tenta, rien que la perfide imagination, la dureté de son caractère et la dépravation de ses mœurs ne lui fit entreprendre" (There was nothing that he said, nothing that he tried, nothing that the perfidious imagination, the severity of his character and the depravity of his morals didn't permit him to commit).[35] The constraints of society that delineate the abject are precisely those that Sade condones transgressing and which resonate most strongly with the desire typified in *Philomena*. In both these texts, subjectivity and power are created through an erotics of transgression, reifying the norms they seek to destroy, eschewing law, religion, and reason.

Sade's articulation of the erotic, which I suggest resonates with medieval models of privilege seen in texts like *Philomena*, is tightly linked to figuring

---

33. See, for a small subset within the expansive scholarship on Sade, David B. Allison, Mark S. Roberts, and Allen S. Weiss, *Sade and the Narrative of Transgression* (Cambridge: Cambridge University Press, 1995); Kenneth Reinhard, "Kant with Sade, Lacan with Levinas," *MLN* 110, no. 4 (1995): 785–808; Jean-Baptiste Jeangène Vilmer and Maurice Lever, *Sade moraliste: Le dévoilement de la pensée Sadienne à la lumière de la réforme pénale au XVIIIᵉ siècle* (Geneva: Droz, 2005); Michael J. Shapiro, "Eighteenth Century Intimations of Modernity: Adam Smith and the Marquis de Sade," *Political Theory* 21, no. 2 (1993): 273–293; Carolyn J. Dean, *The Self and Its Pleasures: Bataille, Lacan, and the History of the Decentered Subject* (Ithaca, NY: Cornell University Press, 2016).

34. Roland Barthes, *Sade, Fourier, Loyola* (Paris: Éditions du Seuil, 1971). See also Pierre Klossowski, *Sade My Neighbor*, trans. Alphonso Lingis (Evanston, IL: Northwestern University Press, 1991); Alison M. Moore, *Sexual Myths of Modernity: Sadism, Masochism, and Historical Teleology* (Lanham, MD: Lexington Books, 2016).

35. Sade, *Oeuvres*, 2:417.

the pleasures of death as an act of creation. In a conversation between Rombeau and Rodin about sadistic torture in *Justine*, Rodin asserts that

> —Si la jouissance de la nature est la création, celle de l'homme qui détruit doit infiniment flatter la nature. Or, elle ne réussit à ses créations que par des destructions. Il faut donc étonnamment détruire des hommes pour lui composer la voluptueuse jouissance d'en créer.
> —Aussi le meurtre est un plaisir.[36]

> —If the pleasure of nature is creation, that of the man who destroys must be infinitely flattering to nature. Because she only succeeds at her creations by destructions. You must therefore completely destroy men in order to afford the voluptuous pleasure of creating them.
> —Murder is also a pleasure.

While Sade's insistence on the pleasures of violence and death postdates our medieval *Philomena*, his articulation of pleasure as transgression (here, pain and murder) echoes a medieval erotic in which grief and desire entwined, in which the natural thrust of life ("un des moyens dont la nature se sert" and "la voluptueuse jouissance d[e] . . . créer") can be found in the destruction of torture (where one must "étonnamment détruire des hommes").

Suffering is formative to desire, in Sade's terms—but in ways that resonate with, rather than break from, medieval teleologies. Indeed, though Sade's work pretends that the violation of cultural norms (in our case, emotional boundaries) somehow makes it possible to turn away from the human and toward the viciousness of nature, away from the control of socialized morals and toward an individual drive, his work actually delineates the boundaries of the culture he seeks to transgress.[37] While traditionally rendered as revelatory of a libertine body devoid of narrative significance—unable to "sign" the link between sexual organ and human desire, between bodies and subjects—the Sadean body is, as I read it, revelatory of Sade's longed-for state of "pure," innovative desire. That is, Sade's desire to render the body as a sexual

---

36. Ibid., 2:557.
37. Indeed, as Barthes points out, the endless iterability of Sade's orgies render his desire as work, bodies coupling and uncoupling as parts of a machine. Barthes schematizes Sade's subjectivity as both produced through and wrangled by the cogs of his desiring machine: "Ce qui est décrit ici est en fait une machine (la Machine est l'emblème sublimé du travail dans la mesure où elle l'accomplit et l'exonère en même temps); enfants, ganymèdes, préparateurs, tout le monde forme un immense et subtil rouage, une horlogerie fine, dont la fonction est de lier la jouissance, de produire un temps continu, d'amener le plaisir au sujet sur un tapis roulant (le sujet est magnifié comme issue et finalité de toute la machinerie, et cependant dénié, réduit à un morceau de son corps)." Barthes, *Sade, Fourier, Loyola*, 129.

machine longs for a way of writing about "pure" desire, and it imagines that "purity" might somehow exist in contrast to "corruption." Sade's insistence on "naturalizing" bodily desire as *transgression* renders explicit the emotional *boundaries* of his community, revealing that the former cannot exist without the latter and figuring the very limits of community explored in the manifold transgressive desires of noble subjectivity in *Philomena*.

We can read along with Sade not because we may ignore the particulars of our medieval historical and cultural contexts, nor because his work offers any direct commentary on *Philomena*, but rather because he is the first to formally articulate as philosophy what Old French fiction seems to propose as narrative strategy: that the language of eroticism is the swan song of death and decay. To function, it must admit the boundaries it seeks to eschew. Sade can help us more clearly enunciate an erotics of grief that—whether or not he acknowledges it—had their origins long before he began to pen *Justine*, and in fact were anything but a novel way to articulate privilege. Sade's own destruction of Justine echoes Tereus's kidnapping, confinement, and repeated rape of Philomena, as both virgins seek first to flee and then to dissuade their rapists, offering men the narrative space to enunciate their feelings and articulate their philosophies of love, power, and destruction as a kind of *libertinage*. Whereas many modern critics and scholars of the Enlightenment render Sade as *devoid* of feeling, reading with medieval affective perspectives reveals Sade's eroticism to be deeply in dialogue with emotion and, ultimately, with the relation between desire, community, and power for the elite.

With their refusal to share in communal frameworks of desire, Chrétien's Tereus and Sade's narrator defy and transgress in similar ways, leading Georges Bataille, who himself wrote an introduction to *Justine*, to comment that "De Sade—or his ideas—generally horrifies even those who affect to admire him and have not realized through their own experience this tormenting fact: the urge towards love, pushed to its limit, is an urge toward death."[38] In *L'érotisme* (1957), a study I regard as of fundamental interest to working with the culture of medieval emotions, Bataille locates desire in the transgression of social, religious, and cultural prohibitions; the desire to transgress is the fundamental boundary of human culture: "in the act of violating . . . we feel the anguish of mind without which the taboo could not exist: that is the experience of sin. That experience leads to the completed

---

38. Georges Bataille, *Erotism*, trans. Mary Dalwood (San Francisco: City Lights Books, 1962), 42. For commentary on the relationship between Bataille and Sade see Allison, Roberts, and Weiss, *Sade and the Narrative of Transgression*, 7.

transgression, the successful transgression which, in maintaining the prohibition, maintains it in order to benefit by it. The inner experience of eroticism demands from the subject a sensitiveness to the anguish at the heart of the taboo no less great than the desire which leads him to infringe it" (38–39). Without sensitiveness, in Bataille the erotic would be brute drive; the sensitiveness to transgression is what makes the erotic possible. So, with Bataille, part of the erotic field of *Philomena* is not only about the transgression of taboo—incest, rape, property, and, as we shall see, infanticide—but also about *articulating* transgression, a "sensitiveness to the anguish at the heart of the taboo." In Bataille's system, it is *narrative* that contextualizes, exposes, and characterizes emotions—especially desire and suffering—to articulate the "sensitiveness" that creates eroticism. In the speeches of both Tereus and Philomela/Philomena, both Ovid and Chrétien imagine that language narrates the relation between "sensitiveness," transgression, and desire at the heart of eroticism, wedding the erotic to a language of power.

Jürgen Habermas reads Bataille's eroticism in dialogue with contextualized, narrated emotion, an expression of "sensitiveness" that both delineates and transcends the boundaries of its emotional community.[39] Or, as Michele Richman puts it in her critique of *L'érotisme*, "the crucial distinction is between sexuality as *biological*, focused exclusively on the reproductive process, and eroticism as a *social phenomenon* which arises within the vacillation between attraction and repulsion, affirmation and negation."[40] In formulating the erotic around the performance of social boundaries, Bataille may help us understand transgressive desire as constituting the emotional center of medieval elite courtly culture, in contrast to emotional centers for other social groups in the medieval period. That is, while transgression may intuitively be liminal and peripheral, as work on gender has shown, it is central to medieval courtly literature.[41]

---

39. Jürgen Habermas and Frederick Lawrence, "The French Path to Postmodernity: Bataille between Eroticism and General Economics," *New German Critique* (1984): 82. Habermas explains that "for Bataille, a completely different perspective . . . is opened up with this idea of unbounding: the self-transcendent subject is not dethroned and disempowered in favor of a superfoundationalist dispensation of Being; rather spontaneity is given back its outlawed drives."

40. Michele Richman, "Eroticism in the Patriarchal Order," *Diacritics* 6, no. 1 (Spring 1976): 47.

41. Peggy McCracken has proposed that the illicit desire of adultery is the backbone of the medieval love story (and therefore not transgressive in functioning outside of medieval courtly structures), and Kathryn Gravdal further suggests that romance is predicated on a foundational narrative of rape. See McCracken, *Romance of Adultery*; Kathryn Gravdal, *Ravishing Maidens: Writing Rape in Medieval French Literature and Law* (Philadelphia: University of Pennsylvania Press, 1991). See also E. Jane Burns, "Raping Men: What's Motherhood Got to Do with It?," in *Representing Rape in Medieval and Early Modern Literature*, ed. Elizabeth Robertson and Christine M. Rose (New York: Palgrave,

Building off of the centrality of transgression articulated in Bataille may help clarify the relation between emotional transgression and the articulation of privilege. If, as we have seen in *Philomena*, an erotics of grief are central to the emotional community in the text, that eroticism also helps articulate the contours of Tereus's (and, later, Procne's and Philomena's) privilege. The sexualization of mourning, the elision of desire and death, is *normative* and *foundational* to articulating noble privilege, what Bataille characterizes as "organized transgression": "If transgression proper, as opposed to ignorance of the taboo, did not have this limited character it would be a return to violence, to animal violence. But nothing of the kind is so. Organised transgression together with the taboo make social life what it is. The frequency—and the regularity—of transgressions do not affect the intangible stability of the prohibition since they are its expected complement—just as the diastolic movement completes a systolic one or just as explosion follows upon compression" (65). Here, the purposeful transgression of prohibitions against incest, rape, and revenge only reinforces the essential taboos of medieval society. Consider, for example, the extensive medieval writings about incest, bloodline, and kin affinity, nowhere more animatedly questioned, discussed, and enforced than among fractures between the medieval nobility and the church. We might think of the "sensitiveness" to violation in *Philomena* as articulating medieval courtly culture's fundamental need to police belonging, genealogy, reproduction, and the expression of power: in effect, the *Philomena* story reads as a catalog of medieval courtly values, even as, in Bataille's sense, it obliterates all of them. *Philomena* not only figures privilege as violation, but the ways it figures violation supposes that other kinds of people are *not* allowed to violate, and therefore emoting works differently for different groups.

The emotional landscape of the medieval text also tells us something about both Sade's and Bataille's relation to the erotic: namely, it offers a critique of their figuring of the erotic as inherently modern. The medieval emotional regime of *Philomena*, in which Tereus imagines he can violate taboo as an articulation of his will, resonates with Sade's project to "étonnement détruire" as a man of nature: essentially, they both imagine privilege as the violation of taboo, and though they fantasize about violation, their "sensitiveness" reveals the strength of the system, their transgressions creating no alternative model for subjectivity, no new power system at all. Reading with

---

2001); Marder, "Disarticulated Voices"; Nancy A. Jones, "The Daughter's Text and the Thread of Lineage in the Old French *Philomena*," in *Representing Rape in Medieval and Early Modern Literature*, ed. Elizabeth Roberston and Christine Rose (New York: St. Martin's, 2001).

Tereus posits Sade's "work," as Barthes casts it, to achieve neither innovative pleasure nor to escape a socially constructed system in which power and desire are bound. Transgression articulates society even as it seeks to eschew it, and Bataille's construction of "sensitiveness" aligns his model of desire with both the medieval eroticism of our text and with the struggle to power enunciated in Sade's transgressions, revealing commonalities in their framing of eroticism, privilege, and subjectivity.[42] That is, Bataille's conception of the modern, desiring subject may find unexpected resonance in medieval models of privilege that imagine emotional exceptionalism through the possibility of transgression, of the warping of the emotional compact that delineates the contours of community and makes the erotics of grief central to the story line of exceptionalism.

Eroticism, Narration, Transgression: The Silencing of Philomena

The heart of our narrative is one of betrayal and violation; it is a story of rape, mutilation, and revenge. It is a story that turns around witnessing and reporting: the *language* of transgressive love. Indeed, by having Tereus drag Philomela to a hut in the woods and rape her while she cries for help, Ovid is framing the rape in terms of speech. Philomela's cries broadcast crisis on multiple levels, simultaneously emphasizing misperformances of fatherhood, kingship, and masculinity and highlighting the twisted polysemy of love. Her cry to her father is a call to the (failing) structures of patriarchy, which should by all accounts forbid versions of masculine desire that would authorize her violation; her cry to her sister exposes a fundamental weakness in female voice in the community of the text; her cry to her gods reveals how easily the emotional limits of religion are abandoned. Their failure to intervene emphasizes the critical breakdown of social structures regulating elite desire.

Yet, crucially, the scene staging the violent polysemy of *amor* also exposes the precarious relation between emotions and narrative, between emotions and how they are reported in language. Whereas the Ovidian account explores the relation between emotions and storytelling, in the medieval

---

42. Several scholars have noted Bataille's dubious commitment to the historical. See, for example, Yves-Marie Bercé, "Bataille et l'histoire des mentalités," in *L'histoire-Bataille: Actes de la journée d'études consacrée à Georges Bataille, Paris, École Nationale des Chartes, 7 Décembre 2002*, ed. Christophe Gauthier and Laurent Ferri (Geneva: Droz, 1996), 25. Bercé elaborates on the anachronistic analysis by critiquing Bataille's assertions that "avant Sade et Freud le monde était à la fois cruel et innocent, c'est à dire que de tels crimes pouvaient bien être commis mais qu'ils étaient inimaginables," 26.

account, Philomena's rape is also a discussion of the felicity of the performative. *Philomena* participates in medieval conversations about the relation between language and truth, and it underscores concerns about the veracity of emotions, in this case another being's true intentions, culpability, and state of mind. In Chrétien, we are invited to witness—and judge—the assault through metonymic indicators of emotions written through the body. The physical signs of emotions perform them for the medieval audience interpellated by the text. She changes color (802), sweats (803), and trembles (803) in her fear and horror. Philomena's bodily distress is meant to stand in for her own narrative, as if emotions could metonymize her truth, again highlighting the frailty of women's speech in the text.

Directly after her assault, in the Ovidian version Philomela threatens *narrative* as her revenge, weaving essential links between an erotics of grief and storytelling that become fundamental to later medieval romances:

> mihi poenas dabis. Ipsa pudore
> proiecto tua facta loquar. Si copia detur,
> in populos veniam; si silvis clausa tenebor,
> implebo silvas et conscia saxa movebo:
> audiet haec aether, et si deus ullus in illo est. (544–49)

> you—someday—
> will pay. I'll cast aside my shame, proclaim
> your crime. If that be possible for me,
> I'll tell my tale where many people crowd.
> And if I'm shut up in these woods, I'll shout
> unto the trees; I'll move the rocks to pity.
> My tale will reach the heavens and—if they
> are still in heaven—it will reach the gods. (trans. Mandelbaum)

In response, Tereus literally mutes her, cutting out her tongue in order to silence her potential narrative, thereby protecting himself from possible repercussions. In the muting, Ovid imagines Philomela as a powerful storyteller, one with potential to recount the relation between taboo and transgression, between elite desire and elite power in ways that potentially destabilize her community. Even as we become voyeuristic witnesses to its internal contradictions, the text still reports an eroticism *hors norme*, as if the fundamental compact of elite exceptionalism were a secret meant to be untold, an unenunciated but central sign for privilege.

When Tereus silences Philomela, we witness a second critical breakdown within the ethics of the text, a muffling of the norms of their shared emotional community. Though in Ovid she is muted for threatening to tell of her rape, her muting is also an attempt to silence systemic inadequacies, specifically around those constraining the misperformance of power. Ovid deploys gendered wordplay around "tyranny" as a way of describing the relation between power, community, desire, and transgression in the scene of mutilation:

> Talibus ira feri postquam commota tyranni
> nec minor hac metus est, causa stimulatus utraque,
> quo fuit accinctus, vagina liberat ensem
> arreptamque coma fixis post terga lacertis
> vincla pati cogit; iugulum Philomela parabat
> spemque suae mortis viso conceperat ense:
> ille indignantem et nomen patris usque vocantem
> luctantemque loqui conprensam forcipe linguam
> abstulit ense fero. radix micat ultima linguae,
> ipsa iacet terraeque tremens inmurmurat atrae,
> utque salire solet mutilatae cauda colubrae,
> palpitat et moriens dominae vestigia quaerit.
> hoc quoque post facinus (vix ausim credere) fertur
> saepe sua lacerum repetisse libidine corpus. (549–62)

[Tereus's] anger was stirred by these words, and his fear also. Goaded by both, he freed the sword from its sheath by his side, and seizing her hair gathered it together, to use as a tie, to tether her arms behind her back. Philomela, seeing the sword, and hoping only for death, offered up her throat. But he severed her tongue with his savage blade, holding it with pincers, as she struggled to speak in her indignation, calling out her father's name repeatedly. Her tongue's root was left quivering, while the rest of it lay on the dark soil, vibrating and trembling, and, as though it were the tail of a mutilated snake moving, it writhed, as if, in dying, it was searching for some sign of her. They say (though I scarcely dare credit it) that even after this crime, he still assailed her wounded body, repeatedly, in his lust. (trans. Mandelbaum)

Whereas Ovid initially naturalizes Tereus's desire to rape through a biological explanation, here he quickly recasts Tereus's sexual lust as a desire for power through the wordplay between the Latin *tyrrani*, from the Greek for "absolute ruler," and its less forceful English translation in Mandelbaum as "anger." For Ovid, emotion and power are co-constitutive; it is no mistake that the Latin text deploys *vagina* to describe the sheath for Tereus's sword, a terrible double entendre with which to describe Philomela's rape and mutilation. Tereus delineates the codes regulating power even as he violates them; the text reveals his knowledge of his deviancy when he names his transgression by silencing it. Whether or not one reads Tereus's actions as normative or transgressive, his actions recognize a socially contextualized model of desire and tie it to the narration of elite affective rules.

The scene of mutilation also initially seems to privilege men's story lines over women's: Philomela is no longer able to tell a story, to create narrative, whereas Tereus's lies beget stories that accord him even more power. The text initially equates abnormal, destructive performances of emotion to the elimination of feminine narrative, reifying emotion's link to power through the stories emotions produce. Here, Tereus literally silences Philomena's narrative of her emotions; later, in his lies to his wife, he silences her again. Perhaps it is Procne who most clearly articulates the link between gender, emotion, and narrative as she contemplates her son and wonders aloud, "Why should the one be able to speak *his* endearments, while the other is silent, *her* tongue torn out?" (619–52, trans. Mandelbaum, emphasis mine).

While in Ovid we hear Philomela's own, long diatribe threatening to tell, in the medieval text Chrétien has already effectively muted her through his own narrative technique, as he does frequently to women's speech in his later romances. Recasting the mutilation through reported action and indirect speech, Chrétien transforms the woman's direct speech to a man's assumptions, inviting attention to the gendered relation between speech and power in the medieval version:

> por ce que cele ne puisse
> Conter a home qu'ele truisse
> Ceste honte ne cest reprouche,
> Dist que la langue de la bouche
> Li tranchera tout a un fes,
> Si n'an sera parlé ja mes. (847–52)

> so that she could not
> tell any man that she found
> this shame or this reproach,
> he says that he will
> cut out her tongue from her mouth all at once,
> so that it will never be talked about.

The medieval text has already silenced Philomena through indirect discourse; *his* assumptions define and narrate *her* emotional response. As Jane Burns and Roberta Krueger have separately pointed out, in the medieval text the rape is a double violation, a silencing not only of Philomena's will but also of her voice.[43] Yet the relation between affect and voice here could also be read another way, as consonant with Kathryn Gravdal's contention that medieval romance is a genre predicated on sexual violence.[44] Here, both the text's silences and its eroticism are uncomfortably productive. The gap between the other's emotion and our perception calls for narrative and begs for a story to help us understand: Why is this person sobbing? What is wrong? Emotions require an answer, a narrative to explain; this is the fundamental disjuncture revealed by the medieval text's uneasiness with performativity, for the misreading of emotions—from Tereus's sincerity to Procne's love for her son—reveals emotions' instability as their dependence on *narrative* to contextualize and explain them.

Philomena provides that explanation when she sends a tapestry visualizing and explaining her assault to her sister, Procne. The tapestry itself is a metatextual object: it functions as a story within a story, weaving together the narrative threads of her rape and mutilation.[45] As Jane Burns remarks, weaving and rape are both depicted as narrative, and "weaving here enables Philomena to speak without speaking. . . . [It] works in this narrative to tell the suppressed story of what can happen to female genitalia, the tale of Tereus's handiwork, repeatedly referred to as his *oeuvre*," a word that literally references a masterpiece and here conflates rape and written text.[46] When sent off to her sister, the tapestry becomes an epistolary object, implying and requiring decoding by a reader who can perceive its meaning. The tapestry becomes a substitute tongue, a stand-in that recounts a story and begs for an emotional connection in return, one all too happily pursued by Procne, who covertly follows the messenger back to the hut where her sister is being imprisoned. It is the moment where Procne arrives at the hut that the text begins to align transgression not only with the masculine but also with the feminine, for like Tereus, Procne becomes *forsenee* (1246). The erotics of grief espoused by the "aim" for which Tereus violates and mutilates his sister-in-law metamorphose into an erotics of grief in which motherhood becomes weaponized, another "aim" full of transgression, grief, and death.

---

43. Burns, *Bodytalk*, 132; Krueger, "*Philomena*: Brutal Transitions," 93.

44. Gravdal argues that, even as it is eroticized, rape is *not* romanticized, but viewed as a political and legal violation, in *Ravishing Maidens*, 158n9.

45. See Judith Segzdowicz Chelte, "Philomela's Tapestry: Empowering Voice through Text, Texture, and Silence," *Dissertation Abstracts International* 55, no. 11 (May 5, 1995); Marder, "Disarticulated Voices."

46. Burns, *Bodytalk*, 116.

The Erotics of Revenge: A Broken, Eaten Heart

Perhaps nowhere do an erotics of grief more starkly articulate the link between emotions, social boundaries, and exceptionalism than in Procne's and Philomena's joint infanticide and cannibalism of Tereus's son, Itys, after the tapestry reaches Procne and she "reads" about her husband's rape of her sister. As we have seen in the scenes of rape and mutilation, the text systematically uses discomfort to draw the reader's attention to the polyvalency of men's desire; here it goes further, to also construct discomfort through women's desires. If power and pain were articulated as facets of Tereus's *amor* in the first half of the text, death and grief are equally important to fleshing out desire in the women's terminal infanticide and cannibalism. Procne's response to her sister's plight associates grief and desire by describing her desire for revenge with emotives such as *pleure* (crying), *dolente* (grieving or sorrowful), and *demente* (lament) (1285–91).

By refocusing the second half of the narrative on the sisters' desires, the text offers a realignment of gender, power, and eroticism. While we might suppose that Tereus's destructiveness limits the collocation of desire and grief as unique to *men's* performances of noble power, the *women's* work in the second half of the romance reveals that the emotional exceptionalism we encounter in Tereus's attitude may revolve more around status than gendered power structures. I do not seek to attenuate the violence against women that structures many medieval texts or patriarchy in general (that is, I do not reclaim or characterize this text as articulating gender equality), but rather I wish to suggest that the text builds a shared culture of exceptionalism that is articulated through emotions, here thematized through an erotics of grief.

The nexus of desire and grief that permeates this culture of exceptionalism is clearly delineated in the fracturing of the mother-son relationship enacted when Procne turns her desire for vengeance toward Itys, in murder and cannibalism. Though I have argued elsewhere that the framing of the murder in terms of motherly love is a kind of sacrifice, as Peggy McCracken has convincingly noted, there are no scenes in which women have access to sacrificial practice in the Bible or other medieval literature: women, it seems, cannot sacrifice their children out of love, because medieval culture imagines children as fundamentally belonging to men.[47] If so, then the transgression of Philomena and Procne as articulated in Chrétien's version—as opposed

---

47. In her reading of blood and lineage in medieval culture, Peggy McCracken notes that "stories about child murder identify sacrifice as the blood right of fathers, as a visible demonstration

CHAPTER 1

to that in Chaucer, where it is the violent rape, but *not* the infanticide and cannibalism, that structures the text's violations—is one that contravenes not only normative practices of love within medieval noble motherhood, but also within patriarchy, doubly stacked to reveal parental love as aligned with the most terrible kind of grief in infanticide.[48] In Chrétien's text, Procne sees Itys and immediately desires his death:

> Morir t'estuet de mort amere
> Pour la felonie ton pere.
> Sa felonie comperras,
> Pour son forfeit a tort morras. . . .
> Et pour ce te vuel decoler. (1301–4; 1309)

> You must die a bitter death
> for the felony of your father.
> You will compensate for his felony
> for his forfeit you will die, wronged. . . .
> And for this I want to decapitate you.

Attentive to the nuanced layering of desire we have uncovered in reading the multivalency of *amor* in our text, discerning readers may argue that *Philomena* thematizes love through an erotics of *death*—rather than its attendant emotion, *grief*. Yet this impulse toward semantic purification is one the text gladly shrugs off in both its definition of a multivalent, sometimes rapist, "love," as well as in its insistence on complicating the performance of noble desire with scenes of love-as-revenge, such as this scene of sororal love enacted as infanticide and cannibalism. Moreover, consonant with the rampant presence of death throughout, the prologue begins by associating desire with *grief*, locating the emotional framework of the text and its community in the words *dol* and *douleur* that mark the narrative's initial attempt to contextualize the text in a community of characters and readers, and its last grief-stricken, enraged metamorphosis. It is not death that frames the articulation of noble desire, but grief: pain, suffering, domination, the discomfort of its insistence on correlating desire with power over others, in the nexus of *dol*.

---

of paternal lineage and patriarchal order that depends on the suppression of the mother's bleeding body." McCracken, "Engendering Sacrifice," 55; see also McCracken, *Curse of Eve*, 60.

48. Though Chaucer explores the nightingale legend in his fourteenth-century *Philomela* in his *Legend of Good Women*, his work focuses on the violent assault and overlooks both the women's heinous murder and their subsequent metamorphoses; only fleeting allusions to those aspects of the Ovidian tale arise in *Troilus and Chriseyde*.

PHILOMENA AND THE EROTICS OF PRIVILEGE

Indeed, in a semantic layering of *amors* resonant with the transgressions already encountered in the rape scene, the text reframes Procne's motherly and sisterly love as vengeful cannibalism, using end-rhyme to align motherly love and the erotics of revenge in *acolee* (hugging) and *decole* (decapitation) and *afolee* (to go mad). She muses,

> Et pour ce te vueil decoler.
> Li enfens la court acoler . . .
> Si com la tenoit acolee
> Li petis enfes par chierté,
> Par dÿablie et par fierté
> Que dÿables li amoneste,
> A a l'enfant coupé la teste,
> Si l'a Philomena baillie,
> Si ont la char apareillie
> Entr'eles .II. moult bien et tost.
> Partie en mistrent cuire en rost
> Et en essiau l'autre partie (1309–10; 1328–37)

> For this I want to cut your head off.
> The child runs over to hug her. . . .
> Although he hugged her to himself,
> the sweet child by charity,
> by devilishness and by pride
> that the devil had put in her,
> she cut off the child's head,
> and so gave it over to Philomena,
> and then they skinned him
> between the two of them very quickly and well.
> They took part of him to begin to cook and roast
> and kept a shoulder from the other part.

Here, Procne imagines love as embodied in the act of eating death. Desire is literally embodied in the flesh—the cooking, serving, and consuming of the flesh of the son enact her own *forsenee* desire: not for sex and its thrust to life, but for revenge and its incipient grief.

In this scene, the women's transgressions liken them to Tereus via emotional twinning: like Tereus, Philomena has finally also become *forsenee* (mad)—she has forsaken the bonds of societal regulation in favor of her individual expression of emotion, by fusing murder, desire, and revenge, by rejecting the communal agreement about both erotic and parental love.

In his discussion of cannibalism in canto 33 of the *Inferno*, Ronald Herzman points out that Dante may well have used the Philomena story as a model for imagining cannibalism's threat to familial love, and I agree with him that "Procne's savagery in carrying out her vengeance equals the savagery of her husband in committing the rape of her sister."[49] Here, the newly expanded semantic capabilities of *amor* undergird not only rape and torture, but murder and cannibalism.

Bataille asserts that "the final aim of eroticism is fusion, all barriers gone"; this fusion is rendered incarnate in the child both desired and devoured, made one by the orgiastic cooking and consumption of his flesh by his family.[50] The fusion of desire and consumption resonates with Bataille's claim that "eroticism[,] which is a fusion, which shifts interest away from and beyond the person and his limits, is nevertheless expressed by an object. We are faced with the paradox of an object which implies the abolition of the limits of all objects, of an *erotic object*" (130). The child murdered and consumed becomes the ultimate "erotic object" of *Philomena*, transcending even the voyeurism of her brutal rape and cleaved, writhing tongue. Admittedly, Itys, a small boy, is not the obvious erotic object of *Philomena*, where the rape of the eponymous protagonist seems the more obvious choice. After all, Itys is too young to be anyone's lover, and as a child he seems initially an awkward fit for the erotic nexus of desire, death, and grief woven so carefully within the text.[51] Yet, when reread within a consideration of affective exceptionalism, Itys best represents not only the transgression of all limits, but also how the text imagines medieval noble desire—and privilege, and subjectivity—as fundamentally rooted in grief. At once kin and flesh, at once desire and love, and death and grief, Itys becomes the symbol of the tightly knit emotional entwining of grief and desire foundational to elitism. The murder and

---

49. Ronald B. Herzman, "Cannibalism and Communion in Inferno XXXIII," *Dante Studies, with the Annual Report of the Dante Society*, no. 98 (1980): 59. See also his discussion of the Greek sources for the *Inferno*'s representation of cannibalism, 59.

50. Bataille, *Erotism*, 130. The scholarship on medieval cannibalism, especially that of the "eaten heart" story lines, which focus on a punishment for adultery that feeds one of the lovers to their partners, aligns anthropophagy with sexuality. See John D. Williams, "Notes on the Legend of the Eaten Heart in Spain," *Hispanic Review* 26, no. 2 (1958): 95. For more on the eaten-heart theme see Madeleine Jeay, "Consuming Passions: Variations on the Eaten Heart Theme," in *Violence against Women in Medieval Texts*, ed. Anna Roberts (Gainesville: University Press of Florida, 1998); John E. Matzke, "The Legend of the Eaten Heart," *Modern Language Notes* 26, no. 1 (1911): 1–8.

51. Whereas we might not characterize the murder of Itys as a sacrifice in its lack of links to ritualized theology, we may think along with the Bataille that "in sacrifice, the victim is chosen so that its perfection shall give point to the full brutality of death. Human beauty, in the union of bodies, shows the contrast between the purest aspect of mankind and the hideous animal quality of the sexual organs" (144).

consumption of a blameless child in the name of love signify the distortion of desire into grief in ways that the destruction of an adult cannot.

The text's devotion to the destructive, distressing forces of the erotic invites consideration of it in the context of violent pornography. While in feminist scholarship, pornography has fostered intense debate about gender and power,[52] Lucienne Frappier-Mazur offers a feminist critique of pornography that theorizes the erotic as sexuality in transgression; she "call[s] erotic those stories which represent a succession of sexual acts connected by a narrative thread, and which are perceived at some point in time as transgressive because they violate both the norms of discourse and of sexual behavior."[53] Reading from this perspective, we can find some overlap with Bataille in considering eroticism deeply linked to transgression and its reification of social structures, and also recognize medieval texts as productive sites for interrogating the complexity of the erotic and its relation to (modern) subjectivity. It is not my purpose to rehabilitate *Philomena*, Bataille, or Sade for a feminist audience, but I do claim that our medieval text is vested in displaying elite women's work as equally integral to an eroticism linked to violence, grief, and death and foundational to the articulation of power. Here, the women's destruction of the father (i.e., Tereus's fatherhood, and its attendant implications for medieval genealogies of power and constructions of patriarchy) by murdering his child suggests a more expansive understanding of the erotics of grief as structuring power across a spectrum of gender positions. The text aligns desire, grief, and annihilation with performances of privileged exceptionalism, even as it stages gendered paradigms of destruction.

Metamorphosis, Punishment, and the Human

After the cannibalistic feast, we are left to wonder whether *anyone* will be punished for the heart-wrenching, manifold transgression of taboo in *Philomena*. Suddenly, however, our enraged protagonists are transformed to fly away, banished from human existence and human language. Irit Kleiman and Susan Small have separately worked on a productive interpretive controversy born of the nightingale's ambiguously voiced cry "oci, oci!" at the end

---

52. Perhaps the most germane discussion is that of Nadine Strossen, who critiques the notion that there should or could be one feminist approach to pornography (that is, a right or a wrong answer) proposed by Catharine A. MacKinnon, *Toward a Feminist Theory of the State* (Cambridge, MA: Harvard University Press, 1989), in Strossen's "A Feminist Critique of 'the' Feminist Critique of Pornography," *Virginia Law Review* 79 no. 5 (1993): 1099–190.

53. Lucienne Frappier-Mazur, "Marginal Canons: Rewriting the Erotic," *Yale French Studies*, no. 75 (1988): 113.

of Chrétien's *Philomena*: should it be considered a directive to "kill, kill"—certainly one interpretation permitted by the Old French verb *ocire*—or should it be understood as a mournful *plaint*?[54]

While the debate over the precise meaning of the nightingale's cry has underscored the complex linguistic formulation of Procne and Philomena's culpability, it can also contribute to our appreciation of Chrétien's work as author.[55] In his tale, the nightingale's "plaint" functions metonymically. Its piercing cry—the melody that shatters lovers' repose and interrupts the tranquillity of the night—offers readers more than mere emotional outburst.[56] It functions as a key to the text's emotional landscape, underscoring how romance depends on the instabilities of emotion. As Roberta Krueger points out, "[if] *Philomena* is indeed Chrétien's, then the founding narrative by one of the first and most influential romancers is not of love and honour, but of deception, rape, incest, mutilation, infanticide and cannibalism."[57] Yasmina Foehr-Jannsens agrees, calling *Philomena* a "hapax."[58]

The text foretells its ultimate silencing of human narrative in metamorphosis by leaving Philomena "sobbing and crying and braying" (*plore et crie et brait*) like an animal robbed of human language after her assault and mutilation (859). While I have characterized the Philomela legend as both a representation of masculine noble exceptionalism predicated on emotional transgression and a silencing of women's narrative in the erotics of revenge, it ultimately invites us a step further, to consider not only the *gendering* of elite power, but the *humanity* of elite power. The text constructs the human through its emotional prohibitions, defining as abject—that is, as *not*

---

54. Chrétien details the metamorphosis: "Por les mauves qu'ele tant het / Chante au plus doucemant qu'el set / Par el boschage: 'Oci! Oci!'" (For those terrible people that she so hates / she sings as sweetly as she knows how / in the woods: "Kill! Kill!") (1465–67). For discussion see Elena Llambas Pombo, "Beauté, amour et mort dans les *Ovidiana* français du XII siècle," in *Le beau et le laid au moyen âge* (Aix-en-Provence: Presses Universitaires de Provence, 2000), 349. See also the introduction to the 1974 Slatkine reprint of the 1909 edition, in which De Boer claims that "Le traducteur . . . raconte brièvement la métamorphose, et finit par une explication du cri, 'oci! oci!' du rossignol, qui n'aurait d'autre sens que d'exhorter les hommes à faire périr tous les 'desleal'" (introduction, c). Chrétien de Troyes, *Philomena, conte raconté d'après Ovide*, ed. Cornelius De Boer (Geneva: Slatkine, 1974).

55. Roberta Krueger, in "*Philomena*: Brutal Transitions" (88–89), agrees with many scholars that it is nearly impossible to unpack Chrétien's words inside the largely redacted version that has been transmitted to us today.

56. See the recent work on the bird's cry in the Old French rendition by Small, "Language of Philomena's Lament."

57. Norris J. Lacy and Joan Tasker Grimbert, *A Companion to Chrétien de Troyes* (Cambridge: D. S. Brewer, 2005), 89.

58. Yasmina Foehr-Janssens, *La veuve en majesté: Deuil et savoir au féminin dans la littérature médiévale* (Geneva: Droz, 2000), 93.

human—a mother who would kill or dismember her child. Procne pauses before murdering her child, and the text pauses with her, to briefly naturalize exemplary motherhood:

> Si com requiert Drois et Nature
> De toute humaine creature,
> Et si com Pitiez le desfent,
> Que mere ne doit son enfent
> Ne ocire ne desmembrer (1315–19)

> As is required by Law and Nature
> Of every human creature,
> And as Pity forbids them from it,
> A mother may not kill
> Or dismember her child

Here, the text imagines maternal infanticide not only as not *natural*—as against both Nature and the Law—but as not *human*, the ultimate transgression of the bounds of community.

Transformed into birds, the triad escapes evaluation by medieval juridical and ecclesiastical authorities, and, thematically at least, Chrétien, too, is able to flee queries about the relation between emotions, community, and culpability. Do rage, transgression, or incestuous desire justify banishment from the human? Do emotional reactions to pain operate independently of social constraint? Do they merit judgment by a feudal legal apparatus, or is one free to execute based on emotional responses to desire and slaughter? The conclusion purposefully sets such questions aside, puzzling most readers and leaving them to judge the characters' and tale's cannibalistic morality in a seeming vacuum, well outside the scope of institutional feudal justice and even textual condemnation:

> il devint hupe coupee,
> Si com la fable le raconte,
> Pour le pechié et pour la honte
> Qu'il avoit fet de la pucele.
> Progné devint une arondele
> Et Philomena rousseignos.
> Encore, qui creroit son los,
> Seroient a honte trestuit
> Li desloial mort et destruit,
> Et li felon et li perjure,
> Et cil qui de joie n'ont cure,

> Et tuit cil qui font mesprison
> Et felonnie et traïçon
> Vers pucele sage et cortoise. (1445–61)

> he became a hoopoe,
> as the fable recounts,
> for the sin and for the shame
> that he had done toward the maiden.
> Procne became a swallow
> and Philomena a nightingale.
> Even today, they who would believe his counsel,
> they will be brought straightaway to shame,
> the disloyal one killed and destroyed,
> and the felons and the perjurers,
> and those who have no care for joy,
> and all those who wrongly imprison
> and commit felony and treason
> against wise and courteous maidens.

Chrétien clearly condemns the rape here, casting it as the central thematic problem of the text, and he uses a juridical vocabulary to contextualize the moral of the metamorphosis with words like *felon, perjure, felonnie,* and *traïçon*. Yet he avoids resolving the problem in juridical terms, and he resists any precise locus of punishment, rendering the erotics of grief an unresolved problematic for elite culture predicated on exception. Similarly, he contextualizes his condemnation within a shared religious community by invoking the lexicon of Christianity and sin with the word *pechié*, yet he also refuses to elaborate either on a theology of sin or proffer a punishment beyond banishment from the human. Instead, both religious and legal transgressions are resolved through metamorphosis, punishing Tereus by transforming him into an ignoble, excrement-eating bird. His punishment may come with a didactic exhortation—to leave maidens unharmed—but it does little to respond to social, juridical, or religious concerns about the horrific variety of taboo and transgression within the text, rendering the metamorphosis disappointing at best.

The metamorphosis, however, has more to offer. In sidestepping questions of culpability and institutional justice, the text permits readers to indulge in other questions, ones with which the text itself seems eager to engage on a much deeper level. Emotions are completely recontextualized here, offering a lesson that is not so much about overt punishment for rape, but rather about the reinsertion of wayward conceptualizations of emotion (an extrajudicial "I") back into a social narrative structure in which feeling practices are policed by community. In *Philomena*, for example, Tereus's abject repulsion at eating his son is neither innate nor instinctual ("natural"), but rather it is part of the fabric of medieval social values ("social"). That is, his emotions (horror, repulsion, anger, and fear) are only produced once he is told about the deed; they are no natural, innate response, but rather they are contextualized by his social conditioning, what Julia Kristeva would call the socializing functions of the "powers of horror."[59]

Itys's murder delegitimizes a "natural" connection between emotions: mothers can kill their children, even with remorse and love in their hearts; fathers can eat their children without feeling any "natural," innate biological horror. In eliding love and death, Itys's killing questions the nobility's relation to emotional regimes governed by the social—where emotions are post-cognitive, expressed with the intention of their reception within a group—rather than the individual, as an expression of privilege within a highly stratified community. Itys's murder questions the permeability of the boundaries of elite exceptionalism, and it highlights grief as foundational to figuring noble privilege.

From the politics of forced marriage to the prevalence of rape and torture; from the fears surrounding infanticide, incest, and cannibalism, to the desires wrapped around sexual and societal transgression; from considerations of the legal definition of justifiable homicide to the ultimate satisfaction of revenge, the gamut of feelings essential to exploring power and privilege is encapsulated in the metamorphosis that begets the nightingale. And, though banished from the human, these metamorphosed nobles certainly still attain narratological and temporal immortality, much in the same way knights' stories are later told and retold: the nightingale's cry "oci, oci" is meant to narrate and reiterate the Philomela legend for lovers who hear its warbling through the window.

Before her final flight from the human, Procne marks the nexus of love, loss, and grief on her body:

Lors se claimme lasse, chieitive,
Et s'a tel duel ne set que face.
Or tret ses crins, or fiert sa face.
Or plore, or crie et or se pasme,
Les deus maudist et la mort blasme. (974–77)

---

59. Julia Kristeva, *Powers of Horror: An Essay on Abjection* (New York: Columbia University Press, 1982).

> Then she bemoans herself as miserable and worthless,
> and she has no idea how to face such grief.
> Now she pulls out her locks,
> now she scratches her face.
> Now she sobs, now she cries and now she faints,
> she curses the gods and blames death.

Like so many women in medieval texts, Procne marks her grief on her body by scratching her face and pulling out her hair; these physical markers not only commemorate her own pain, but they also predict and interpellate a reading public, a community that can understand, contextualize, and react to her narration of emotion. As we shall see in chapter 2, which focuses on the widows of romance, women's bodily narratives recount much more than their own grief—they become sites of narration, read and decoded by others as desirable in ways that transcend the boundaries of the somatic and the personal.

CHAPTER 2

Widows and the Romance of Grief

> Who am "I" without you?
> —Judith Butler, *Precarious Life*

While *Philomena* deploys transgression to expose the polyvalency of *amor*, perhaps nowhere is love's layering more complicated than in romance, specifically when women mourn their dead lovers. One of the most curious moments of romance occurs in Chrétien's twelfth-century Old French *Erec et Enide*, the story of an impoverished beauty, Enide, who is ennobled by her marriage to one of King Arthur's valiant knights, Erec, who becomes so enamored of his wife that he dallies at her side and risks his reputation. When Enide informs Erec that he has fallen from favor, Erec seeks revenge by dragging her along on episode after episode of dangerous chivalric encounter. In one episode, Enide believes she has witnessed an errant knight defeat and kill her husband in hand-to-hand combat; in her grief, she falls wailing to the ground and, shrieking, scratches her face bloody and pulls out entire clumps of her hair. She marks her anguish and despair—her grief—onto her body. Another knight hears her cries and,

---

This chapter draws on a preliminary essay, "Chrétien's Romance of Grief: Widows and Their Erotic Bodies in Yvain," in *Masculinities and Femininities in the Middle Ages*, ed. Fred Kiefer (Turnhout, Belgium: Brepols, 2010), as well as feedback from conversations at the Center for the History of Emotions in Sydney and Melbourne. I am also indebted to the careful research detailed in Anita Guerreau-Jalabert, *Index des motifs narratifs dans les romans arthuriens français en vers (XIIe–XIIIe siècles)* (Geneva: Droz, 1992).

finding her wailing, is immediately aroused; he accosts her and informs her that if she refuses to become his wife, he will rape her.

In its insistent, attentive detailing of Enide's self-destruction, the episode invites the reader to gaze upon her self-mutilations to pose the essential question: Why is Enide at all desirable in this moment? What it is about her sniveling, scratched, and mutilated rendition of grief that inspires uncontrollable lust in the onlooking man? This moment certainly invites a reading of gender, in that, like in *Philomena*, Enide's distress and despair are what fuel a man's lust; women's suffering seems to generate men's desire. Feminist readings of romance have convincingly documented how the performance of gender and power are entwined in the genre, and Jane Burns's study of Enide's speech is a forceful analysis of how voice, gender, and power coalesce to imagine the masculine as inaugurated through the suppression of the feminine in many Old French texts.

Yet while this moment reveals much about how gender operates and what it does, it is not simply about aligning grief and suffering with the feminine, as I will show. Often read as objects of men's desire, widows like Enide are also desirable because women's mourning entails *narrative*. This chapter explores how emotional and gender practices entwine to articulate the contours of the story of noble privilege. I focus on grief as a kind of storytelling, one eroticized as it narrates power for the powerful. I explore why, at the moment of death, romance conflates grieving, desire, and narration.

Who May Grieve? Widows and Exemplary Grief

Though puzzling, the prevalence of scenes like Enide's in medieval romance invites not only attention to grief, but also an examination of romance's characterization of grief as entailing desire. Literary sources repeatedly bear witness to grief as integral to medieval love: in some texts, lovers literally die of lovesick grief,[1] and elsewhere scenes of lovers grieving are ubiquitous.[2] Grief is a particularly central emotion to medieval romance because it constitutes the relationships of attachment: it is the lack felt when uncoupled

---

1. See, for example, *La continuation Perceval Gerbert*, 1613–861; *Deus amanz*, 153–250; *Tristan Thomas* fr. 5, 1541–815; *Yonec*, 393–454, 455–554.

2. See similar scenes in *L'âtre périlleux*, 2070–492; *Le Bel Inconnu*, 2751–925; *Chaitivel*, 71–143; *Claris et Laris*, 20836–1110; *Cligès*, 1535–2199; *La conte du graal*, 6293–416, 8160–467; *Fergus*, 4455–830; *Floriant et Florete*, 375–512, 7009–244; *Lancelot*, 4157–532; *Les continuations Perceval* 1, 504–944, 10063–534, 19420–606; *Les continuations Perceval* 2, 21579–658, 26552–824; *La continuation Perceval Gerbert*, 1613–861, 8906–9285, 10982–1526; *Hunbaut*, 1779–889; *Les merveilles de Rigomer*, 2641–858, 4035–686; *Meriadeuc*, 7544–807; *Yder*, 519–2877, 3552–749, 3750–4415; *Yvain*, 1144–544. And, of course, the *Tristan* romances and Chaucerian tales also elide love and grief.

for either an evening or an eternity; it is an emotion expressed in the context of mourning the loss of partnership; it is one of the emotions used to describe lovesickness; it is men mourning for other men's lost prowess, as many have noted.[3] At once an emotion and a story line uniting lovers, grief is fundamental to figuring the affection that binds courtly narrative.

In his study of death and sexuality in medieval Occitan literature, Simon Gaunt contends that Sigmund Freud's *Mourning and Melancholia* is foundational to reading medieval grief with sexuality, for Freud conceptualizes grief as libidinal, even as he pathologizes the emotions surrounding loss as unproductive.[4] Freud initially recognizes both mourning and melancholia as stemming from a libidinal attachment to the lost object: "The loved object no longer exists, and it proceeds to demand that all libido shall be withdrawn from its attachments to that object. This demand arouses understandable opposition—it is a matter of general observation that people never willingly abandon a libidinal position, not even, indeed, when a substitute is already beckoning to them."[5] In short, grief is meant to be transitory, a way of disentangling desire for the dead.

In this vein, Enide's grief should be transformative, leading her to overcome her libidinal attachment to Erec. Yet it is precisely this stasis that attracts medieval men and destabilizes Freud's claims about the psychology of grief's libidinal roots. Enide's unrelenting attachment to Erec interrogates the dichotomy Freud seeks to establish between *mourning* as a healthy, fugacious part of death and *melancholia*, which he aligns with the stagnancy of pathology and which in his model becomes excessive, indulgent, unproductive.[6] Freud's melancholia—which aligns with the count's protests that Enide is

---

3. Marie-Noëlle Lefay-Toury, *Mort et fin'amor dans la poésie d'oc et d'oeil aux XIIe et XIIIe siècles*, Nouvelle bibliothèque du Moyen Âge (Paris: Champion, 2001); Leslie Abend Callahan, "The Widow's Tears: The Pedagogy of Grief in Medieval France and the Image of the Grieving Widow," in *Constructions of Widowhood and Virginity in the Middle Ages*, ed. Cindy L. Carlson and Angela Jane Weisl (New York: St. Martin's, 1999), 245–63; Jeff Rider, "The Inner Life of Women in Medieval Romance Literature: Grief, Guilt and Hypocrisy," in *The Inner Life of Women in Medieval Romance Literature*, ed. Jeff Rider and Jaimie Friedman (New York: Palgrave, 2011), 1–25; Basil Dufallo and Peggy McCracken, *Dead Lovers: Erotic Bonds and the Study of Premodern Europe* (Ann Arbor: University of Michigan Press, 2006).

4. Gaunt also reads the link between sexuality and death with Lacan, whose seminal work on grief and libidinal attachments he details in *Love and Death in Medieval French and Occitan Courtly Literature: Martyrs to Love* (Oxford: Oxford University Press, 2006).

5. Sigmund Freud, *The Standard Edition of the Complete Psychological Works*, ed. Anna Freud, trans. James Strachey, vol. 14 (London: Hogarth Press and the Institute of Psycho-Analysis, 1974), 244.

6. Pointed to in *Mourning and Melancholia* within the discussion of narcissism and hysteric excess, when he describes the pathological stasis of melancholy: "The melancholic's erotic cathexis in regard to his object has thus undergone a double vicissitude: part of it has regressed to identification, but the other part, under the influence of the conflict due to ambivalence, has been carried back to the stage of sadism which is nearer to that conflict" (14:251–52).

mourning *too much*—is both excessive and particularly *feminine* in its pathology.[7] Taken in concert with a long history of somatic models of emotion rooted in Galenic medicine, Freud's work contributes to dichotomizing—rather than complicating—gender by aligning unproductive, cold melancholic excess with femininity, and active, hot cleansing grief with masculinity.[8] Yet the ubiquity of grief within romance invites a reconsideration of Freud's paradigm, for our medieval texts imagine grieving as particularly fecund, a place of possibility: here Enide's mourning not only entails the sexual desire of an errant count, but also fulfills a commemorative function that immortalizes Erec's worth. In medieval romance, mourning is a profoundly interesting and productive state of being that destabilizes Freud's emotional hierarchies.

Indeed, other models may offer more intriguing and productive resonances with the erotics of medieval grieving. Roland Barthes, for example, recharacterizes Freud's mourning/melancholia dichotomy when he writes of the *productivity* of grief's stasis: "It is said that mourning, by its gradual labor, slowly erases pain; I could not, I cannot believe this; because for me, Time eliminates the emotion of loss (I do not weep), that is all. For the rest everything has remained motionless."[9] And, "The indescribableness of my mourning results from my failure to hystericize it: continuous and extremely peculiar indisposition."[10] Barthes theorizes a space in which grief can make time stand still, continually reinscribing both pain and memory, loss and commemoration; his determination to feed his grief and mark its place resonates with the gestures of mourning present in medieval literary encounters with chivalric death—a productive, active state of emotional

---

7. See his construction of hysteria and its alignment with women's pathological excess in Sigmund Freud, *Dora: An Analysis of a Case of Hysteria*, ed. Philip Rieff (New York: Touchstone, 1997). And of course, feminist critiques of Freud's gendering of pathology abound, most notably in Juliet Mitchell, *Psychoanalysis and Feminism: A Radical Reassessment of Freudian Psychoanalysis* (New York: Penguin Books, 2000); Madelon Sprengnether, *The Spectral Mother: Freud, Feminism, and Psychoanalysis* (Ithaca, NY: Cornell University Press, 1992); Jane Gallop, *The Daughter's Seduction: Feminism and Psychoanalysis* (New York: Palgrave, 1982); Judith P. Butler, *Gender Trouble: Feminism and the Subversion of Identity* (New York: Routledge, 1999).

8. Freud's insistence on the somatic alignment of a "predisposition" to melancholia suggests a "natural" alignment with mourning and gender, which I resist in this chapter. Similarly, for a reconsideration of Freud's somatics of grief within the context of homosexual couples and AIDS, see Judith Butler, "Melancholy Gender—Refused Identification," *Psychoanalytic Dialogues* 5, no. 2 (1995): 165–80.

9. Barthes cited in Kathleen Woodward, "Freud and Barthes: Theorizing Mourning, Sustaining Grief," *Discourse* 13, no. 1 (1990): 97–98.

10. Roland Barthes, *The Mourning Diary* (London: Notting Hill Editions, 2010), 84.

stasis.[11] Barthes's model indulges in *creation*—narration—within the stymied paradigm of loss, mourning, and melancholia. His journal is the product of the stasis of mourning, and his writing is the productive testament to the lost other, akin to the productivity of mourning for the elite in medieval texts.

Like Barthes's luxuriating in his grief's productivity, medieval texts linger lovingly over mourning women and their grief, using repetition and reiteration as narrative strategies to stretch out the time of storytelling, repeating and embellishing the scenes of women's destruction, the narratives of grief and valor they write onto their bodies as signs of their distress. The plethora of scenes detailing women's grieving suggests that romance is intimately bound up in the productivity of grieving, an erotics of both women's suffering and the possibilities it proffers for storytelling, as not only literary, but historical women's bodies suggest.

Historical Women Working Grief

Erec et Enide's curious sexualization of grief is part of a long literary tradition that suggests women's grief had historical importance. Ancient Greek warfare gave women ample reason to mourn, and indeed their sorrow is central to the emotional axes of texts such as *The Iliad, Antigone, The Trojan Women*, and, much later, Ovid's *Heroides*. From Aeschylus's Cassandra, to his and Sophocles's representations of Electra, as Anne Klinck suggests in *Laments for the Lost*, "in ancient Greece, as in medieval England, unrestrained lamentation by women, meeting a deeply felt psychological need, persists . . . even while proscribed by authority."[12] Lamentation was purposefully excessive and consistently went beyond prescribed boundaries to mark the depths of both individual and collective loss.[13] And excessive, public grief was integral

---

11. In a similar vein, Barthes's insistent gazing at photographs narrates and maintains his relationship with his mother. Woodward ("Freud and Barthes," 102) asserts that "in his theorization of mourning, Freud insists that the end result of the process be that we give up the 'lost' object in the world, that we sever the bonds of love. In *Camera Lucida*, Barthes, on the other hand, explores photography as a 'wound' (21), as a way of refusing to allow the pain of his mother's death to subside and of asserting his attachment to her."

12. Anne Klinck, "Singing a Song of Sorrow: Tropes of Lament," in *Laments for the Lost in Medieval Literature*, ed. Jane Tolmie and M. Jane Toswell (Turnhout, Belgium: Brepols, 2010), 11.

13. Hans van Wees cites Solon's legislation banning women's excess as exceeding the borders of social control, spurring men's violence, which had become a contest for lamentation; the need for the legislation simultaneously makes obvious the relation between lament and praise. Van Wees argues that "the intensification of funerary display of grief is evidently part of a development affecting female behavior more generally: as the masculinity of self-control is being discovered, women are beginning to act out a new role as the 'emotional' sex." "A Brief History of Tears: Gender

to the functioning of a community at war, as Sappho recognizes when she exhorts women to "beat your breasts, girls, and rend your garments!"[14]

Both the Greeks and the Romans imagined grief as integral to figuring heroism. In the *Iliad*, Hecuba's sobbing contrasts her personal emotional needs to the depths of Hector's commitment to Greek ideals of civic duty. Likewise, Virgil's Dido laments Aeneas for loving and leaving her, and the intensity of her despair paradoxically helps to figure him as heroic, a man who abandons personal, sexual love in pursuit of his civic duty (4.305–30 and 4.365–87). Mediterranean literature abounds with examples of women's grieving that contrasts excessive public displays of ostensibly private (female) emotions with public, heroic (male) duty, deploying emotional practices to uphold not only individual men's reputations, but also to recognize emotions as able to figure the limits of their communities.[15]

While of course there are vast differences between the figuring of identity in the classical period and the ideals of medieval feudal and courtly communities, grief has a functional relationship to narrating men's valor.[16] For example, as Klinck points out, in *Beowulf*, community is not threatened, but rather is reinforced by women's grief, and, as in many of these ancient models, "the most intense lamentation [is] assigned to women."[17] Fictional women are vocal, violent mourners in medieval literature, art, and culture; in some medieval cultures, women were employed professionally as keeners, or remunerated mourners.[18] Women were the primary grief workers

---

Differentiation in Archaic Greece," in *When Men Were Men: Masculinity, Power and Identity in Classical Antiquity*, ed. Lin Foxhall and J. B. Salmon (New York: Routledge, 1998), 44.

14. Sappho F 168, from *Sappho et Alcaeus: Fragmenta*, ed. Eva-Marie Voigt (Amsterdam: Athenaeum, 1971), 136.

15. On women's mourning and the ancient Greek tradition see in particular the study of ancient Greek attitudes toward grief and gender in Gail Holst-Warhaft, *Dangerous Voices: Women's Laments and Greek Literature* (New York: Routledge, 2002), 100. See also Rush Rehm, *Marriage to Death: The Conflation of Wedding and Funeral Rituals in Greek Tragedy* (Princeton, NJ: Princeton University Press, 1994).

16. Loring Danforth, for example, identifies a kind of inherent ambivalence between love for and decay of the dying corpse throughout the Mediterranean, and he sees this ambivalence as expressed through the ritualized lamentations contained within the same exact song sung at both weddings and funerals. *The Death Rituals of Rural Greece* (Princeton, NJ: Princeton University Press, 1982), 74–79.

17. Klinck, "Singing a Song of Sorrow," 12.

18. Christina S. Brophy, *Keening Community: Mná Caointe, Women, Death, and Power in Ireland* (Boston: Boston College, 2010); Julie Le Blanc, "Lamentations of the Past: An Echo of the Medieval Irish Keening Women (with Audio-Cassette–Not Received by Library)" (PhD thesis, Trinity College Dublin, 2001); Kaarina Hollo, "Laments and Lamenting in Early Medieval Ireland," in *Medieval Celtic Literature and Society*, ed. Helen Fulton (Dublin: Four Courts, 2005), 83–94; Kristen Mills, "Grief, Gender and Mourning in Medieval North Atlantic Literature" (PhD thesis, University of Toronto, 2013).

of medieval culture.[19] Grieving women are everywhere, from images of that most iconic griever, the Stabat Mater associated with the Virgin Mary's mourning of Christ, to the women who adorn church walls and miniatures and figure in medieval art as mourners of their dead husbands, sons, and lovers.[20] Undoubtedly, the Crusades, the plague, and warfare left women much to mourn, and public spaces were a place to model coping with loss in many different media. These diverse representations conceptualize grieving as both bearing witness to the individual life of the dead and as deploying affective practices to reaffirm the strength of community.

Christine de Pizan (1364–c. 1430), a widowed twenty-five-year-old mother who wrote to provide for her family, offers a model of how one medieval woman deployed laments to figure grief in a way that benefited herself, her immediate community (her family), and the public image of widowhood. In the poetry through which she earned a living, Christine deploys grief to evoke sympathy from her audience, creating community through a shared understanding of widowhood and its attendant emotions. As she laments her deceased husband, Christine describes her new relation to community. Her lamentations run throughout several works, but in "Seulete sui" she depicts widowhood as a solitary, vulnerable endeavor, and she complains that she has lost the male other through which she interpellates her self:

Seulete sui et seulete vueil estre,
Seulete m'a mon douz ami laissiee;
Seulete sui, sanz compaignon ne maistre
Seulete sui, dolente et courrouciee,
Seulete sui, en langueur mesaisiee,
Seulete sui, plus que nulle esgaree,
Seulete sui, sanz ami demouree.[21] (1–7)

I am alone and alone I wish to remain,
alone my sweet love left me;
I am alone, without companion or master,

---

19. See Louise Mirrer, *Upon My Husband's Death: Widows in the Literature and Histories of Medieval Europe* (Ann Arbor: University of Michigan Press, 1992); Yasmina Foehr-Janssens, *La veuve en majesté: Deuil et savoir au féminin dans la littérature médiévale* (Geneva: Droz, 2000); Wendy Pfeffer, "Constant Sorrow: Emotions of the Women Trouvères," in *The Representation of Women's Emotions in Medieval and Early Modern Culture*, ed. Lisa Perfetti (Gainesville: University Press of Florida, 2005), 119–32.

20. Julia Kristeva, "Stabat Mater," trans. Arthur Goldhammer, *Poetics Today* 6, no. 1/2 (January 1, 1985): 133–52.

21. Anne L. Klinck, *Anthology of Ancient and Medieval Woman's Song* (New York: Palgrave Macmillan, 2004), 87–88.

> I am alone, sorrowful and angered,
> I am alone, languishing uncomfortably,
> I am alone, more than anyone abandoned,
> I am alone, without my love I must stay. (trans. mine)

Christine brings her narrator into being through anaphoric repetition of the diminutive *seulete* (little loner), constructing her poetic identity both through her relation to society and through her gender. That is, she repeatedly reiterates not only her enduring loneliness, but also how loneliness defines her relation to community: here she has none, she is the abject, female loner, defined through a void, a vulnerable lack. The sibilance of the *s* in *seulete, sui, sanz* and the endings of *courroucie, mesaisiee* reinforces the sinister difficulties facing widows and seeks to elicit the reader's sympathy.

In her anaphoric insistence on calling herself into being as "alone" in "Seulete sui," Christine recognizes grief's power to narrate (or destroy) subjectivity through relationships with the other. This is what Judith Butler characterizes as existing through and being *confounded by* another. She writes of grief, "For if I am confounded by you, then you are already of me, and I am nowhere without you. I cannot muster the 'we' except by finding the way in which I am tied to 'you,' by trying to translate but finding that my own language must break up and yield if I am to know you. You are what I gain through this disorientation and loss. This is how the human comes into being, again and again, as that which we have yet to know."[22] Butler articulates what the polysemy of our doleful *seulete* suggests—that emotions are both constitutive of the self and find their necessary resonance in relation with the other. Questions about the relation between grief, narrative, and subjectivity posed separately by both Butler and Barthes find resonance in the emotional interrogation posed here by the widow's lament: how do "I" exist if I don't have the emotional community of "you" against and through which my emotional practices resound? Grief interrogates the articulation of a narrative of the self when the emotional interlocutor is lost.

Deprived of the "you" for her "I," Christine's voice recognizes widowhood as a linguistic blow to women's subjectivity, consonant with what Cindy Carson and Angela Jane Weisl have described in another context as socio-linguistic abnegation: "That widowhood describes a specifically female position is born out in language; the word *veuve* has no male equivalent (*veuf* is not attested until the sixteenth century); widowhood had a social, rather than private, meaning, connoting a woman without social standing,

---

22. Judith Butler, *Precarious Life: The Powers of Mourning and Violence* (New York: Verso, 2006), 49.

economic means, or legal representation. However, it also constituted an emancipation and the choice not to remarry."[23] Not only loneliness, but also sadness (*dol*) and anger (*courroux*) complement Christine's characterization of widowhood. And empowered, angry widowhood is an identity position Christine strategically deploys in the debate epistles (in particular, in her last, longest response in MS Harley 4431), yet it is the one she refuses in "Seulete sui."[24]

Whereas the widowed femininity strategically showcased by the terminal, feminine rhymes throughout the poem and highlighted by the "ete" of *seulete* should be a place of liberation, instead Christine constructs it as her emotional imprisonment, a subject position wherein she is muted, like her feminine rhyme.[25] As Yasmina Foehr-Janssens suggests, Christine's deployment of sorrow is relational to her subjective and linguistic disenfranchisement by the men around her.[26] Widowhood is a silent place, an "I" ever searching articulation and resonance with the community of "you," but doomed to never succeed. With its recognition of its own disenfranchisement from the "confounding other," "Seulete sui" seems to conform to the emotion rules articulated within a contemporary medieval conduct manual written for a young bourgeois housewife by her older husband, *Le mesnagier de Paris* (1383), which advises that women adapt their emotions to the pleasure of the men around them. *Le mesnagier* interweaves performances of exemplary femininity with the correct performance of a household community whose harmony is dictated by men's feeling rules.[27] Both texts imagine

---

23. Cindy Carson and Angela Jane Weisl, eds., *Constructions of Widowhood and Virginity in the Middle Ages* (New York: St. Martin's, 1999), 9. Carson and Weisl point to the widow in *Sir Amadace* (109–20) as exemplary of her social construction.

24. See Earl Jeffrey Richards, "'Seulette a Part'—the 'Little Woman on the Sidelines' Takes Up Her Pen: The Letters of Christine de Pizan," in *Dear Sister: Medieval Women and the Epistolary Genre*, ed. Karen Cherewatuk and Ulrike Wiethaus (Philadelphia: University of Pennsylvania Press, 1993), 138–70.

25. See a similar but broader argument about Christine's subjectivity in N. Kıvılcım Yavuz, "'Seulette suy et Seulette veuil estre': The Allegory of Emplacement in Christine de Pizan's *Cité des dames*," in *Selves at Home, Selves in Exile: Stories of Emplacement and Displacement; Proceedings of the Seventh Cultural Studies Symposium, Ege University, Izmir, May 2002*, ed. Ayşe Lahur Kirtunç et al. (Izmir: Ege University, 2003), 101–6.

26. She explains, "Même les manifestations de la douleur s'effacent, car les larmes gardent toujours la trace d'une révolte latente. La lente élaboration d'un héroïsme féminine aboutit . . . à la production d'une figure hiératique, inaccessible aux troubles passionnels, mais dépouillée aussi de toute sensibilité humaine." Foehr-Janssens, *La veuve en majesté*, 101.

27. *Le mesnagier de Paris* (Paris: Livre de Poche, 1994). See also Glenn Burger's discussion of the *Mesnagier* and the intersection of affect and community in marital love in chapter 3 and in the conclusion to *Conduct Becoming: Good Wives and Husbands in the Later Middle Ages* (University of Pennsylvania Press, 2018), 196.

that the correct deployment of appropriate emotional codes—here, about aggrieved widowhood—into the appropriate social milieu will result in a felicitous reading and ultimately bring praise to the woman emoting her lover's worth as commemorative grief.

It is tempting to read widowed women's grief as confinement, disempowerment, disenfranchisement, and passivity—to underscore in real social practices the kinds of muting and disenfranchisement depicted in the near rape of our fictional, silenced Enide, or in the abnegation assumed by Christine's narrator in "Seulete sui." However, as Patricia Ingham has recently argued in her rereading of the place of gender and mourning in Anglo-Saxon culture, women's mourning is *active* work. Ingham critiques recent feminist scholarship that seeks to complicate the association of mourning and femininity as simultaneously repeating the same tropes it seeks to avoid, namely that women must be understood as *passive* in medieval culture. By assuming that women's mourning is a passive activity, writes Ingham, we are missing out on theorizing "the work of women's mourning *for* Anglo-Saxon culture."[28] Mourning performs important emotional work through which communities are created and bound together, and women are its active agents.

And indeed, Christine's work resists characterization as disenfranchisement. While one could read Christine's overt positioning of grief as alienating, grieving is also rife with connection, and thus poetically fecund. Christine's narrator stays hooked into—and indeed defines herself through—mourning in ways that resonate with Barthes's observations on grief's *productivity*. As her subsequent, active engagement in the *Querelle* over the depiction of rape in the *Roman de la Rose* reveals, Christine is no passive victim; in the larger context of her career, it is reasonable to suggest that she deploys mourning here to profit from poetry about widowhood, grief, and an ongoing, productive libidinal attachment to her lost man. Perhaps for Christine, this anaphoric mourning loop is not only poetically productive, but also lucrative: when she deploys grief to forge emotional connections with her readership, grief feeds both her poetry and her children.

Without much evidence for reader reception, such readings are only speculative, but we can surmise that, like most poets, Christine deploys feelings to create an emotional relationship with her readers, implying at least an emotional, if not an economic, sense of community. I agree with

---

28. Patricia Clare Ingham, "From Kinship to Kingship: Mourning, Gender, and Anglo-Saxon Community," in *Grief and Gender: 700–1700*, ed. Jennifer C. Vaught and Lynne Dickson Bruckner (New York: Palgrave Macmillan, 2003), 18.

David Hult that Christine consciously deploys "her weakness to a strategic advantage."[29] The poem's survival and success suggest that the popularity of its emotional framing found resonance among her readership, becoming a parallel emotional community for our now-doubled Christine de Pizan, our Christine-as-narrator. Her paying public becomes the new "you" who reaffirms the relation between grieving, narrative, and an economy of desire, and her strategic deployment of gendered emotion codes throughout her writings (most notably in the *Epistre au dieu d'amour* and the *Querelle*) offers context for understanding medieval emotion as in consonance with performances of gender. Christine's manipulation of convention to elicit sympathy offers a prescient glimpse into how performances of grief and gender could be entwined and deployed in certain emotional communities within which they were expected to find resonance, here reading communities that were by the nature of medieval literacy inherently elite.[30]

Such examples suggest that mourning be considered neither passive nor invisible: grieving can be read as an active process that is deployed by women in tandem with strategic performances of gender, especially exemplary widowhood. Women's despair imagines grief as both powerful sentiment and practical rhetorical tool, and it thereby recognizes emotions as performing concrete relationships, sometimes with an audience. The relation between grief and eroticism that emerges in medieval literature depends on its willing consumption by the public of romance, by a community of elite listeners who imagine that women's grief has a story to tell.

"To Love Is to Narrate": Grief and the Erotics of Storytelling in Romance

If Christine de Pizan's story is one beset by bereaved solitude, the story of femininity in romance is engulfed in an erotics of grief that entwine gender performances with the writing of elite renown and the broadcasting of its

---

29. David F. Hult, "The *Roman de la Rose*, Christine de Pizan, and the Querelle des femmes," in *The Cambridge Companion to Medieval Women's Writing*, ed. Carolyn Dinshaw and David Wallace (Cambridge: Cambridge University Press, 2003), 188.

30. Nadia Margolis, "Christine de Pizan's Life in Lament: Love, Death, and Politics," in *Laments for the Lost in Medieval Literature*, ed. Jane Tolmie and M. Jane Toswell (Turnhout, Belgium: Brepols, 2010), 265–81; Earl Jeffrey Richards, "Christine de Pizan and the Freedom of Medieval French Lyric: Authority, Experience, and Women in the Republic of Letters," in *Christine de Pizan and Medieval French Lyric*, ed. Earl Jeffrey Richards (Gainesville: University Press of Florida, 1998), 1–24; S. H. Rigby, "The Wife of Bath, Christine de Pizan, and the Medieval Case for Women," *Chaucer Review* 35, no. 2 (2000): 133–65.

story lines to an eager listening public. One of the complex knots that binds the center of romance's story line entwines performances of elite masculinity and femininity that are interwoven in service of chivalric renown. The eroticization of grief occurs, I argue, when women's emotions are imagined as deployed to figure men's worth.

Grief is a narrative broadcast through and written on bodies—wounded bodies, disfigured bodies, defiled bodies. In the throes of her grief, Enide claws at her face, writing despair onto her body as public testimony for all to read. As she bemoans her loss, Enide tears out her hair and rends her garments, tropes so widespread that we may identify them as formulaic:

> En haut s'escrie et tort ses poinz;
> De robe ne li remest poinz
> Devant son piz a dessirier;
> Ses crins commence a detirier,
> Et sa tendre face desire. (4603–7)

> She cried out at the top of her voice, wringing her hands and tearing away every thread of the dress at her breast. She began to pull her hair and claw her delicate face. (Staines, 58)

Enide's despair becomes an interpretive apparatus designed to transform her private feelings into publicly legible emotions and assign value to Erec's near-death—her *dol* is a set of signs (the rending of her garments, the tearing of her hair, the scratching of her face) that is multivalent. These signs require a community of readers to be decoded; within romance, they become keys to a communal language of emotion that describes the value of elite masculinity. Enide's *dol* not only invites consideration of the legibility of women's grief and performances of elite femininity, but, eroticized and consumed by onlooking men, it also informs depictions of feudal masculinity and become an invitation for a story.

This invitation to write the story of grief through the body is extended to women throughout romance. Though the scene is particularly well described in *Erec et Enide*, Enide is by no means exceptional in her grief: torn-out hair, scratched countenances, and shredded garments figure in a number of other Arthurian tales, such as the *Atre périlleux* (2070–492); the *Bel Inconnu* (2751–925); *Cligès* (1535–2199); *Conte du graal* (6293–416, 8160–467); *Continuations Perceval* I (504–944; 10063–534); *Continuations Perceval Gerbert* (1613–1861, 10982–1526); *Continuations Perceval Manessier* (32598–979); *Hunbaut* (1779–889); and the *Merveilles Rigomer* (2641–858, 4035–686), suggesting that women's performances of grief are integral to romance.

Indeed, the grieving at the heart of *Erec et Enide* is expanded in Chrétien's later work *Le chevalier au lion* (*Yvain*) in a sustained passage of over four hundred lines (1144–544), where the recently widowed Laudine is aggrieved by the surreptitious intrusion of her husband's adversary and murderer, Yvain, into her castle. Laudine's grieving follows other contemporary depictions, and she disfigures herself to mark her loss:

> A la feÿe s'escrioit
> Si haut qu'ele ne pooit plus,
> Si recheoit pasmee jus.
> Et quant ele estoit relevee,
> Aussi comme femme desvee
> S'i commenchoit a deschirer,
> Et ses chaveus a detirer.
> Ses chaveus tire et ront ses dras,
> Et se repasme a chascun pas,
> Ne riens ne le puet conforter,
> Que son seigneur en voit porter
> Devant li en la biere mort,
> Don ja ne quide avoir confort:
> Pour ce crioit a haute vois. (1146–76)

She cried out at the top of her voice, then fell in a swoon. When she had been set back on her feet, she began, like a madwoman, to tear at herself and pull her hair, clawing her hands and ripping her clothing and fainting at every step. Nothing could comfort her when she saw her lord carried dead before her on the bier. Believing that she could never be consoled, she was screaming in anguish. (Staines, 184)

In this passage, women's grief is written on a body rife with potential—it is at once a site of commemoration and a site for dangerous melancholy. The emphatic qualifiers *ne* and *si* amplify the steadfastness of Laudine's grief, which functions as an obsequy even as its disfiguring wounds threaten to disrupt the sexual economy of her medieval community in ways that repetition suggest could become grotesque.[31] Overplayed, Laudine's disfiguring grief threatens to take her out of the sexual economy of future noble marriage;

---

31. Laudine's self-mutilation-as-commemoration seems to participate in a larger medieval tendency toward commemoration, as Mary Carruthers has pointed out, and what Caroline Walker Bynum has examined in a religious context as ecstatic suffering to praise and commemorate Jesus's sacrifice. See Mary Carruthers, *The Book of Memory: A Study of Memory in Medieval Culture*, 2nd ed.

underdone, it undercuts her deceased husband's legacy and denigrates her own worth as his wife.

The connection between women's grief and their bodies is born out in the twinning of eroticism and narration, which becomes more explicit as these narratives progress from describing women's sorrow to witnessing their grief, in the moment the male gaze eroticizes it within an economy of chivalric renown. When an errant count comes across our sobbing Enide, who is by now on the verge of suicide, for example, he reads her grief as inviting a story not about what *she feels* (made most obvious by the knife she is pointing at herself, highlighted by variations on the same essential cry running through *Philomena*, "oci"), but about what has happened to *her man* ("anquerre del chevalier"):

> A tant ez vos grant aleüre
> Un conte a grant chevalerie,
> Qui de mont loing avoit oïe
> La dame a haute voiz crïer.
> Deus ne la vost mie oblïer;
> Que maintenant se fust ocise,
> Se cil ne l'eüssent sorprise,
> Qui li ont tolue l'espee
> Et enz ou fuerre reboutee.
> Puis descendi li cuens a terre,
> Si li commença a enquerre
> Dou chevalier, qu'ele li die,
> S'ele estoit sa fame ou s'amie.
> "L'un et l'autre," fet ele, "sire.
> Tel duel en ai, n'en puis plus dire.
> Mais poise moi que ne sui morte." (4670–85)

Behold a count came galloping along with a large troop of knights. From afar he had heard the lady's loud screams. God had not intended to abandon her, for by now she would have killed herself had she not been taken by surprise: the knights snatched the sword from her and put it back in the scabbard. The count then dismounted and began by asking her about the knight, and whether she was his sweetheart or his wife. "Both the

---

(Cambridge: Cambridge University Press, 2008); Caroline Walker Bynum, *Jesus as Mother: Studies in the Spirituality of the High Middle Ages* (Berkeley: University of California Press, 1982).

one and the other, sir," she replied. "Such grief is mine I don't know what to tell you. I am in agony not to be dead." (Staines, 58–59)

Enide's cries become a narrative hook, attracting and creating more interaction through their legibility by the errant knight. Indeed, the end rhyme of the passage constructs an audible relationship between knighthood (*chevalerie*) and the act of listening (*oïe*) for the narrative of ladies' cries (*crier*). For Enide, the cries are meant to amplify and perpetuate her sorrow, but for the knight and the audience of romance, they are also simultaneously narrative, highlighted by the pairing of *die/amie*: in romance, to narrate is to love.

This is Enide's invitation to become a storyteller, a curious moment of possibility within Chrétien's romances, which continually seek to mute women's voices.[32] Many of Chrétien's tales problematize women's narratives by aligning storytelling with patriarchy, focusing on the generative place of the author as a metaphoric narrative father, a feature fully explored in scholarship on the lexicon of *semence* in the later *Roman de la Rose*. Yet here we have an explicit invitation for a woman to narrate—and she is invited to tell the story of another man's glory. Here, women's cries are engraved on their bodies and become aligned with storytelling, and they attract men who want stories about other men.

The *erotics* of grieving in romance are most crystalline in *Yvain*, when the eponymous protagonist sneaks into his vanquished adversary's castle to spy on and lament Laudine's self-mutilation. Here, Chrétien best renders the alignment between women's grief and men's desire, a grief eroticized in the locus of storytelling about elite death:

Grant duel ai de ses biax cheveax
Qui fin or passent, tant reluisent;
D'ire m'esprennent et aguisent
quant je li voi romper et trenchier,
N'onques ne poent estanchier
Les larmes qui des iex li chïent.
Toutes ches choses me dessïent.
Atout che qu'il sont plain de lermes,

---

32. Consider, for example, how in the episode of the "Joie de la cour," Enide's female cousin's narrative is silenced and passed over, for Chrétien has already recounted that himself. Likewise, much of the intrigue of *Erec et Enide* revolves around the ways that Enide is forbidden from speaking, for she told a *bad story* about Erec in the intimacy of their marriage bed. E. Jane Burns, *Bodytalk: When Women Speak in Old French Literature* (Philadelphia: University of Pennsylvania Press, 1993); Roberta L. Krueger, *Women Readers and the Ideology of Gender in Old French Verse Romance* (Cambridge: Cambridge University Press, 1993).

> Si que che n'est ne fins ne termes,
> Ne furent onques si bel oeil.
> De che qu'ele pleure me doeil,
> Ne de riens n'ai si grant destreche
> Comme de son vis qu'ele bleche,
> Que ne l'eüst pas deservi,
> C'onques si bien taillé ne vi,
> Ne si fres, ne si coulouré.
> Et che me par a acouré
> Que je li voi sa gorge estraindre.
> Chertes, ele ne se set faindre
> C'au pis qu'ele puet ne se faiche;
> Ne nus cristaus, ne nule glache
> N'est si bele ne si polie. (1466–87)

I lament so deeply her beautiful hair, which shines more brightly than pure gold. I am tormented with anger and rage to see her tear and pull it out. The tears falling from her eyes can never dry. This is not at all to my liking. Although her eyes flow with an endless stream of tears, yet there were never eyes so beautiful, and her tears bring me agony. Still nothing distresses me more than to see her tear her face, by no means deserving of such treatment. I have never seen such a beautifully formed face, so fresh and so delicately colored. And this, that she is her own enemy, is what rends my soul. She cannot refrain from harming herself in the worst of ways, yet no crystal or mirror is so bright and polished. (Staines, 274)

Through Yvain's description, we have this secondary source, a visual—and highly legible—account of her dismay, in her scratched face and fistfuls of hair. Paradoxically, the sites where Laudine marks her grief are precisely the places that Yvain finds the most arousing—when her eyes are bloodshot and tear-filled, he finds that he has "never seen such beautiful eyes"; when she destroys her face, he has never one "so well sculpted seen"; when she is unable to restrain her grief-induced mutilation, he has never seen "a mirror . . . so bright and polished." In describing beauty as blood and gore, the scene points to the ways that Chrétien uses bodies—and specifically, the disfigured and destroyed bodies of women—as reflections, literally here, "mirrors," of the men they mourn.

Though Laudine may be figuratively muted like most of the women in Chrétien's romances, Yvain nonetheless reads her as refracting a visible, legible story of widowed abjection with the mutilation she inscribes onto her body. Laudine annihilates the markers that normally distinguish a valuable noble woman in medieval society: her beautiful countenance, her sublime golden-blond hair, and her sumptuous clothing.[33] In the process, she should be destroying her desirability, for, as a knight in one romance notes, deformity, poverty, and ugliness are not attractive qualities in a woman.[34] Yet her self-mutilation is misread by other characters as an invitation to sexuality—her abjection is paradoxically the pinnacle of her desirability, eroticized, as Yvain's gaze suggests. Oddly, as with Enide, Laudine's wounds of grief are what *constitute* her desirability; they are what inspire the sexual lust of the male onlookers who read her wounds as desirable, her pain as erotic, and her grief as narrative.

Laudine encodes and broadcasts her emotional pain through the mutilation of her own body; her self-inflicted pain, her self-*torture*, are another manifestation of what Elaine Scarry has described in another context as the attempt to make a "radically private [experience] . . . enter the realm of public discourse" as the private body in grief becomes a speaking, narrating body for a reading, interpreting, and receiving public.[35] Widows' emotions, mapped through violent self-mutilation onto their own faces, become a mnemonic narrative of their partners' valor, participating in what Mary Carruthers identifies as a medieval culture of commemoration.[36] In passage after passage, the destruction of the female body figures the value of a man's memory and rewrites grief as praise. The diegetic and the mimetic merge in the storytelling of the wounded female body.[37]

Scenes in medieval romance in which women's disfiguring despair is transformed and eroticized into storytelling are far from anomalous or particular to Chrétien. Women's wailing is widely depicted as an invitation for narrative, both in the canonical Arthurian narratives and in the lesser-known

---

33. See especially the relationship between class, status, and sumptuous clothing detailed in E. Jane Burns, "Speculum of the Courtly Lady: Women, Love, and Clothes," *Journal of Medieval and Early Modern Studies* 29, no. 2 (1999).

34. See Perceval's comments on the ugly maiden in Chrétien's *Conte du Graal*, lines 4542–73.

35. Elaine Scarry, *The Body in Pain: The Making and Unmaking of the World* (Oxford: Oxford University Press, 1987), 6.

36. Carruthers, *Book of Memory*.

37. As Katharine Goodland points out, "female lamenters are believed to commune with the spirit of the dead at the same time that they articulate the emotions and anxieties of their respective communities. Gestures of self-mutilation—tearing the hair and rending the face—align the mourners with the dead: just as death disfigures the body, so the mourners disfigure themselves." Goodland, "'Us for to Wepe No Man May Lett': Accommodating Female Grief in the Medieval English Lazarus Plays," in *The Representation of Women's Emotions in Medieval and Early Modern Culture*, ed. Lisa Perfetti (Gainesville: University Press of Florida, 2005), 92.

romances.[38] In the relatively obscure anonymous thirteenth-century Old French *Li chevaliers as deus espees*, for example, which tells the encounters of Gauvain and an unknown "knight with two swords," a knight hears a woman's cries. The inscrutable, yet intelligible narration of grief he hears from afar requires resolution, and in approaching, he seeks the story of distress:

> Et il s'areste et escouta
> Vne uois faire trop grant duel.
> Et il ua auant, car son uoel
> Seust, por coi tel duel faissoit
> La uois, car point ne se taisoit. (7251–55)[39]

> And he stopped and listened
> to a voice that was making too great grief.
> And he went ahead, because he wanted
> to know why the voice was making such great grief,
> because it wasn't stopping at all. (trans. mine)

Here, the woman and her suffering are metonymized, reduced to the singularity of *la voix*—the voice that wails, that invites investigation and that, once found, requires explanation. Her "voice" not only attests to her suffering, but it also becomes an erotic draw, the possibility of a story. The voice becomes an invitation to narrate, to find out what is wrong.

Similarly, in *Claris et Laris*, a quest-based thirteenth-century Old French Arthurian romance grouped loosely around a friendship between the titular protagonists, a maiden's grief attracts one of the errant knights, named "the Ugly Strong One" (Li Laiz Hardiz), who in turn demands to know the story of the man she mourns:

> Desus seoit une pucele
> Plourant, sa main a sa maissele;
> Trop merveilleus duel demenoit
> Pour .i. chevalier, que tenoit
> Mort et tue en son giron. . . .
> Demande li a belement,
> Se li chevaliers durement

---

38. See *Chaitivel*, 71–143; *Claris et Laris*, where the woman kills herself once her request is completed, 20836–1110; *La continuation Perceval 1*, 19420–606; *La continuation Perceval 2*, 26552–824; *La continuation Perceval Gerbert*, 8906–9285, 10016–192; *Fergus*, 4455–830; *Lancelot*, 4157–532; and *Yder*, 2519–877, 3552–749, 3750–4415.

39. *Li chevaliers as deus espees*, ed. Wendelin Foerster (Halle: Max Niemeyer, 1877), 225.

Iert navrez, que ele tenoit,
Et quel part ele le menoit ?[40] (9786–90; 9796–99)

On top of that a maiden was sitting
Crying, her hand on her cheek;
Too marvelous grief was she exhibiting
For one knight, whom she held
Dead and killed in her lap. . . .
He asks her nicely
Whether the knight was mortally
Wounded, whom she held,
And where she was from?

The maiden explains that she will soon perish from her grief, but that it has one last function: to tell a story that will inspire vengeance (9807–10). Whether meant to narrate a dead man's glory or inspire other men to avenge a wronged, fallen knight, grief is romance's storytelling: grief propels narrative transfers from one man to another, and women's grief has potential.

In a rereading of *Erec et Enide* at the intersection of eroticized grief and storytelling, the female body is both palimpsest and parchment, a dead man's story that interpellates a reader and functions as a site for future potential narration for the passing knight. Grief creates a narrative economy inside the text itself, with writers (that is, women like Enide and Laudine), readers (that is, the men their grief attracts), and material to discuss (that is, their lovers' dead bodies). This narrative economy might be reformulated as a reading community, a group of people sharing and making meaning together by interpreting signs, particularly emotions. In using Enide's self-mutilation to create a textual community of authors and readers, the passage frames Enide's grief not as a *private* performance for herself, but rather as a *public* text, open to interpretation by others.[41] Rather than identifying traditionally gendered formulations of space in this contrast, we can instead seek a layering of grief's erotic and narrative potential within the culture of romance, rendering both women's emotions and their bodies as participants in figuring the narrative of noble identity concomitantly in multiple spaces.

---

40. *Claris et Laris*, ed. Corinne Pierreville (Paris: Champion, 2008).
41. See comparable scenes in *L'âtre périlleux*, 2070–492; *Le Bel Inconnu*, 2751–925; *Cligès*, 1535–2199; *La conte du Graal*, 6293–416, 8160–467; *La continuation Perceval 1*, 504–944, 10063–534; *La continuation Perceval Gerbert*, 1613–1861, 10982–11526; *Erec et Enide*, 4280–558; *Hunbaut*, 1779–889; *Les merveilles de Rigomer*, 2641–858, 4035–686; *Yvain* 1144–544.

Women's bodies become sites of narrative potential, where embodied grief not only produces narratives of commemoration (memory) but also reiterates the values of the living (community). Yet how well do these commemorative narratives—written on bodies, and not committed to parchment—withstand the test of time? In the face of the count's unbearable lust and his assertions that he has "never beheld such beauty," the female body seems a mutable tablet on which men's desires efface women's emotions. After all, although Enide can write the story of her grief by marking her own body, once that grief is eroticized and consumed by another man, it becomes illegible, as impermanent as her destroyed beauty. In his work on death in Old French romance, Simon Gaunt wonders whether, by extension, death itself is gendered and performed differently, with a different sense of permanence for medieval men than for medieval women.[42]

We might ask, then, what is the work of Enide's and Laudine's scratched countenances for the culture of romance? Enide's grief is eroticized in the moment that her grief for Erec creates the possibility of narrative *for another man*. The erotic draw of her narrative is directly proportional to her wailing, her screams, her tears—she figures men's glory through her despair, and it is this despair that is intensely erotic to other men, for it functions as a promise.[43] Women's grief is a promise that both narrates the worth of the dead man present and offers future renown to onlooking men who act as bravely as the man being mourned. Women's grief promises future mourning to onlookers; it promises narration as commemoration; it promises men immortality. Women's grief is eroticized in romance because it promises a transferal of commemoration and valor from the wounded body of the dead warrior to onlooking men. After all, it is only after he has heard and witnessed Enide's grief, listened to the story of Erec's accomplishments and seen Erec's wounded body that the count exclaims, "I would like to marry the lady despite her displeasure. I have never beheld such beauty, nor have I so coveted a woman!" (4654–700).

The perceived transience of women's grief—both refused and effaced by its translation into men's desire—suggests that women's narratives somehow, as Ingham puts it, "facilitate the very cultural future that they, as mourners, are understood to be refusing."[44] That is, in twelfth-century romance, women's work in mourning seems to both promote dead men and

---

42. See chapter 5, "Talking the Talk / Walking the Walk: Gendering Death," in Gaunt, *Love and Death in Medieval French and Occitan Courtly Literature*.
43. See J. L. Austin, *How to Do Things with Words* (Oxford: Clarendon, 1975).
44. Ingham, "From Kinship to Kingship," 30–31.

rewrite their own circulation into an economy of eroticism, even as women often stridently refuse the sexualized misreading of their emotional narrative, as Enide and Laudine both do. In twelfth-century romance, women's grief writes emotional stories about men *for other men's erotic consumption*; women's grief is foundational to the narrative of chivalric glory, and it is eroticized in service of the sacrifice of men's bodies that is essential to the functioning of feudalism.

Grievable Bodies and the Romance of Courtly Masculinity

Marie de France's twelfth-century Anglo-Norman *lai Chaitivel* explores the relation between grief and gender in a narrative that looks awry on the male gaze that dominates Chrétien's work. *Chaitivel*, known within the text also as *Les quatre doels* (The Four Mournings), features a beautiful lady who hosts a tournament to select a husband. But disaster strikes, and instead of celebrating, she must subsequently mourn the loss of three suitor-knights and the concomitant grave injury of a fourth, now known as Chaitivel because of his genital wound. In a speech about her own allure, the lady identifies narrative (the *lai*) as a vehicle for permanent commemoration not only of her men, but of herself:

> "Ja mes dame de mun parage
> tant nen iert bele, pruz ne sage,
> tels quatre ensemble n'amera
> ne en un jur si nes perdra,
> fors vus tut sul ki nafrez fustes,
> grant poür de mort en eüstes.
> Pur ceo que tant vus ai amez,
> vueil que mis doels seit remembrez.
> De vus quatre ferai un lai
> e Quatre Doels le numerai."
> Li chevaliers li respundi
> hastivement, quant il l'oï:
> "Dame, faites le lai novel,
> si l'apelez Le Chaitivel!" (195–208)[45]

---

45. Marie de France, *Lais de Marie de France*, ed. Laurence Harf-Lancner (Paris: Livre de Poche, 1990), 258.

CHAPTER 2

> "Never was a woman of my standing
> so beautiful nor valorous nor wise
> such that she loved four men at the same time
> and lost them all on the same day,
> except he who was made to suffer,
> and for whom we greatly feared death.
> Because I have loved you so much,
> I want my grief to be remembered.
> Of all four of you I will make a story
> and 'Four Griefs' I will call it."
> The knight responds to her quickly,
> when he hears it:
> "Lady, make the new story,
> and call it the Wounded One!"

Here, the focus is on the woman and her emotions; it is on her process negotiating—and *eroticizing*—grief. Both the lady and her wounded knight imagine that grief begets narrative and that storytelling is the natural successor to injury and loss. In the lady's formulation, narration is a force that will continue to commemorate permanently, beyond the lives of individual people, and it is meant to tell of the lives of the glamorous, the beautiful, and the powerful—and, specifically, powerful women. The lady's move to narrative is not simply about the men's prowess as fighters. Rather, she seeks to record her grief—*mis doels*—for eternity, commemorating not only men's sacrifice but, more prominently, *her* beauty and pain.[46] Marie's *lai* imagines women's grief as active, productive work—it is emotional work for their own eternal commemoration. It can also be work to uphold narratives of beauty, wisdom, and desirability, writing and broadcasting the story of elite femininity through an erotics of loss. Loss is eroticized in the moment where men sacrifice themselves for her; her suffering attests both to her affective attachment to these lost lovers *and* eroticizes her own worth.

---

46. In other *lais*, death is associated with narrative, too: dead lovers are buried in the same grave as a way to narrate the depth of their commitment to each other, even when there is no speaking body to mourn them (*Deus amanz*, 153–250); likewise in *Yonec* the burial becomes a legible sign entwining love and death eternally with the story of the swan-lover and his lady (455–554).

In romances authored by men, men's alignment with grieving differs. In the passage where Yvain spies on Laudine's grieving, the male gaze frames the relationship between grief and desire around Yvain's pain and arousal by Laudine's grief. As we saw, he complains at length in a passage I summarize here:

> grant duel ai de ses biax cheveax . . .
> D'ire m'esprennent et aguisent
> quant je li voi romper et trenchier. . . .
> C'au pis qu'ele puet ne se faiche;
> Ne nus cristaus, ne nule glaçhe
> N'est si bele ne si polie. (excerpted from 1463–85)
>
> I lament so deeply her beautiful hair. . . . I am tormented with anger and rage to see her tear and pull it out. . . . She cannot refrain from harming herself in the worst of ways, yet no crystal or mirror is so bright and polished. (Staines 274)

Using the same lexicon of grieving ("I lament," "anguish," "torment"), Yvain marks not pain, but desire. The more Yvain sees Laudine disfigure herself, the more aroused he becomes by her beauty; he grieves as she grieves, but his grief eroticizes hers in service of his own desire. As she mutilates her body as an expression of her pain as a memory of her dead husband, his desire grows.

The pain/pleasure association resonates eerily with the rape-like lust of the count who wants Enide to marry him, and it certainly resonates with the hypersexualization of widows in the fabliaux, as I discussed in the introduction. While some scholars claim that romance itself is predicated on rape, Yvain's lust is not for *unrequited* possession (that is, for forced domination), but rather to possess for himself the heart of a lady who is willing to destroy her beauty in order to express her lover's worth. The ways that Laudine destroys herself are the very same ways that Yvain finds her attractive—an erotics of self-mutilation, a displaced lust for loss. This self-destruction, so prized by Yvain, not only makes Laudine's unknowable psychological distress readable (that is, a kind of translation made intelligible by men's gazing and witnessing), but it also memorializes her dead husband (that is, a kind of dissemination of the narrative of chivalric renown). In effect, Yvain conflates Laudine's bodily expression of her grief with his desire for a woman who will vociferously narrate the lost glory of her lover. In this way, his expression of lust is not for the woman before him, but for the glory of another man, a transference underscoring the homoerotics of death in chivalric romance.

In insisting both on the permanency of Laudine's grief and its eroticization by Yvain, the episode constructs grief as a chiasmatic commemoration in which the depth of the widow's grief writes the height of her dead man's glory. Not only does Laudine experience grief, but her grief is broadcast and received, "read" and desired by onlookers and consumed as part of a narrative economy of her dead husband's glory. Both Laudine's depiction of grief and Yvain's reading of it offer a key to understanding the spectrum of desire undergirding chivalric masculinity within the romance. And it is this narrative—the self-destruction of grief for another man, written by and through the body of a woman—that Yvain finds irresistible. The self-destruction so prized by Yvain not only makes Laudine's unknowable psychological distress readable, but it also memorializes her dead husband for a courtly readership. In its extended dedication to tying desire to destruction, lust to grief, this passage in *Yvain* completes the work that *Erec et Enide* began, finally fully tying female desirability to a semiotics of grief about other men.

Taken together, these readings suggest that men's desire and women's grief are imagined as entwined in romance, both performing important work for their community of elites, internally within the text and within the elite readership of romance. Widows like Enide and Laudine—who are often read as objects of men's desire—are not merely rape bait, as some have suggested. Rather, romance imagines widows as desirable for their grief, and depicts women's mourning as desirable—eroticized—because of its relation to narratives that propel models of exemplary feudal masculinity through stories of renown. Likewise, men's desire for these widows is simultaneously a desire for other, dead men, and for the abject grief that is eroticized precisely for its promise of immortality. At its heart, the commemorative process of grief that is so desirable to onlookers is one that is ultimately about the immortality achievable only through storytelling.

The impermanence of women's wounds invites us to consider not only who may *grieve*, but also who or what is *grievable* within the community of medieval romance. We might return to query, with Judith Butler, what kinds of losses may be mourned, what kinds of lives are valuable. In *Precarious Life*, Butler identifies a critical tension surrounding grief: "Some lives are grievable, and others are not; the differential allocation of grievability that decides what kind of subject is and must be grieved, and which kind of subject must not, operates to produce and maintain certain exclusionary conceptions of who is normatively human: *what counts as a livable life and a grievable death?*"[47] Butler's concerns are the politics of the post-9/11 American response to the war on terror, but her question elucidates the nexus of privilege, gender, and class at play in contextualizing grief in any era, and it invites us to consider not only who may grieve, but also who may be mourned, what lives have worth. In a medieval context, I read her questions as drawing attention to the interplay of class, narrative, and gender within the community of readers of the text. The literary texts that have been transmitted to us seem to respond that (1) it is only noble bodies that are grievable in romance; (2) both men's and women's bodies can mark that grief, but that women's *plaies d'amour* are impermanent; and (3) grief is fundamental to courtly masculinity.

Of course, noble women are not the only ones who grieve in romance—after all, men suffer for love, too. Men's mourning is imagined as a sickness, a malady destined to be cured. Consider the twinning of death and love by the lovesick male *amant* in *Le Bel Inconnu,* who complains to his lady, "Vostre amors *m'a donné la mort*" (your love *has given me death*) (4083–88, translation and emphasis mine).[48] Written by Renaud de Beaujeu, the thirteenth-century Old French *Bel Inconnu* stages a kind of prototypical lovesickness repeated in romances from *Floire et Blancheflor* to *Tristan et Yseut,* from *Le roman de la violette* to *Lancelot,* and his association of love with the grief surrounding death is particularly poignant when he says that her love is killing him. Earlier, in Chrétien's work, Yvain's excessive lovesickness is also described as a kind of festering disease, a dangerous and liminal performance of elite masculinity called into being in relation to the violent eroticism of Laudine's grief:

> Bien a vangiee, et si nel set,
> La dame le mort son seignor;
> Venjanche en a prise gregnor
> Que ele prendre ne l'en peüst
> S'Amors vengie ne l'eüst,
> Qui si douchement le requiert
> Que par les iex el cuer le fiert;
> Et cist cols a plus grant duree
> Que cols de lanche ne d'espee:
> Colz d'espee garist et saine

---

47. Butler, *Precarious Life,* xiv–xv.
48. Renaud de Beaujeu, *Le Bel Inconnu: Roman d'aventures,* ed. Gwladys Perrie Williams (Paris: H. Champion, 1929). Emphasis mine.

> Mout tost, des que mires y paine;
> Et la plaie d'Amours empire
> Quant ele est plus pres de son mire.
> Cele plaie a mesire Yvains
> Dom il ne sera jammais sains,
> C'Amors s'est toute a lui rendue. (*Yvain*, 1366–82)

> Without knowing, the lady had avenged well her lord's death. She had obtained greater revenge than she ever would have accomplished had Love not avenged the death by attacking Yvain so gently, striking his heart through his eyes. This wound lasts longer than one made by lance or sword, for a sword cut is soon healed and made whole when a physician tends it. But the wound of Love worsens the nearer its physician. (Staines, 273)

Here, love is violence, love threatens death: it is described as a wound, a *plaie* that cuts deep into the body of the lover. It is a wound that heals even more slowly than battle scars because it is unrequited—and, implicitly, misdirected. Reinscribed by every glance and sigh until eased in sexual fulfillment, the *dol* and *douleur* of the lovesick *amant* are modes of grief as intensely felt as those inscribed on the wounded bodies of disheveled widows.[49] The wound of the sword heals to become a narrative of glory, yet despite all care and attention, the wound of love is continually reinscribed, a continual reopening of the body.

Men's grief for women is both constitutive of the courtly condition *and* a temporary, impermanent reminder of their emotional distress: lovesickness, unlike battle scars, is meant to go away, through the healing balm of sexual conquest at the heart of the romance endeavor. In *Philomena*, for example, Tereus's tormented sighs are only heard for so long before he takes possession of Philomena's body—his lovesickness, if it must be called that, is predicated on its moment of future abnegation in sexual completion, yet it underwrites the entire narrative, ultimately allying desire with death. Lancelot also pines for Guinevere throughout *Le chevalier de la charrette*:

> Pansers li plest, parlers li grieve.
> Amors mout sovant li escrieve
> La plaie que feite li a;
> Onques anplastre n'i lia
> Por garison ne por santé,

---

[49]. See, for example, this typification in Gaunt, *Love and Death*.

> Qu'il n'a talant ne volanté
> D'emplastre querre ne de mire,
> Se sa plaie ne li anpire (1335–42)

> Thinking pleased him; speaking pained him. Often Love reopens the wound he inflicted, and the patient never applies a dressing for his recovery and good health, for he has no intention or desire of seeking a remedy or doctor unless his wound grows deeper. (Staines, 186)

All these passages imagine that men's mourning—their *dol* and *douleur*, their *plaie*—is tightly caught up in the ache of their desire; their wounds are transitory witnesses to a lady's desirability, forgotten once assuaged. They suffer for an object not yet attained; they fret over the object of their sexual conquest; they feel death's threat as a symbol of their lady's erotic draw.[50] Yet for none of these men is lovesickness a permanent state, and their extended grief is shown to be anticipatory of sexual completion, as suggested here by the use of the conditional (*se*) and words of questing (*querre*) that suggest future possibility rather than present foreclosure.[51]

Tristan et Yseut, perhaps the most memorable romance predicated on the alignment of death and love, of grieving and desiring, is the story of a misdirected and ill-fated love triangle between a king; his nephew, Tristan, whom he sends to fetch his new bride; and the beautiful Yseut. The extant manuscript evidence attests to the romance's popularity, and in every version and translation of the tale, the lovers' affair is documented in ways that align *dol* and *amor*, especially in the moment when the love potion's malediction is explained to the lovesick couple: "'In that cup you have drunk not love alone, but love and death together.' The lovers held each other; life and desire trembled through their youth, and Tristan said, 'Well then, come Death'" (Gottfried, *Tristan*, book 4).[52] And again, in the Thomas *Tristan*,

> De nostre amur fine et verai
> Quant ele jadis guarri ma plai,
> Del beivre qu'ensemble beuimes
> En la mer, quand suppris en fumes.

---

50. Which in some readings constructs the woman as an object, as in Slavoj Žižek, "Courtly Love, or, Woman as Thing," in *Metastases of Enjoyment: Six Essays on Women and Causality*, edited by Slavoj Žižek (London: Verso, 1994), 89–112.

51. There are, of course, some exceptions in which lovers do die for each other, but it is rare for a man to die of lovesickness. See in particular *La continuation Perceval Gerbert*, 14557–998; see also ibid., 1613–1861; *Deus amanz*, 153–250; *Tristan Thomas* fr. 5, 1541–1815; *Yonec*, 393–454, 455–554.

52. *Tristan et Yseut*, ed. Christianne Marchello-Nizia (Paris: Gallimard, 1995), 538.

> El beivre fud la nostre mort,
> Nus n'en avrum ja mais confort;
> A tel ure duné nus fu
> A nostre mort l'avum beü.[53] (2645–52)

> Of our fine love and you will see
> when she has already healed my wound
> from the beverage that we drank together
> when we were surprised at sea.
> In this beverage was our own death,
> and neither of us will ever have relief from it;
> at that time at which it was given to us,
> we drank in it our own death.

The potion guarantees Tristan and Yseut's fateful demise, and it figures their love through death, to the point where, as Tristan points out, "they could uncouple our bodies but not our love" (noz cors feseient deservrer / Mais l'amur ne porent oster) (Thomas, 2667–68). Likewise, in her version of the Tristan story, the *Lai de chèvrefeuille*, Marie de France uses a variant of *dol* to imagine love as suffering, commenting that "he who loves loyally / is very aggrieved and taken in thought / when he does not have his desires" (ki eime mut lealment / Mut est dolenz e trespensez / Quant il nen ad ses volentez) (22–24).[54] Tristan and Yseut's love is perhaps one of the most problematic in romance, in that the potion offers no solution, no possible resolution or escape—there is no felicitous outcome where their desires are finally sated, except, literally, in death. It is no surprise, then, that the romance systematically equates love with suffering, grief, and death. And here, digital humanities work can offer some confirmation of what careful reading supposes: in the ARFTL TFA database, of the sixty-six occurrences of *dolur* in their Béroul *Tristan* version alone, *amur* and *amor* collocate with *dolur* in the same sentence over half the time (twenty-five and nine times, respectively). Love and suffering are entwined.

Lovesickness is well explored in the scholarship on medieval physiology, yet it is often treated as gendered male, though many medieval texts offer complicated examples where both men and women mourn as an expression of love.[55] Discussing the German tradition associated with Gottfried's

---

53. Ibid., 194–5.
54. Ibid., 213.
55. Mary Frances Wack, *Lovesickness in the Middle Ages: The Vatican and Its Commentaries* (Philadelphia: University of Pennsylvania Press, 1990); Esther Zago, "Women, Medicine, and the Law

Tristan, for example, Katja Altpeter-Jones suggests lovesickness is aligned with masculinity and that women's active work is in *healing*—rather than *suffering*—the wounds of love.[56] Yet, within the broader context of the romances in consideration here, that gender equation is belied by the function of the love wound itself: the love wounds our grieving women write onto their bodies create the mark of an emotional community, imagined as particular to noble love; women's wounds mark courtly community through an erotics of grief.

Yet when grief threatens to become permanent, that stasis becomes threatening to the functioning of medieval communities predicated on masculinities secured through confrontation with other men. Consider how in *Floire et Blancheflor*, Floire's ceaseless mourning of his supposedly dead Blancheflor becomes problematic, as it takes him out of an economy of homosocial interaction with his peers:

> Quant Flores ot qu'ele estoit morte,
> molt durement se desconforte,
> la color pert, li cuers li ment,
> tos pasmés ciet el pavement.[57] (691–94)

> When Floire heard that she was dead,
> he was very heavily aggrieved,
> lost his color, his heart was unsteady,
> and he fell in a swoon to the pavement.

Flore's excessive fainting recalls the extended scenes of women's grief typified by Enide and Laudine. His mother's criticisms of Blancheflor, his love / grief object, suggest that he is directing his libidinal energy toward an inappropriate match, and his excessive grief becomes a performance of masculinity that his mother recognizes as damaging, and for which she sharply

---

in Boccaccio's *Decameron*," in *Women Healers and Physicians: Climbing a Long Hill*, ed. Lilian R. Furst (Lexington: University Press of Kentucky, 1997), 64–78.

56. Altpeter-Jones writes, "There is, in other words, a peculiar dynamic inherent in medieval texts about love and the suffering love causes: men tend to love and suffer in disproportionate numbers while women suffer only occasionally. In addition, their suffering differs conceptually from that of men. German Minnesang, for example, offers a voice almost exclusively to loving and suffering men; and while Reimpaardichtung and Versnovellen portray men and women as in love and as suffering when the fulfillment of desire is impossible, these texts tend to reserve depictions of the suffering of love as an actual somatic ailment or wound for male lovers alone." Katja Altpeter-Jones, "Love Me, Hurt Me, Heal Me: Isolde Healer and Isolde Lover in Gottfried's *Tristan*," *German Quarterly* 82, no. 1 (2009): 8.

57. Robert d'Orbigny, *Le conte de Floire et Blancheflor*, ed. and trans. Jean-Luc Leclanche (Paris: Honoré Champion, 2003).

criticizes him. We learn, through men's excessive lovesick grief for women in texts such as *Floire et Blancheflor*, *Yvain*, *Erec et Enide*, and *Lancelot*, among many others, that men's grief is meant to be ephemeral, effaced by the chase and conquest of the lady as part of their courtly identity; stasis brings unacceptable stagnation among other men. If anything, lovesickness is meant to bear witness to an emotional education in elite affect: imagined as fleeting and curable, men's lovesickness is sometimes explicitly aligned with their quest to become a good ruler, as in the twelfth-century Greek romance *Belthandros and Chrysandza*, where Belthandros must explicitly become a good lover by suffering in order to assume his throne.

Taken another way, the negativity surrounding men's lovesick grief for women seems to suggest that women are not the correct objects of grief—they are not its mournable subjects. Their bodies are impermanent sites for narrating glory, their love often gazed upon as transient by errant knights who hear their cries of distress as an invitation to sex. In romance, women's bodies are markers for men's glory, and as such they are imperfect objects of adoration and commemoration in a community geared toward appreciation of the male, noble subject. I suggest that romance's interest in declaring noble men's bodies the appropriate target of erotic grief coincides with the intersection of grief, eroticism, and narrative.

We may already intuit that, in medieval literature, women are supposed to mourn men; a long tradition of public grieving dating to the Greeks supports the intersection of war culture, public grief, and masculinity. Women's grief writes the narrative of romance: love, writ and wailed large through grief, proclaims noble men's valor. Grief for men—and pointedly, not for women—is at the core of the romance endeavor, for ultimately it is the consumption of narratives about damaged bodies—the *plaie* that mark their bravery on their bodies—that is the story of men's worth. Men's bodies become the grievable objects of *all* grief in romance, whether in the sighs of the ladies longing for them, the wails of women mourning them, or the libidinal transference from a man watching a woman mourn them.[58] Medieval texts show that, at its most productive, women's grief *is* narrative. As such, medieval romance interrogates Freud's model of pathologizing melancholia as an unproductive form of feminine hysteria, proffering instead a

---

58. Ingham ("From Kinship to Kingship," 19), incisively writes that "the gendering of the loss of family means that the fiction of a transcendental community beyond the grave, beyond the particularities of specific families, bodies, or lives can remain tied to men and to brotherhoods. This putatively more sophisticated view of sovereignty is thus founded upon a tradition of managing grief by way of gender, and dependent upon the important activity of female mourning."

model wherein the emotion is fundamental to framing the desires that bind human communities and make lives matter, in Butler's terms.

The threat of death and the frequent mourning that permeate romance offer a forum for commentary on the social nature of medieval emotions. Grief is eroticized within romance because it serves the ends of feudalism: mourning is done for appropriate bodies, appropriate sacrifice, appropriate loss, and rewarded with appropriate renown, through the promise of narrative. The most valiant men are desired and mourned in service of their political and social systems; women's tears and men's envy combine to write the narrative of courtly glory based on men's sacrifice in combat.

I have argued here that in romance, grief functions as a kind of narrative, one that serves as an expression of sorrow and loss, writ large on the bodily signs of the mourner, embodied and broadcast through tears, sighs, the rending of garments, the pulling out of hair. Yet an attentiveness to emotions invites a reconsideration of the gendered polemics of grief: what if it is not the gendered paradigm of the emotion that is eroticized—that is, the desirability or sexualization of the *mourner*—but the gendered paradigm of the libidinal *object* of that emotion? I suggest that our readings of the erotics of grief in romance create a space for imagining grief to be available as an emotion to both men and women, one that must have a proper erotic object and which, if writ permanently, is meant to be in service of chivalric masculinity. In the next chapter, I consider how the erotics of grief function in the homosocial world of men mourning on the battlefields of chansons de geste, from a lachrymose Charlemagne to a morose Arthur.

Chapter 3

Masculinity, Mourning, and Epic Sacrifice

> But in the place of this event, place is given over, for the same wound, to substitution, which repeats itself there, retaining of the irreplaceable only a past desire.
>
> —Jacques Derrida, *The Work of Mourning*

In the last chapter, I explored how in romance, women's grief was eroticized as a promise of narration for men. Yet the pervasive loss and mourning that structure the chansons de geste nuance our understanding of the relation between the erotics of grief, genre, and gender. I argue that we might reread chansons de geste as songs about men's work in the erotics of grief, and perhaps nowhere is this more prominent than in the *Chanson de Roland*, a recounting of the sacrifice of one of Charlemagne's most trusted men, Roland, in order to save his army by calling for reinforcements. Its first two *laisses* have been endlessly dissected because they offer a world in a verse, foreshadowing the success of Christian conquerors in what the text casts as a morally justified (if historically compromised and wildly propagandistic) triumph over Saracen adversaries.[1] Yet the last *laisse* of the poem, perhaps also its most provocative, is much less discussed. The *Roland* concludes not with the public glory of battlefield triumph, but rather with the private sorrow of death, as Charlemagne wails, "'Deus . . . si penuse est

---

1. Susan P. Millinger, "Epic Values: The Song of Roland," in *The Middle Ages in Texts and Texture: Reflections on Medieval Sources*, ed. Jason Glenn (Toronto: University of Toronto Press, 2011), 141–52; Susan L. Rosenstreich, "Reappearing Objects in *La chanson de Roland*," *French Review* 79, no. 2 (December 1, 2005): 358–69.

ma vie!' / Pluret des oilz, sa barbe blanche tiret" ("Oh god . . . my life is full of toil!" / Tears fall from his eyes and he tugs at his white beard) (4001–2).[2]

Charlemagne's closing tears showcase some of the core questions of epic that are highlighted particularly well in the *Song of Roland*: Whose sacrifice is valuable, memorable, worthwhile? What is the best way to honor a life? The ultimate lines of the *Song of Roland* offer a response: we should grieve, most publicly and openly. Taking the last *laisse* of the poem as an interpretive key casts Charlemagne's world as shrouded in loss, with moments of deep and enduring sorrow punctuated by triumph; the last *laisses* render the *Chanson de Roland* a meditation on the relation between grief, elite masculinity, and narrative.

In a genre where men's most abiding legacy is their triumph over other men, the framing of the *Song of Roland* in sorrow seems enigmatic at best. Yet privileging Charlemagne's wretched outburst in the epilogue over the boastful vaunting proffered by the prologue may invite a rereading of chansons de geste. Specifically, and as the *Roland* suggests, turning toward emotions allows us to reevaluate the landscape of hypermasculinity within epic, and it invites us to query the relation between emotion and manliness in one subset of medieval nobles, those who are dedicated to conducting warfare. Whereas scholars such as Virginie Greene have considered how *women* mourn for men in both romance and epic, by focusing, for example, on Aude's famous lament for Roland, *men's* mourning other men is equally integral to figuring community in chansons de geste.[3]

In this chapter, I explore the homosocial emotional world of medieval men in battle in texts such as the *Song of Roland*, *Aliscans*, *Le roman de Rou*, and *La mort le roi Artu* to better understand how grief, desire, and masculinity intersect in service of elite culture predicated on sacrifice. I argue that the emotional community of the chanson de geste is undergirded by complex performances of masculinity tied to eroticizing grief in service of narrating elite community.

The Genre and Its Emotions

The *Chanson de Roland* is but one example of hundreds of texts loosely grouped under the generic rubric of "epic," or, for the medieval French-speaking

---

2. Citations are taken from *La chanson de Roland*, ed. and trans. Ian Short, 2nd ed. (Paris: Livre de Poche, 1990). Translations are from *The Song of Roland and Other Poems of Charlemagne*, trans. Simon Gaunt and Karen Pratt (Oxford: Oxford University Press, 2016).

3. Virginie Greene, "Le deuil, mode d'emploi, dans deux romans de Chrétien de Troyes," *French Studies: A Quarterly Review* 52, no. 3 (1998): 259.

world, chansons de geste. Yet these generic terms are at best slippery, encompassing texts whose only certain commonality is their commitment to representing feudal warfare. As Thomas Greene has pointed out, for every pattern that emerges in epic, one or several texts will contradict it.[4] Chansons de geste seem concerned with the struggle for feudal justice, which can take the form of infighting among neighbors, far from the violent combat abroad among those seeking Christian justice for Jerusalem. Epics from all eras test the boundaries of fighters' masculinity in order to imagine and deploy images of the hero for a larger cause that resonates with their audience; here I will use the chanson de geste to discuss the Old French literary tradition and epic to refer to the subject matter of promoting heroism through depictions of war. Lynn Ramey has recognized epic as inherently political, arguing that it articulates not only the more obvious and public feudal goals of a patron's family, but also the private and personal financial desires of the bard telling the tale.[5] In scholarship rethinking the relation between medieval studies and the construction of nationalism, epics have been reread to better understand the working of what might loosely be described as studies of dynastic imperialism.[6]

When we think of emotions in epic material, it is often to reify their extremes: the absence of fear, the absence of cowardice; or to condemn their presence: excess of pride or rage. Epic seems to suggest that men are successful if they harness *appropriate* emotions to fuel their combat; hysteria, fear, and sadness seem to have little overt place within the performance of masculinity in the face of the violence that structures the genre.[7] Initially, epic appears to lend itself to *denying* men's emotional ties to the battlefield, especially those thought to be "weak" or "excessive"—qualifications most

---

4. Thomas M. Greene, "The Natural Tears of Epic," in *Epic Traditions in the Contemporary World: The Poetics of Community*, ed. Margaret Beissinger, Jane Tylus, and Susanne Lindgren Wofford (Berkeley: University of California Press, 1999), 189.

5. Lynn Tarte Ramey, *Christian, Saracen and Genre in Medieval French Literature: Imagination and Cultural Interaction in the French Middle Ages* (New York: Routledge, 2013), 36.

6. Ibid.; Millinger, "Epic Values." See the late nineteenth-century studies of epic with which the field of medieval French studies was co-constructed in works such as Joseph Bédier, *Les légendes épiques*, vol. 3 (Paris: H. Champion, 1929). The scholarship underscores the colonial and nationalist paradigms inflecting these earlier readings. See, as a brief sample, Patricia Clare Ingham and Michelle R. Warren, *Postcolonial Moves: Medieval through Modern* (New York: Palgrave Macmillan, 2003); Patrick Geary, *The Myth of Nations: The Medieval Origins of Europe* (Princeton, NJ: Princeton University Press, 2003); and my own *Exchanges in Exoticism* (Toronto: University of Toronto Press, 2014).

7. And, as Gaston Paris writes in his introduction to the epic, "La poésie primitive se divise en deux grands courants: la poésie lyrique et la poésie épique. La première est l'expression de sentiments, la seconde est le récit d'événements." *Histoire poétique de Charlemagne par Gaston Paris* (Paris: Franck, 1865), 1.

often relegated to condemning feminine emotional excess in women who are their wives or captives.

Indeed, the *Roman de Rou*, a ca. 1170 verse chronicle of the dukes of Normandy composed by Wace, seems to suggest that in chivalric cultures, inefficient or extraneous emotions have little place. In one illustrative episode, William de Tancarville, the king's seneschal, instructs the king, who is mourning the loss of his son,

> "Sires, levez sus,
> Alez mengier, ne targiez plus.
> Vos anemiz sereint liez
> Se lungement dol faisiez;
> Lié sereient de vostre annui,
> Se il vos saveient marri.
> Femes deibvent plaindre è plorer,
> Femes se deibvent dementer,
> Maiz vos vos debvez conforter.
> Jà por plainte ne vivront
> Cil ki morent è ki mort sont.
> Filz ne pot pere rescovrer,
> Ne pere filz por dol mener;
> En plorer n'a nul rescovrier;
> Levez tost sus, alez mengier.
> Forz est dol, la perte grant,
> Jamez en fereiz nul semblant."
> Por ço ke li chamberlenc dist,
> Leva li Reis, et liet s'asist,
> Son mengier rova aprester;
> Sez Baronz fist od sei disner,
> Ne fist pas sembland véiant gent
> Ke del filz out marement.[8] (15353–75)

> "Sire, get up, go eat, do not tarry any longer.
> Your enemies will be happy
> if you grieve for a long time;
> they will be pleased by your pain,
> if they will know that you are despondent.

---

8. Robert Wace, *Le roman de Brut. Tome 2 / par Wace, poète du XIIe siècle; Publié pour la première fois d'après les manuscrits des bibliothèques de Paris, avec un commentaire et des notes par Le Roux de Lincy* (Rouen: É. Frère, 1836).

> Women are meant to complain and cry,
> women are meant to go mad,
> but you must comfort yourself.
> Never will those who die and are dead
> come back to life because of crying.
> Sons cannot be recovered by fathers,
> nor should sons be distracted
> by mourning their fathers.
> In crying nobody has ever
> recovered anything; get up now, go eat.
> Strong is grief, and the loss great,
> but never will you be able to make another one like him."
> Because the seneschal said this to him,
> the king sat up in the bed,
> and sent off to have his food made ready;
> he had his barons dine with him,
> and he did not appear to have extreme trouble
> by the death of his son before his people.

Several lessons about the relation between gender, community, and emotions emerge from the seneschal's condemnation of the king's emotionality. First, emotion is described here as a political practice. Grief (especially excessive, private grief) is just as debilitating for a man's power as the kinds of excessive sexual desire that waylay—and emasculate, as Enide points out—men beside beautiful women in romance. The seneschal reminds the king that not only does his grief take him away from his *men*, but that his *enemies* can also read and judge his power through his emotions (as in "lié sereient de vostre annui"). Here, emotions are imagined as a calculated practice of power best showcased in public and deemed dangerous when they threaten to remove a man from homosocial bonding.

Second, the seneschal describes the elite emotional landscape as consonant with contemporaneous moral discourses on temperance and patristic teachings prohibiting earthly grief. In the *Rou*, we learn that the emotions of chansons de geste function within and have resonance with contemporaneous moral teachings, placing the genre within a broader social, moral, and religious context, and inviting a reading of epic sorrow within noble fighting communities.

Third, we learn that emotional displays are not only *produced within* a community, they are also *received by* that community, particularly received as socially gendered. In this passage, for example, the seneschal sputters accusatory fricatives that highlight the disjuncture between the king's performances of emotion and gender ("*Femes* deibvent plaindre è plorer, *Femes* se deibvent dementer"). Reading with the seneschal, we learn that kingship must epitomize masculinity—and the corollary is that he may not perform excessive grief. Grieving becomes feminizing, a sign of weakness, bringing joy and levity (*liez* and *lié* in the Old French) to enemies, destroying the king's performance of masculinity and power in his community.

In aligning grieving with the feminine, the seneschal's words resonate with the critique of wailing in *Raoul de Cambrai*, another contemporaneous (ca. 1200) Old French chanson de geste in which the object of men's affection—and the reasons for their warfare—are confounded, caught up in a man's love for his wife rather than his homosocial affection for his comrades.[9] When Bernier is upbraided by his superiors in *Raoul de Cambrai*, we see a schooling that, like in the *Rou*, proscribes amorous grieving and ties men's emotions instead to the community of feudal battle:

De ces biax eix conmença a plorer.
"B[erniers] dist il, por le cors saint Omer
este vos feme por grant duel demener?
Ja nus frans hons ne se doit demanter
Tant con il puisse ces garnemens porter." (6189–93)

He began to shed tears from his beautiful eyes.
"Bernier," said [Guerri], "by the relics of Saint Omer,
are you a woman to give yourself to such sorrow?
Never should such a noble man give himself to grief
as long as he can carry his arms!"

The first impulse is to read this passage as maligning excessive emotional display by associating it with a negative femininity. For the seneschal, and, ostensibly, the king who heeds him, there is no point in crying; it will never bring back the dead: "jamez en fereiz nul semblant," he says. The seneschal's advice seems to confirm received notions about grief as an emotion whose display should be reserved for women. It is, pointedly, *not* men's work.

However, the passage offers another interpretive layer, an invitation to imagine the *correct* performance of men's emotions—and not just physical combat—as essential to the performance of epic masculinity.[10] Though

---

9. *Raoul de Cambrai*, ed. and trans. William Kibler and Sarah Kay (Paris: Livre de Poche, 1996).
10. As Patricia Ingham points out, even though women's emotional work in grief is often (mis) read as passive, it clearly accomplishes important work both in epic and romance; as such, it is a

certainly dismissive of women's emotions, the passage simultaneously reminds readers that, in the ethos of this text, emotional work is for men; men's grieving is integral to articulating the emotional community of elite sacrifice. The emotional equivocation here may not be one of pejorative feminization, but rather one that underscores the work of *men's emotions for other men* on the battlefield, an admonishment to turn away from feelings directed outside the arena of combat in favor of the love they feel for their comrades and lords. From the perspective of a masculine emotional community, the passage becomes an acknowledgment that men's emotions are *integral* to epic—and that they must be performed and channeled appropriately.

The emotional lesson proffered in this passage from *Raoul de Cambrai* also provides clarity about the *Rou*, where we can now see that when the seneschal instructs the king in the futility of emotions, he is constructing emotions as integral to the proper performance of both gender and power—essentially tethering emotions to the performance of noble masculinity. It makes sense that within the ethos of epic there should be lessons about how to feel like a warrior and about how community is constituted through men's feelings. Yet Charlemagne, who should be one of the ultimate markers for elite, powerful masculinity within the world of the chanson de geste, remains enigmatic, just as Arthur remains puzzling as he broods for a good story throughout much of romance. The unsettling, terminal *laisses* of Charlemagne's wracking sobs in the *Roland* only underscore the potency of our question: why does medieval epic condone a Charlemagne who weeps so profoundly? Or, put another way, what is so powerfully erotic about men's tears?[11]

Epic Repetition, Epic Grief: The Erotics of Narrating Loss

In the last chapter, I explored Roland Barthes's feelings of grief on the occasion of his mother's death—his grief is atemporal, a stasis; yet it is a grief that

---

mistake to dismiss the work of either men's *or* women's grief in medieval communities. "From Kinship to Kingship: Mourning, Gender, and Anglo-Saxon Community," in *Grief and Gender: 700–1700*, ed. Jennifer C. Vaught and Lynne Dickson Bruckner (New York: Palgrave Macmillan, 2003), 19.

11. Though there is no textual or theoretical *need* to establish separate, gendered sets of grief, as Bonnie Wheeler observes, "grief is almost but not entirely a male prerogative in the poem [the *Song of Roland*]." Here, I follow the separation in order to tease out not a naturalized gendering of grief, but rather how grief is imagined as performing power, from any gendered position. See Wheeler, "Grief in Avalon: Sir Palomydes' Psychic Pain," in *Grief and Gender: 700–1700*, ed. Lynne Dickson Bruckner and Jennifer Vaught (New York: Palgrave, 2003), 66.

is simultaneously creative, spurring narrative precisely because he luxuriates in it long after his mother's passing. Barthes's grief is both problematic and productive: in staying with the moment of abjection, Barthes claims a paradoxical subjectivity as a writer empowered by loss. He links the moment of grief with the moment of commemoration, rendering the moment of loss (of mother, of identity as son, and, to some extent, self) one of subjectivity, of calling the self into being through writing.

Writing of Barthes's own death in *The Work of Mourning*, Jacques Derrida offers a different theory of grief, temporality, and subjectivity—one that exposes his fear of the imperfection of commemoration, which he characterizes as the fundamental flaw of human memory when he imagines the moment of commemoration as one of failure. As Pascale-Anne Brault remarks, Derrida theorizes a kind of mourning that insists on our lack of narratological specificity, in that grief's iterability denies us a singular moment of subjectivity:

> Because of the possibility, indeed the ineluctability, of iteration, we should perhaps not assume that we can ever identify with absolute certainty the object of our mourning. For we might think we are mourning one friend when we are in fact mourning another . . . or perhaps all our mournings are but iterations of the one death that can never be identified—the first death, the total, undialectical death—so that what is mourned is a singularity that exceeds any proper name, making posthumous infidelity the very work of mourning.[12]

Infidelity—that very gesture he wishes to avoid—thus structures Derridean thinking about his grief for his friend and interlocutor. For Derrida, iterability is tantamount to infidelity, for it denies the singularity of both the life and the death. He identifies a primal fear, that "I am gone, no one will any longer be able to testify to this: nothing will remain but an indifferent Nature. This is a laceration so intense, so intolerable."[13] That is, I am gone, and will never be remembered; my memory will be a fleeting remembrance of my presence on Earth, my life vanishing after the moment of my death. This is the greatest fear of epic's great warriors, from Achilles to Hector to Roland to Vivien, who all seek to die a good death *and be remembered for it*.

But, more importantly, Derrida identifies a terror that not only are our deaths impermanent, so are our lives, what he identifies as the "ghostly power

---

12. Pascale-Anne Brault, introduction to *The Work of Mourning*, by Jacques Derrida (Chicago: University of Chicago Press, 2001), 17.
13. Derrida, *Work of Mourning*, 37.

of the supplement" in his tribute to Barthes.[14] In focusing on the iterability of the supplement, Derrida identifies the iterability of death as a destabilizing force, inviting consideration of the epic's insistence on repetition—which the literature has explored in the guise of narrative time and emphasis, and which I will instead consider with Derrida as an investigation of the effects of the iterability of death, and its emotional product, grief. For Derrida, the specter of death is its iterability into nothingness, reifying no one, and nothing, as memorable. He writes, "It is not a question here of vanquishing literature but of preventing it from neatly and cleverly sealing up the singular and flawless wound (nothing is more unbearable or laughable than all the expressions of guilt in mourning, all its inevitable spectacles)."[15] Iteration, here, is a sign of the wound, of our intrinsic inability to repeat—faithfully, and forever—all that came from another's life. The central angst, then, comes from his fear that all attempts to commemorate—to narrate—will also be moments where, in his words, "I disfigure, I wound, I put to sleep, or I kill."[16] Essentially, he grapples with an "excess of fidelity [that] would end up saying and exchanging nothing. It returns to death. It points to death, sending death back to death."[17] Iterability—of people, of wounds, of the scene of death, even of words and concepts—becomes a minefield.

Insensitive to the paranoia of existentialism, grief is constantly, uncomfortably reiterated in medieval epic through endless scenes of violent, bloody death. There is an interesting and even crucial insistence on death, not only for the sake of reifying battle and sacrifice as central tenets to medieval feudal service, but also, I claim, as a way of stitching medieval heroic masculinity to emotion. Specifically, endless (re)iteration ties warring men to the emotions of death, namely grief and rage. As such, the proliferation of battlefield encounters in texts like *La chanson de Roland, La mort le roi Artu, Girart de Roussillon, Le roman de Rou,* and countless other medieval epics transcends the mere mechanics of battle to provide a space to figure and foreground *men's* feelings, as a language for masculinity. Epic provides a space to entwine noble masculinity with the iterability of grief, and this iterability is foundational to cultures steeped in sacrifice.

Yet iteration leaves us with an essential, paradoxical question. As Derrida's later work points out and as medieval epics query, if grief is in fact

---

14. Ibid, 41.
15. Ibid, 44.
16. Ibid, 44.
17. Ibid, 46.

(re)iterable, wherein lies its originality? If all grief is an iteration of the same loss—the encounter of the individual with the timelessness of all death—then in what way is *any* death unique? Put another way, iterability invites the question: in what way is the individual life grievable, memorable, *narrate-able*? Derrida's question is important for medieval texts, in that it not only recognizes the urge to celebrate life by grieving the dead, but it also raises the specter that no death is unique—and therefore, no life, either. This threat, I claim, is at the basis of epic's urge to spawn example after example of bravery in combat, of heroic and deadly encounter. At its heart, epic tries to escape from the dynamics of forgetfulness through iteration, but its iterability belies a medieval recognition that all fades, eventually, from memory and narration.

Contrasting Derrida and Barthes permits a dialogue to emerge between two philosophies of the relation between emotions, their embodied subjectivity, and narration. Though different in approach, both Barthes and Derrida essentially invite us to consider how emotions create narrative. This narrative questions whether subjectivity is possible, and if so, whether it can commemorate individual men's lives. This is a crucial question within the *Iliad*, where one of the central problems with Achilles's outrageous treatment of Hector's corpse is not only that it renders his body unable to be properly *grieved*, but also that it can no longer properly *narrate* Hector's bravery, that it is unable to serve as a marker, a palimpsest, of the story of his valor. Hector has an *ungrievable* body; without burial and obsequies, he cannot be remembered, and therefore his life is unexceptional. Hector's kin are confronted with the ugly iterability of warrior death, with the meaninglessness of an "ungrievable" life, in Judith Butler's sense:

> So his whole head was dragged down in the dust.
> And now his mother began to tear her hair. . . .
> she flung her shining veil to the ground and raised
> a high, shattering scream, looking down at her son.
> Pitifully his loving father groaned and round the king
> his people cried with grief and wailing seized the city.[18] (trans. Fagles, 22.477–82)

Like the mourners in our medieval epics, the duty of these ancient mourners is to produce meaning from death; they must grieve Hector's corpse in order to ascribe meaning to death, and hence, to life. The *Iliad* insists on tying the

---

18. Homer, *The Iliad*, trans. Robert Fagles (London: Penguin Books, 1990).

moment of grieving to that of creating meaning, binding death to narrative. And, in the Greek tradition, it is not just any person who must grieve for the best warrior, but the best kings, the best chorus, the best of the entire polis. The good life is a grievable life.

The Greek poem reminds us that epic expects commemoration to be predicated on status—that these questions about emotion are deeply wedded to class. Like the *Iliad*, in which grief is tied to narrating elite heroic masculinity, in the *Song of Roland*, the creation and diffusion of commemorative narration are depicted as one of the duties of medieval kingship. In the opening *laisses* of the poem, for example, Charlemagne's dreams presage Roland's fateful death; it is a moment in which emotion and narrative are already entwined:

> Li emperere s'en repairet en France;
> Suz sun mantel en fait la cuntenance.
> Dejuste lui li dux Neimes chevalchet
> E dit al rei: "De quei avez pesance?"
> Carles respunt: "Tort fait kil me demandet!
> Si grant doel ai ne puis muer nel pleigne.
> Par Guenelun serat destruite France." (67)

> The emperor is returning to France;
> Under his cloak he gives way to his emotion.
> Duke Naimon rides up alongside him
> And says to the king: "What are you worried about?"
> Charles replies: "It is wrong to ask me about this.
> My distress is such that I cannot help but vent it.
> France is going to be ruined by Ganelon!" (trans. Gaunt and Pratt, 30)

Here, Charlemagne is "read" by Naimon as in distress, as "made heavy" by emotion, and emotions require explanation, they require narrative. Charlemagne explains that his fear is not only for the loss of *his* kin, but also for the threat it poses to his own subjectivity, in a synecdoche where "France" stands in not only for his kingdom, but his own position as its ruler, his way of knowing himself. His grief presages his own downfall and renders the tone of the text that of a dirge, despite his eventual victory. More importantly, however, his grief begets the questions that pepper the tale: What has happened? Who has died? Over and over, grief is tied to a question imagined to both inspire and require a narrating cure.

The *Roland*'s excessive, insistent repetition of death invites a consideration of whether commemoration can actually produce meaning/permanency through narrative. After Roland's (long-feared) death, when Charlemagne reawakens from his grief-induced faint, the new iteration of this passage marks both his own loss *and* the worth of his baron:

> "Ami Rollant, prozdoem, juvente bele,
> Cum jo serai a Eis, em ma chapele,
> Vendrunt li hume, demanderunt noveles;
> Jes lur dirrai, merveilluses e pesmes:
> 'Morz est mis nies, ki tant me fist cunquere.' . . .
> E! France, cum remeines deserte!
> Si grant doel ai que jo ne vuldreie estre!"
> Sa barbe blanche cumencet a detraire,
> Ad ambes mains les chevels de sa teste.
> Cent mille Francs s'en pasment cuntre tere. (209.2915–32)

> "Roland, dear friend, worthy flower of youth,
> When I am back at Aix, in my chapel,
> My vassals will come to me to ask for news.
> What I shall have to say is dreadful and cruel.
> 'My nephew, who won so much land for me, is dead.' . . .
> Alas, fair France, how bereft you are now!
> I am so grief-stricken, I no longer wish to live."
> He begins to tear out his white beard,
> And with both hands, the hair on his head.
> A hundred thousand Franks fall in a faint on the ground. (trans. Gaunt and Pratt, 97–98)

Bolstered by the force of his men's hyperbolic emotional display, Charlemagne's lament continues into the next stanza, which terminates in a reiteration of his sorrow through a repetition of specific sites of bodily self-destruction, here removal of his hair and, again, the pulling out of his beard (210).

In the very next *laisse*, the Duke of Nîmes constructs this grief as destructive and discouraging for the army Charlemagne is supposed to lead; yet it is grief, and not "ire" or rage, that leads him to success, in vengeance. Grief's productivity becomes explicit when Charlemagne's motivations to finish the battle against the traitorous Ganelon are explained:

> Carles li reis en ad prise sa barbe,
> Si li remembret del doel e del damage;
> Mult fierement tute sa gent reguardet,
> Puis si s'escriet a sa voiz grand e halte:
> "Barons franceis, as chevals e as armes!" (214)

> King Charles has begun to stroke his beard.
> He is remembering his grief and all he has lost.
> He gazes upon his army with a fierce glint in his eye.
> Then he cries out in a strong and clear voice:
> "Frenchmen, barons, mount your horses, to arms!" (trans. Gaunt and Pratt, 100)

This passage envisions an embodied connection between emotions, memory, and chivalry. An embodied and visible sign of his age, wisdom, and power, Charlemagne's famous white beard metonymizes his emotional well-being—and the well-being of the entire camp—throughout the narrative. His beard becomes a place of memory, with strands that narrate loss in ways that remind us of the threads of memory woven into Philomena's tapestry. Supposedly destroyed through mourning, Charlemagne's beard instead becomes a visible marker, a testament to an un-seeable internal emotional reality. Like Philomena's disheveled hair or Enide's handfuls of locks, Charlemagne's beard is a witness to the veracity of his powerful emotional performance.[19] As such, his stroking of his beard not only metonymizes Roland's loss and worth, but it makes that loss visible and legible to others through the body, much in the way widows' tears function in romance, aligning grief with a corporeal reality.

The genius of this *laisse* is that it transforms stagnant commemoration into productive revenge. It becomes the pathway that connects the moment of sorrow with the workings of chivalry, twinning commemoration with action, sorrow with prowess. Whereas Nîmes might castigate Charlemagne for his grief, this *laisse* reveals grief as central to spurring men to engage in medieval feudal battle within chansons de geste. Grief becomes the narrative of battlefield glory, where the visible markers of emotion are eroticized by the onlooker's desiring gaze. And such descriptions are reiterated throughout many *laisses*, where the signs of his grief are many: "clouded eyes" (2896); "he starts to pull out great handfuls of his hair" (2906); one hundred thousand Franks are in "floods of tears" (2908); days will be spent in "tears and sorrow" (2915); he pulls out his white beard (2930, 2943); and the formulaic repetition of "I am so grief-stricken, I no longer wish to live" (2929, 2936; translations Gaunt and Pratt).

---

19. On the power of hair and dishevelment in figuring rape see the analysis and references to other critical studies in Irit Ruth Kleiman, "A Sorrowful Song: On Tears in Chrétien de Troyes's *Philomena*," in *Crying in the Middle Ages: Tears of History*, ed. Elina Gertsman (New York: Routledge, 2012), 208–29.

Whereas epic repetition normally highlights martial prowess by slowing down time, here the repetition of Charlemagne's emotions is put to a decidedly different purpose: it creates potential, eliding the time of emotion with the time of narration. Here, narrative repetition proffers a possibility of renown to every man who hears sacrifice retold.[20] Charlemagne's hyperbole eroticizes Roland's sacrifice, invoking his nephew as the apogee of chivalric service and simultaneously destroying any possibility for others to emulate him, as no kinsman could ever be his equal. Charlemagne becomes an unwilling narrator, yet he imagines this as his new duty: telling the story of his grief. "What a tale is [his] to tell," indeed.

Charlemagne's repeated indulgence in the depths of his despair is a surprisingly productive affective state, one that resonates obliquely with Barthes's project of mourning his mother through narrative and that interrogates the felicity of Derrida's assertions about infidelity. His epic and repetitive grieving recall Barthes's immobility, what Barthes cites as a productive, luxurious moment of stasis, faintly echoing a mourning Achilles holed up in his tent, without whose grief work the *Iliad* would be a decidedly different text. Charlemagne's grief writes the story of Roland's worth, and even as the story line threatens to stagnate, Charlemagne is content to reiterate the depths of his despair. This model of iterative lamentation resonates with the productivity of Barthes's lamentation of his own mother, in that both see felicity in narrating grief over and over. For the former, the felicity is tied to the reception of that narrative: we the readers, his own soldiers, even the soldiers at Hastings, are all consuming Roland's glory through Charlemagne's grief.

Derrida might worry about the repetition in the stasis, rather than the stillness. The repetition of grief in medieval epic seems to interrogate Derrida's assertion that the iterability of death reminds us of the iterability of life, and hence the lack of value in either. While the *Chanson de Roland* certainly depends on repetition, Roland's death, and its subsequent two millennia of commemoration, seem hardly forgotten. What medieval epic proposes—and what Derrida struggles vehemently to resist—is that the story of grief is more important than the individual life it seeks to recount. Death's iterability serves to highlight a medieval feudal system that is self-perpetuating through the emotions its narratives produce.

The fact that Roland is not only extolled in this monumental story line, but that the *Chanson de Roland* is then later retold to soldiers facing a different

---

20. It is of note that when Marsile dies a few lines later, his tale takes no flight; it is ungrievable: "Marsilie turns his face to the wall; / Tears fall from his eyes and he bows his head. / He has died of grief and is weighted down by sin" (trans. Gaunt and Pratt, 122).

foreign encounter at the battle of Hastings, only redoubles the power of iterability: both the death and its initial retelling only serve to spur more men to feudal bravery. Even if fictional, Roland's death still carries weight; the *Roland* teaches us that it is not the historical life lived to which we must be faithful or even attentive, rather it is to the accreted symbolism and meaning assigned to that life by those who retell it. We know that Roland, if he even existed, did not fight Muslims at the pass in Roncesvalles; we know the *Roland* as medieval anti-Muslim propaganda—already a reformulation of that first sacrifice, even in its first literary incantation. Although totally unfaithful to the historical struggle, in reimagining Roncesvalles, the *Roland* nevertheless produces and promises meaning through the emotions it provokes. Charlemagne's grief still promises both Roland and the *Roland* their staying power and renown; it is still a grief that produces desire in other men and takes its power from its iterability in (re)narration. The fiction of the tale is not, at least for the medieval text, its problematic—the distortion, the propagandistic infidelity of the postmortem speech about the life or the battle, is not its weakness. Rather, it is its interpretive strength: according to Charlemagne's repetitive wailings in the *Roland*, feudal life is given meaning not by attention to historical realism, but by grief's ability to provoke an emotional recognition among fellow warriors and listeners—here, the desire is to be mourned like a Roland.

Rendering Loss Productive: Mourning and the Narratological Genealogies

Guillaume d'Orange is an entirely different twelfth- and thirteenth-century cycle from the *Roland*'s retelling of Charlemagne's encounters at Roncesvalles, and it is arguably the most extensive and important epic cycle written in Old French, as Joan Ferrante has pointed out.[21] The cycle principally describes the life of Guillaume d'Orange (d. 812), also known as Guillaume Fierabrace (it also conflates his story with many other Guillaumes), and its many branches and continuations describe a genealogy of men's glory and power in military campaigns within what are now France and Spain and that were loosely associated with Charles Martel and Louis the Pious. Despite differences in compositional timing, dialect, and subject material, men's emotions are as much at the heart of Guillaume's world as they are

---

21. *Guillaume d'Orange: Four Twelfth-Century Epics*, trans. Joan Ferrante (New York: Columbia University Press, 2001).

on Charlemagne's battlefields. Whereas we might agree that the *Roland* is organized almost exclusively around the homosocial community of battle, the cycle of *Guillaume d'Orange* vacillates between battlefield and bedroom.[22]

Despite its looser relation to war, the cycle still foregrounds a homosocial world. One of the chansons de geste of the cycle, the late twelfth-century Picardian *Aliscans*, portrays men's relationships in ways that resonate with the emotional landscape of the *Roland*.[23] Depicting a fierce (if fictional) battle at Aliscans between Guillaume's Christian army and an imaginary Saracen adversary, the epic ties into the larger cycle's glorification of Guillaume's kin. Its intense and extended focus on the death of Guillaume's nephew, Vivien, serves to highlight the family's loss, framed both as an untimely, unfortunate death (for the nephew) and as a personal sacrifice of lineage (for Guillaume). In a description that spans no fewer than *fourteen* stanzas, Vivien's death happens in epic time, a tragic defeat highlighted by the generic conventions of repetition and hyperbole deployed by Guillaume to extol his dying kinsman in a kind of emotional epanorthosis:

> Niés Vivien, de vostre hardement
> Ne fu mais hom puis ke Diex fist Adan.
> Or vos ont mort Sarrasin et Persant;
> Terre, car ouevre si me va engloutant! . . .
> Li quens Guillaumes va durement plorant
> Et ses .II. poins l'un et l'autre torgant;
> Soventes fois se claimme las, dolant.
> De sa dolor mais ira nus parlant,
> Car trop le maine et orible et pesant.[24] (709–19)

> Nephew Vivien, of your powerfulness
> there has been no man since God made Adam.
> Now the Saracens and Persians have killed you;
> Earth, open up so that you may swallow me! . . .
> Count William cries heartily

---

22. Given the size of the *Guillaume* corpus, it is not surprising that critics have focused on a variety of themes. Less work, however, has explored the role of emotions in the *Guillaume*, though he is often characterized as easily flying off the handle, or enraged (as in William Ian Miller, "Threat," in *Feud, Violence and Practice: Essays in Medieval Studies in Honor of Stephen D. White*, ed. Belle S. Tuten, Stephen D. White, and Tracey L. Billado [Farnham, UK: Ashgate, 2010], 16).
23. *Aliscans* exists in eight manuscripts, but the larger cycle exists in several translations.
24. Citations from the *Guillaume d'Orange* cycle taken from *Le cycle de Guillaume d'Orange*, ed. and trans. Michel Zink (Paris: Livre de Poche, 1996).

> and he twists his fists one against the other;
> many times he calls himself exhausted, wretched.
> Of his sadness no one will speak again,
> because it will be too intense, difficult, and weighty.

The manifold iterations of Guillaume's intense grief figure his nephew's valor through inversion and litotes: the more he wails, the greater his loss, and, by extension, the greater the worth of the man he mourns. Here, Guillaume's weeping figures his nephew's valor through his own loss of both kinship and martial valor; by extension, he mourns a masculinity grounded both in class (nobility, through genealogy) and in physical prowess (here, cast explicitly as "power"). *Aliscans* frames one man's exploits as another man's grief, privileging emotion over accomplishment.

The fourteen verses devoted to depicting Vivien's death develop a theory of grief that turns away from men's actions and toward men's emotions as central to the elite community at stake in these battles. Iteration after iteration, *laisse* after *laisse*, Guillaume lauds Vivien's accomplishments on earth, but in each stanza, he returns to figure Vivien's death as *his* loss. Guillaume's grief is given a kind of accreted status, in which his emotion could carry and signify worth beyond its affective quality. Over the next twelve stanzas, grief figures chivalric valor. Through grief, we learn that Vivien's destroyed, dying body smells good (like "baumes ne encens," 724), and that though he was a fierce warrior, he had full control over his reasonable emotions (732–37), among other praiseworthy attributes. Grief figures worth, and it makes narrative space to write Vivien's terrible sacrifice as the story of chivalric valor, one to be eroticized as it is consumed by the audience of both Guillaume within the tale and the noble audience consuming the bard's song.

Repetition permits the slow and deliberate presentation of these details, and it simultaneously foregrounds the writing of this narrative of valor as grief displayed on and through the person of the count. The third stanza sees him kiss his nephew on the lips ("sa tenre bouce d'est douce com canele," 763), while sighing, weeping and looking to Heaven, before turning to elaborate on his nephew's worth in terms of the gifts he was given when dubbed. He kisses his nephew "very sweetly" (*molt doucement*, 777) again before beginning to cry anew in the fifth stanza, this time aligning his grief for his nephew with his own lost generosity as well as with the pressing threat of reconquest and divestment of all his own earthly goods; in a later *laisse* his grief links the death to the loss of his vassals. It is not his nephew's death, but his own grief that is recounted and elaborated; it is not the death but the grief that propels and narrates the story; it is not the death but the grief that it provokes that is endlessly presented and consumed to further another man's narrative.

The passage is so emotionally charged that when Vivien finally expires in Guillaume's arms, like the count, the narrative breaks down, too, sputtering out in aposiopesis:

> L'ame s'en va, n'i puet plus demorer.
> En paradis le fist Diex hosteler,
> Aveuc ses angles entrer et abiter.
> Voit le Guillaumes si [commence à] plorer (865–70)

> His soul flies away, he can remain there no longer.
> God welcomed him to stay in Paradise,
> To enter and abide with his angels.
> Guillaume sees it, and so begins to cry.

When narration fails, grief does not; the grief that can no longer even speak carries the weight of one man's affection for another, expressed quite vividly through the kissing, sighing, and crying in the face of abject loss. Here, grief carries an erotic charge, figuring the possibility not only of male-male affection but also the promise of remembrance.

If the iterative encounters are not so much about eroticizing the *act* of killing, but rather about eroticizing the *emotions* of men's chivalric commemoration, current critical attention to the feudal dynamics—that is, the law—within the poem should be supplemented.[25] Endless (re)iteration of emotion reveals it to be foundational to the construction of medieval epic's depiction of governance, and therefore foundational to the discussion of medieval elite feudal communities. Reading with the medieval offers some nuance: whereas Derrida argues that iteration invites scrutiny of difference (and in the case of grief, reveals the instability of remembrance), iterability here draws attention to and *constructs* a kind of men's emotional community.

---

25. See, for example, Mario Bastide, "Les actes de parole dans *Aliscans*." *L'information littéraire: Revue paraissant cinq rois par an* 45, no. 5 (1993): 5–13; Dominique Boutet, "La pusillanimité de Louis dans *Aliscans*: Idéologie ou topos de cycle? Topique, structure et historicité," *Moyen Âge: Revue d'histoire et de philologie* 103, no. 2 (1997): 275–92; Bernard Guidot, "*Aliscans*: Structures parentales ou filiation spirituelle?," in *Les relations de parenté dans le monde médiéval*, ed. Centre Universitaire d'Études et de Recherches Médiévales d'Aix (Aix-en-Provence: Université de Provence, 1989), 25–45; Romaine Wolf-Bonvin, "À la cour de Laon: Le *furor* sarrasin de Guillaume (*Aliscans*, laisses LXI–LXX)," in *Chanter de geste: L'art épique et son rayonnement. Hommage à Jean-Claude Vallecalle*, ed. Marylène Possamaï-Perez and Jean-René Valette (Paris: H. Champion, 2013), 473–89; François Suard, "L'espace épique dans *Aliscans*," *Op. Cit.: Revue de Littératures Française et Comparée* 2 (November 11, 1993): 5–13.

Returning to our reading of the *Roland*, in the very next *laisse* Charlemagne's grief becomes *the matière* of epic concern: like in *Aliscans*, it is a mourner's *emotions*, rather than a warrior's *actions*, that become prominent:

> "Ami Rollant, de tei ait Deus mercit!
> L'anme de tei seit mise en pareïs!
> Ki tei ad mort France ad mis en exill.
> Si grant dol ai que ne voldreie vivre,
> De ma maisnee, ki por mei est ocise!" . . .
> Ploret des oilz, sa blanche bar[b]e tiret.
> E dist dux Naimes: "Or ad Carles grant ire." (210)

> "Roland, dear friend, may the Lord have mercy on you!
> May your soul find its place in paradise!
> The man who killed you has ruined France.
> I am so grief-stricken, I no longer wish to live,
> Because so many of my household have died for me." . . .
> His tears well up, he pulls on his white beard.
> And Duke Naimon said: "Charles' sorrow is deep!" (trans. Gaunt and Pratt, 98)

As we have seen in passage after passage, the depths of Charlemagne's grief inversely figure Roland's glory. Yet, perhaps counterintuitively, they also broadcast Charlemagne's power, figured through loss rather than gain, through death rather than through conquest. Many have read Roland's sacrifice as a glorification of Charlemagne's power; however, Charlemagne's great grief at the loss of his vassal is an emotional performance that not only recognizes Roland's sacrifice but also concomitantly figures his own worth. Grief, then, has a double narrative function: it both commemorates the worth of the dead (Roland) and reifies the power of the living (the emperor, through the warriors who sacrifice themselves in service to him). Charlemagne's performance of medieval feudal kingship through grief reveals emotion to be at the heart of performing feudal power structures. Emotions serve feudal politics, and grief is as central to the narration of noble masculinity as feudal power; grief is eroticized because, in the construct of elite homosocial masculinity, other men witness and recognize grief's power to depict them as strong and valorous.

The moments where kingship is shown to be *deficient* also reveal the centrality of the erotics of commemoration within medieval epic. Perhaps most intriguing are the moments where men *do not* conform to the ideals of lamentation and commemoration proposed by poems like the *Roland* or the

Aliscans and turn instead toward an ascetic proscription against any excessive affect. *La mort le roi Artu* offers an important test case of what happens when medieval noblemen *do not* grieve other men in Old French epic, when kings become ungrievable subjects. *La mort le roi Artu* is an anonymous thirteenth-century Old French Arthurian chanson de geste detailing the demise and fall of Arthur's house at the hands of his incestuously conceived son and nephew, Mordred.[26] Whereas Howard Bloch has identified the problematic of *La mort* as rooted in Arthur's adherence to archaic *legal* structures,[27] where kinship and kingship are too closely aligned, I argue that *La mort* showcases a deterioration of men's *emotional* regimes, a devolution of their emotional—as well as political—landscape. *La mort le roi Artu* offers a counterpoint to the *Roland*, in that though the texts are distant in composition and historical underpinning, both imagine a world defined and fueled by men's emotions. An imaginary staging of the downfall of medieval kingship, *La mort* is of interest to us because it explores the relation between men and their emotional communities at the moment of implosion, the moment of destruction. Essentially, it offers a glimpse into what happens when men's emotions go haywire, and it reinforces the relation between elite emotions and elite communities.

While many have focused on the legal and structural problems of feudal governance exposed by Arthur, for my purposes *La mort* is most interesting for its lessons about the emotional structuring of feudal relations.[28] As a late addition to the many iterations of Arthurian legend, *La mort* is of course only one vision of Arthur's court, and only one fantasy of Arthurian chivalry, much as the *Roland* is only one version of Charlemagne's governance. Yet,

---

26. *La mort le roi Artu: Roman du XIIIe siècle*, ed. Jean Frappier (Geneva: Droz, 1996).

27. Bloch elaborates that "the death of Arthur and destruction of the Round Table along with its baronage of 'bons seigneurs' looks like the failure of feudal organization to deal with the problems of a new more centrally oriented era." R. Howard Bloch, "From Grail Quest to Inquest: The Death of King Arthur and the Birth of France," *Modern Language Review* 69, no. 1 (1974): 40.

28. Bloch characterizes the differences between the *Roland* and *La mort* in terms of their reflection on the relation between kingship, religion, and justice; whereas the former upholds many of the codes of the feudal system, the latter depicts its tenets as falling apart:

> Unlike the *Chanson de Roland*, where God intervenes at crucial moments to save the hero and thus reaffirm men's faith in his abiding presence, the two trials of *La Mort* only serve to undermine credence in the fundamental tenets of feudal justice: that the righteous, though not necessarily the most powerful, man emerges victorious and that human error and chance play no part in the functioning of the legal process. The *Deo judicio* no longer punishes wrong-doing, nor does it vindicate injury swiftly and clearly. It has failed in its chief capacity, which is the designation of intrinsic but unobvious guilt through an irreducible contradiction of parties. Trial by combat has ceased, even, to distribute justice fairly. Arvalan and Lancelot, the guilty parties in the two legal actions, elude prosecution; Mador and Gauvain fail to obtain redress. (Ibid., 50)

like the *Roland*, *La mort* imagines emotions as central to feudal masculinity. Whereas the *Roland* imagines emotional control to structure chivalry and produce its narratives of renown, *La mort* investigates what happens when structures of control fall apart and emotional excess spurs action. For *La mort* stages men whose emotional landscape is in turmoil, where *nothing* is repeated, because every emotion, every reaction is a break in the feudal code. If we can characterize the *Roland* as depicting men's grief as contextualized within community, endlessly valorizing sacrifice in battle, then *La mort* imagines men who neglect to honor one another. Fittingly, *La mort le roi Artu* is widely considered the end of Arthurian narration.

If, as I suggest, there is a link between grief and the erotics of commemoration, Arthur's death in *La mort* should offer a test of grief's narrative function. If the betrayals of Arthur by Lancelot and Arvalan are the most obvious failings of the courtly code, then Arthur's own death can be read as a critique of the court's dependency on storytelling: his death becomes a failure to narrate. *La mort* represents a crisis not only of feudalism but also of narrative structure, and it reveals how both are tied to figuring and reproducing elite community. Arthur's death is obscured, left unobserved, just as he wishes, and it therefore becomes ungrievable:

> Lors commence [Artus] a penser, et en ce pensé li viennent les lermes as euz; et quant il a esté grant piece ne ce pensé, si dist a Girflet: "Il vos en couvient aler de ci et partir de moi a tel eür que, jamés que vos vivoiz, ne me verroiz.". . . Et quant Girflet voit qu'il n'i prendra plus, il monte et se part del roi; et si tost comme il en fu partiz, une pluie commença a cheoir moult grant et moult merveilleuse qui li dura jusqu'a un tertre qui estoit bien loing del roi demie liue. (249–50)

> Then he [Arthur] began to think, and in thinking tears sprang to his eyes; and when he had been thinking for a long while, then he said to Girflet: "It is necessary that you go away from here and leave me in such a way that, in your lifetime, you will never see me again." . . . And when Girflet saw that he would get no further, he mounted his horse and so left the king; and as soon as he was gone, rain began to fall very heavily and marvelously and lasted until he came to a hillock far away, which was a good half league away from the king.

Insistent on obscurity, the passage marking Arthur's death brings into question not only the meaning of his life, but of the courtly system organized around it: will he be commemorated and praised, or will his failure to discern betrayal be his lasting legacy? Using imagery that underscores the lack of clarity (*pluie*, and *ne me verroiz*), Arthur's speech mimics the narrative obscurity of his court. Arthur, in all his blindness, insists on dying alone, away from the very men who could have remembered him; the obscurity in the passage reflects the darkness and decay of the court and, ultimately, of his own legacy. Rather than choosing a death visible—and narratable—by all, Arthur falters toward an uncertain, un-narratable obscurity, fleeing to the arms of the sister/lover whose relationship ultimately caused the downfall of his feudal system. His unobserved and unlamented death forecloses further narration. As such, it is the ultimate marker of Arthur's failure: once keen for a good story of other men's renown, Arthur now spurns any possibility of documenting his own death by foreclosing his only male companion's grief, whose tears are replaced by the fateful showers that enshroud the departing king. Arthur's failure to be grieved is not only indicative of a rupture in the feudal political system; it is also revelatory for our study of emotions, in that it ties men's emotions to storytelling—roping narratives, the erotics of loss, and masculinity together. Its failure reveals how courtly culture deploys narrative to eroticize sacrifice.

In resisting the social, commemorative, and erotic functions of other men's grief, Arthur's death in *La mort le roi Artu* offers a counterexample that reinforces the narrative model proposed by the *Roland* and reiterated in *Aliscans*.[29] When read against the tenets of *La mort*, the more felicitous deaths in *Aliscans* and the *Chanson de Roland* stage successful models of feudalism as dependent upon acts of grieving and commemoration that celebrate the dead as a promise to the living. The promise of narration celebrates death for the courtly audience that consumes stories of men's glory. As Albrecht Classen points out, in *The Lament*, a Middle German poem of destructive loss, for example, men's *bodies* are not differentiated (they are all hacked to pieces in vv. 714–17), but rather their *reputations* are the things that "receive particular attention and are lamented in short speeches glorifying their deeds."[30] Comparing the relation between grief and narrative, between men's emotions and the "success" of their postmortem feudal memories told in stories, suggests that these texts align in an economy of publicly consumable narrative. At one end of the scale, *La mort* imagines a world

---

29. Other medieval poems also imagine grief to stage utter destruction, such as the Middle German poem *The Lament*. As Albrecht Classen has pointed out, the *Lament* stages the devastation left by war and is focused exclusively on the pain of the living, with no thought for the dead. Classen, "Death Rituals and Manhood in the Middle High German Poems *The Lament*, Johannes Von Tepl's *The Plowman*, and Heinrich Wittenwiler's *Ring*," in *Grief and Gender, 700–1700*, ed. Jennifer Vaught and Lynne Dickson Bruckner (New York: Palgrave, 2003), 33–47.

30. Ibid., 38.

where emotions are irrational, irrelevant, and silenced at the moment of feudal implosion; on the opposite end of the scale, the *Roland* imagines perfect service as complemented by very public men's grief. Though varied in content and depiction of and relation to emotion, the narrative community of Old French homosocial combat seems to suggest that feudalism imagines there is something heady—erotic, even—about being mourned by highly placed men. At the liminal edge of emotion and service, we see a model of feudalism that depends on men who mourn other men through story lines of grief.

The Erotics of Men's Grief

The examples from epic construct a homosocial economy of erotic grief that works in kind with the ways women's grief is eroticized in romance. In romance, we see that grieving creates a kind of economy of desire: men desire to be grieved by women, and in that sense, their combat offers a place where injuries invite women to narrate men's glory through an erotics of grief. As the criticism suggests, we are accustomed to thinking of women as grief's emotional workers—the literature examines the role of the widow, defends women's work in grieving as active and purposeful, and explores the connection between women and grieving, as we saw in chapter 2. We have already explored how women's grief commemorates men, but reading with the erotics of grief in epic identifies an expectation that, in elite communities, men must grieve other men, too. Together, both men's and women's grief have an important place in broadcasting the emotional needs of feudalism: the erotics of their grief serve to valorize and commemorate sacrifice.

Men's grief not only structures the genre, but it also creates an economy of desire. Indeed, if men's grief is as integral to epic as I have suggested, then it is also possible that men's grief *creates* desire for other men's recognition. Consider how Roland and Oliver repeatedly discuss their sacrifice as both an impediment to the enemy's victory and a vehicle for their extensive, public mourning by other men:

> "Sire Rollant, e vos, sire Oliver,
> Pur Deu vos pri, ne vos cuntraliëz! . . .
> Ja cil d'Espaigne n'en deivent turner liez.
> Nostre Franceis i descendrunt a pied,
> Truverunt nos e morz e detrenchez,
> Leverunt nos en bieres sur summers,

> Si nus plurrunt de doel e de pitét,
> Enfüerunt en aitres de musters;
> N'en mangerunt ne lu ne porc ne chen."
> Respunt Rollant: "Sire, mult dites bien." (122.1747–52)

> "My lord Roland, and you too, my lord Oliver,
> In God's name I beseech you, pray do not argue!
> The men of Spain must not be allowed to leave happy.
> Our Frenchmen will dismount from their horses here:
> They will find our dead and dismembered bodies,
> They will place us on biers strapped to packhorses,
> And they will weep for us in their pity and grief.
> They will bury us in consecrated ground near churches,
> Ensuring we are not devoured by wolves, pigs, or dogs."
> Roland replies: "My lord, you speak very well." (trans. Gaunt and Pratt, 60)

and

> Morz est li quens, que plus ne se demuret.
> Rollant li ber le pluret, si l' duluset;
> Jamais en terre n'orrez plus dolent hume. (150.2021–23)

> The count is dead, for he is no more.
> Valiant Roland laments and weeps for him.
> Never on earth will you hear a more grief-stricken man. (trans. Gaunt and Pratt, 69)

and again:

> Li quens Rolant, quant veit mort sun ami,
> Gesir adenz, a la tere sun vis,
> Mult dulcement a regreter le prist:
> "Sire cumpaign, tant mar fustes hardiz!
> Ensemble avum estét e anz e dis;
> Ne m' fesis mal, ne jo ne l' te forsfis.
> Quant tu es morz, dulur est que jo vif!";
> A icest mot se pasmet li marchis (151.2024–31)

> Now Roland can see that his friend is dead,
> Stretched out on the ground, with his face down.
> He began most tenderly to lament him:
> "My lord, companion, alas for your great boldness.

> We have spent many days and years together:
> You never did me wrong, nor did I ever let you down.
> Now you are dead, it pains me to go on living!"
> On saying this, the marquis passes out (trans. Gaunt and Pratt, 69)

Here, men's grief eroticizes the witnessing function of narrative. The passages write an equation between death, eternity, and narrative, balanced in the middle by grief, and they reveal a kind of economy of desire, in which men long for recognition by other men. Essentially, these three passages align men's acceptance of the price of battle—self-sacrifice—with their desire to be formally immortalized through the narrative of grief.

The economy of men's desire for men's grief draws from an ancient Mediterranean tradition. From Achilles's deep and raging mourning of Patroclus to Priam's grief for Hector, men's mourning is fundamental to epic. Achilles's excessive mourning glorifies the homosocial bonds among his warrior community:

> A black cloud of grief came shrouding over Achilles.
> Both hands clawing the ground for soot and filth,
> He poured it over his head, fouled his handsome face
> And black ashes settled onto his fresh clean war-shirt.
> Overpowered in all his power, sprawled in the dust,
> Achilles lay there, fallen. . . .
> Tearing his hair, defiling it with his own hands.
> And the women he and Patroclus carried off as captives
> Caught the grief in their hearts and keened and wailed,
> Out of the tents they ran to ring the great Achilles,
> All of them beat their breasts with clenched fists,
> Sank to the ground, each woman's knees gave way.
> Antilochus kneeling near, weeping uncontrollably,
> Clutched Achilles' hands as he wept his proud heart out—
> For fear he would slash his throat with an iron blade. (trans. Fagles, 18.25–38)

Achilles's battle is one of emotions; his grief is no less intense than that of the wailing women of medieval romance—after all, he mars his face, tears out his hair, and fouls his garments—and its intensity figures other men's glory. The battlefield is as much a place for negotiating men's interpersonal emotions as it is a place for testing their physical prowess or showcasing particular political structures. The test of the epic is not how well men fight, but how well they broadcast their emotions to other men. Their rage and despair, their desire for revenge, are all encoded onto the tools of warfare, facilitating the promise of writing their glory on the battlefield. The muse is to sing the *rage*—and not the prowess—of Achilles, after all.

Such narratives teach their listeners that successful Mediterranean battle entwines warrior masculinity with emotion, particularly grief and love. From Aeneas's insistence that he be remembered as exemplary of Roman duty, to Vivien's service toward his uncle, battle inspires men to seek the commendation of other men. Death and its emotional socialization in grief become a means for remembrance, the tool for men's eternal glory in the desires of other, living men. Epic teaches men to desire other men's words, instructing them to desire the wounds and the death that engender them. They need other men in order to figure their own glory; they need combat to show their strength; they need a glorious death—and a thorough weeping—witnessed and reiterated by other men to ensure their immortality through narrative.

The distress of Achilles, the dragging of Hector's defiled body before the dogs, Roland's terrifically staged self-sacrifice, and even Arthur's muted disappearance all serve as a concerted reminder that proper mourning depends on ritual. Deviating from death's ceremonies creates chaos; valuable deaths must engender both grief and remembrance, and not merely disappearance. As scholars who work on the anthropology of medieval death rituals suggest, the treatment of death not only honors the dead but also defines community among the living.[31] That is, without ceremonial mourning and remembrances, the legacy of the dead becomes a wounding of the community, rather than an exemplar of chivalric service and sacrifice.

We see this best in a simple word cloud constructed from the Oxford *Chanson de Roland*, where a very pointed narrative center emerges (figure 3.1).[32]

The word cloud shows the word *dist* to be central to the epic song; it is predicated on the power of the spoken word, as deployed by men in forming and extolling men's sacrifices, in negotiating their relationships, and in preserving their memories, as represented by the prominence of the other

---

31. Classen, "Death Rituals"; Louise Mirrer, *Upon My Husband's Death: Widows in the Literature and Histories of Medieval Europe* (Ann Arbor: University of Michigan Press, 1992); Neil Small, "Theories of Grief: A Critical Review," in *Grief, Mourning, and Death Ritual*, ed. Neil Small, Jenny Hockey, and Jeanne Katz (Oxford: Oxford University Press, 2001), 153–58; Anna Walecka, "Incest and Death as Indices of the Female Hero in Romance," *Romance Languages Annual* 4 (1992): 159–65; Ingham, "From Kinship to Kingship."

32. The cloud represents the thousand most prominent words of three letters or greater scrubbed for the most common Old French words (*li, les, il, la, et, por, uns,* etc.). Wordle.com, July 30, 2020.

CHAPTER 3

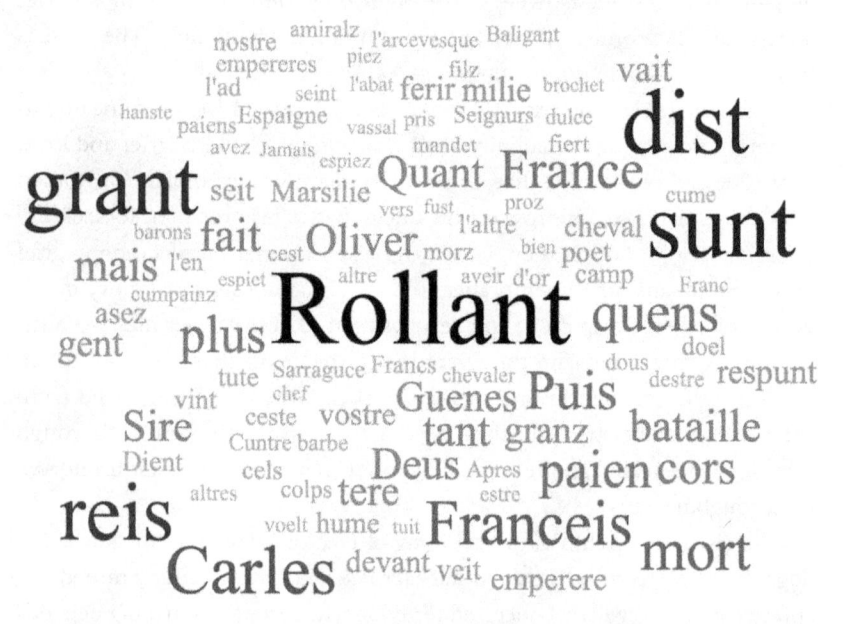

[Word cloud figure showing words from the Oxford Chanson de Roland, with prominent words including: Rollant, dist, sunt, grant, reis, Carles, Franceis, mort, Deus, Oliver, Puis, Guenes, Sire, France, Quant, bataille, paien, cors, quens, plus, mais, fait, gent, asez, respunt, tere, colps, Dient, vint, chef, ceste, vostre, tant, granz, Cuntre, barbe, altres, voelt, hume, tuit, devant, veit, emperere, cels, Apres, estre, dous, destre, doel, Franc, camp, poet, bien, cheval, l'altre, morz, cest, altre, aveir d'or, cumpainz, espiet, l'en, barons, seit, Marsilie, vers, fust, proz, cume, nostre, amiralz, l'arcevesque, Baligant, empereres, piez, l'ad, seint, l'abat, ferir, milie, brochet, vait, hanste, paiens, Espaigne, vassal, pris, Seignurs, dulce, avez, Jamais, espiez, mandet, fiert, tute, Sarraguce, Francs, chevaler*]

FIGURE 3.1. Relation between narration and identity in the Oxford *Chanson de Roland* (WordItOut.com, thousand-word cloud, limited to four or more letters per word and scrubbed for most common Old French articles)

men's proper names and titles (king, Rollant, Blancandrins, Oliver, etc). The *dist*—the story line told through the spoken word—recognizes men's identities as dependent on their narratives, as well as their bodies (*cors*), one of the more prominent non–proper nouns in the cloud. The word cloud suggests the warrior's death is therefore not complete until it is socially narrated—*dist*—by men's emotional outbursts, where grief becomes a way of extolling him to his community. Not only do epic warriors desire and require other men's grief, but they also require that that grief be narrated to and intelligible by others.

As Roland's death and Vivien's passing suggest, only certain kinds of deaths become narratable, legible by other men. Death's legibility seems to cleave along boundaries of class and status. Men desire other men's recognition, and they crave other men's tears—yet those tears are particular to the class and status of the warriors being grieved, most notably between the nobility and its supporting serfs. The texts suggest that while homosocial longings for grief are not exclusive to the nobility—indeed, the emotional desire for exceptionalism, for the good death that will be remembered, is imagined to structure ordinary men's encounters on the battlefield, the supporting cast, so to speak, of thousands of fainting men—it is a privilege to be commemorated, grieved. Consider the endless iterations of battlefield encounters at Roncevaux: it is not the commoners' deaths that are mourned, but the exceptional, noble men who are extolled, mourned, and narrated. The other 90 percent of the army becomes a remainder, the modern-day extras of the movie industry—bodies, but not people, who have died, and whose deaths only serve to heighten the erotic draw of the narrative of certain men's exceptionalism.

In Butler's terms, these commoners are the ungrievable; the disposability and iterability of these deaths resist retelling. These deaths are the unexceptional, the unnarratable—they are the effaced deaths of those whose sacrifice inversely figures the glorification and individuality of the nobility. The ungrievable deaths reveal that class identity is at stake in the emotional community of epic, where only *elite* men's emotions are validated by other men. Men's grief is a longed-for commemoration of elite men's sacrifice, because, unlike for the countless sacrificed serfs, elite deaths are imagined to be exceptional, narratable, memorable. In epic, men's grief constructs and divides communities: it constructs an erotics of the heroic death and elite masculinity and concomitantly labels it as exclusive to certain performances of class.

Chivalric men's desire for grief resonates with what Georges Bataille calls the urge toward "not death": "the death of not dying is precisely not death; it is the ultimate stage of life; if I die because I cannot die it is on condition that I live on; because of the death I feel though still alive and still live on."[33] That is, warrior men's confrontations provide not only the opportunity to not die in dying; they also provide the longed-for opportunity for immortality, in ways that are markedly different from the promise proffered by contemporary theology. It is not only a contest to the death, therefore, but it is the desire to live forever through narrative that we see at the heart of men's emotional landscape eroticizing death in epic. The twinning of men's death and men's desire is fundamentally related to the project of narratological immortality on the battlefield where men write their glory upon each other's bodies.[34]

Reading Old French epic suggests that death on the battlefield is thus an eroticized end for any soldier. But the erotic economy of elite grieving will

---

33. Georges Bataille, *Erotism: Death and Sensuality*, trans. Mary Dalwood (San Francisco: City Lights Books, 1962), 241.
34. For Wheeler, grief makes a palimpsest of the body in epic, where "grief is thus written on the body, expressed in gendered signs that are older than the *Iliad*." "Grief in Avalon," 66.

only have currency among certain kinds of men, and only extraordinary men will be mourned *and* named *and* narrated by their superiors. As the *Roland* proposes and the *La mort le roi Artu* confirms, death is even better when witnessed and retold; glory happens only when someone is there to extol a man's sacrifice. The erotics of men's grief depends on the commemoration created through witnessing and broadcasting, through the communal performance, reception, and eroticization of the narrative of elite masculinity predicated on men's homosocial grief.

The emotional lessons of medieval chansons de geste might help us reformulate Derrida's question about the meaning of his friend's death. Though one of many iterations of loss—a blip on the screen of human existence—still Barthes's death is forever inscribed within a certain social system by Derrida's emotional outpouring of narrative, an erotics of French intellectualism by a fellow French theorist, perhaps. Though repetition and iterability may indeed mean that we are always unfaithful to our dead, our medieval texts suggest that perhaps our goal is not to preserve, but to uphold a system—in Derrida's case, to uphold a version of intellectualism, so that it is not so much the individual life that grieving seeks to validate, but the system itself that it rearticulates. That is, though they purport immortality for the fallen, the erotics of grief articulate a system, not a life; a set of values, rather than an individual. For medieval nobles of epic, men's grief is eroticized because it serves the courtly ideals of feudalism. For Derrida, the erotics of the pen ensure that it is the system of thinking—rather than Barthes himself—that is endlessly iterable, through the commemorative narrative of his loss, witnessed and broadcast.

CHAPTER 4

Toward a Mediterranean Erotics of Grief

In previous chapters, I argued that grief is eroticized in service of privilege in medieval literary texts ranging from fable to romance, from chansons de geste to fabliaux. These texts depict elite communities and emotional practices as co-constructed. Yet, the erotics of grief not only thematize privilege in medieval texts from a wide variety of genres and languages, but also have deeper roots in the Mediterranean. As I argued in *Exchanges in Exoticism*, the widespread practice of exogamous, cross-cultural marriage among the medieval elite after the Fourth Lateran Council offered a space for cross-cultural contact, exchange, and hybridity—marriages became a site for negotiating disparate but entwined practices of power among the Christian elite of the medieval Mediterranean.[1] Cross-cultural marriage functioned as political and cultural strategy and presupposed shared, common values among an elite privileged enough to forge and profit from these kinds of partnerships. By extension, in this chapter,

---

A preliminary version of a portion of this chapter appeared in an edited volume on Byzantine romance: "Romance and the Love of Death in the Medieval Mediterranean," in *A Handbook to the Late Byzantine Romances*, ed. Ingela Nilsson and Adam Goldwyn (Cambridge: Cambridge University Press, 2017), 299–320.

1. Megan Moore, *Exchanges in Exoticism: Cross-Cultural Marriage and the Making of the Mediterranean in Old French Romance* (Toronto: University of Toronto Press, 2014).

I explore what I characterize as a kind of Mediterranean elite affective diaspora, in which emotional exceptionalism goes hand in hand with the construction of elite communities, privileging elite status over geo-cultural specificity. Medieval literature depicting cross-cultural encounter portrays emotional norms—and sometimes even their violation—as a way of reaffirming community. Here, that community is organized around commonalities of elite power throughout the Mediterranean.

Perhaps nowhere is the negotiation of privilege better articulated than in narratives structured by pejorative depictions of the "other" found in the literature of encounter, such as the epic, the *romans antiques*, and especially travel narratives. One of the best known and most widely reproduced travel narratives is John of Mandeville's *Travels*, a fictionalized and highly popular early fourteenth-century account of an Englishman's travels during the Crusades, transmitted in several versions and languages in over seventy-five manuscripts.[2] Here, I read Mandeville's judgments of foreign practices—and specifically of interest to us, the emotions these practices produce—as delineating the contours of the privileged self.

The *Travels* narrate a knight's voyage to the East, and it is in the Mediterranean that he first witnesses the moral and emotional alterity that courses throughout the narrative. One episode, which takes place in Satalia (Antalya) on the shores of modern-day Turkey, details a man's grief-filled lust for his dead wife. In this episode, the traveler recounts that

> all that country was lost through the folly of a young man. For there was a beautiful damsel whom he loved well, and she died suddenly and was laid in a tomb of marble; and on account of the great love he had for her he went one night to her grave and opened it and went in and lay with her and then went on his way. At the end of nine months a voice came to him one night and said, "Go to the grave of that woman and open it, and behold what you have begotten on her. And if you go not you shall have great evil and suffering." And he went and opened the grave, and there flew out a very horrible head, hideous to look at, which flew all round the city; and forthwith the city sank, and all the district round about. And around there are many dangerous passages.[3]

---

2. In this chapter I focus on the Old French manuscripts, specifically BNF Fr. 2810.
3. John Mandeville, *The Travels of Sir John Mandeville*, trans. C. W. R. D. Moseley (London: Penguin, 2005), 55–56.

In some versions of this morbid tale, a serpent slithers out and ravages the kingdom, while in others it is a gorgon-headed monster who plagues the nearby gulf. Yet all imagine travel as a way to sort through a complicated nexus of desire, encounter, and privilege that is at once dangerous and erotic, a way of figuring the self in relation to monstrous alterity. The text relies on a layering of both geographic and emotional encounter, creating what I will call "affective travel." In Mandeville, affective travel repeatedly draws a contrast between abject emotional practices of "eastern" lands and commendable regimes of a vague medieval "west."

The fourteenth-century Satalian episode described in Mandeville has a diffuse and pervasive presence: it seems to originate in Medusa mythology[4] and is already present in thirteenth-century Arthurian romance; it circulates so widely and with such staying power that it is even cited in fourteenth-century Templars' confessions as an explanation of why some heretics worship heads.[5] Its iterability invites further consideration. Indeed, seeking to unravel the puzzling pervasiveness of the gorgon-head motif in premodern literature from ancient Greek to Old French to Boccaccio and Shakespeare, Paolo Rinoldi complains that "ironically, the puzzle seems to be composed for a moment, before dissolving again."[6]

---

4. Recently Alberto Vàrvaro has argued that the Satalian episode reflects a more generalized interest in the power of the head to figure violence in the Middle Ages; he attributes the apparition of the legend in twelfth- and thirteenth-century Norman dialect texts to be a product of the circulation of narratives based on happenings during the Crusades. Yet, if we contextualize the Satalian episode within its Mediterranean emotional community, we are invited to consider it not only as an emotional or cultural "other"—that is, as a crusader tool for expressing political and cultural alterity—but also as a delineation of the contours of desire-as-power in elite communities of the Mediterranean. See Alberto Vàrvaro, *Apparizioni fantastiche: Tradizioni folcloriche e letteratura nel medioevo—Walter Map* (Bologna: Il Mulino, 1994), 138–51.

5. One account of notary Antonio Sicci's deposition by Parisian inquisitors explains the myth's influence on Templars:

> Au sujet de l'article faisant mention de la tête, j'ai plusieurs fois entendu raconter ce qui suit dans la ville de Sidon. Un certain noble de cette ville aurait aimé une certaine femme noble d'Arménie; il ne la connut jamais de son vivant, mais, quand elle fut morte, il la viola secrètement dans sa tombe, la nuit même du jour où elle avait été enterrée. L'acte accompli, il entendit une voix qui lui disait: "Reviens quand le temps de l'enfantement sera venu, car tu trouveras alors une tête, fille de tes oeuvres." Le temps accompli, le chevalier susdit (praedictus miles) revint au tombeau et trouva une tête humaine entre les jambes de la femme ensevelie. La voix se fit entendre de nouveau et lui dit: "Garde bien cette tête, parce que tous les biens te viendront d'elle." (Quoted in Salomon Reinach, "La tête magique des templiers," *Revue de l'histoire des religions* 63 [January 1, 1911]: 31)

6. "beffardamente, il puzzle sembra comporsi per un attimo, prima di dissolversi nuovamente." Paolo Rinoldi, "Boccaccio e il 'gouffre de Satalie,'" *Studi sul Boccaccio* 36 (2008): 105–6.

Rinoldi's metaphor of blurriness is particularly apt, for as we have seen in our readings in earlier chapters, emotional boundaries are forever shifting as a negotiation of community.[7] Scholars have read travel literature as a rich archive of information about the other[8] and geo-sexual alterity,[9] but the relation between travel, community, and *emotion* remains largely unexplored. The Satalian episode—like many in travel literature—offers insight into medieval constructions of the other, but it also invites further consideration of the relation between emotion and travel. Travel permits an encounter with and exploration of affective bonds, and in the folios of medieval travel narratives, we find narrator-travelers whose commentary on emotional practices abroad constructs by extension an imagined emotional community for the home self.[10]

Literature depicting medieval encounter thus figures not only cultural alterity, but also the affective boundaries of its own reading community. In travel literature, the borders between self and other are, as Rinoldi explains, shifting, creating a kind of "narratological blurriness" that reveals, rather than obscures, emotional practices as transcendent, multilayered depictions of shared affective regimes. Practices of emotional exceptionalism abroad on a vague, Mediterranean frontier become a way of describing exceptionalism at home, a kind of emotional current deployed to convey notions of

---

7. As Malcom Barber points out, the frequent reappearance of the Satalia vignette in western medieval literature "seems to be linked to more frequent use of transport by sea by both pilgrims and crusaders, since Satalia is evidently the Gulf of Antalya in southern Asia Minor." Barber's interest in the Satalia account is in its use as leverage against Templars in fourteenth-century heresy trials, but others have focused on this narrative for its relation to myths denigrating the alterity of the Greek-speaking diaspora. Malcolm Barber, *The Trial of the Templars* (Cambridge: Cambridge University Press, 2012), 212.

8. Sebastian I. Sobecki, "Mandeville's Thought of the Limit: The Discourse of Similarity and Difference in *The Travels of Sir John Mandeville*," *Review of English Studies* 53, no. 211 (2002): 329–43; John Tulk, *Marco Polo and the Encounter of East and West* (Toronto: University of Toronto Press, 2008); Paul Zumthor, "The Medieval Travel Narrative," trans. Catherine Peebles, *New Literary History* 25, no. 4 (1994): 809–24; Albrecht Classen, "Marco Polo and John Mandeville: The Traveler as Authority Figure, the Real and the Imaginary," in *Authorities in the Middle Ages: Influence, Legitimacy, and Power in Medieval Society*, ed. Sini Kangas, Mia Korpiola, and Tuija Ainonen (Berlin: De Gruyter, 2013), 229–48; Dana Oswald, *Monsters, Gender and Sexuality in Medieval English Literature* (Suffolk, UK: D. S. Brewer, 2010).

9. Kim M. Phillips, "Oriental Sexualities in European Representation, c. 1245–c. 1500," in *Old Worlds, New Worlds: European Cultural Encounters, c.1000–c.1750*, ed. Lisa Bailey, Lindsay Diggelmann, and Kim M. Phillips (Turnhout, Belgium: Brepols, 2009), 53–74; Irina Metzler, "Perceptions of Hot Climate in Medieval Cosmography and Travel Literature," in *Medieval Ethnographies: European Perceptions of the World Beyond*, ed. Joan-Pau Rubiés (Farnham, UK: Ashgate, 2009), 379–415.

10. See the discussion on the centrality of alterity in establishing Mandeville's "home" in Jeffrey Jerome Cohen, "Pilgrimages, Travel Writing, and the Medieval Exotic," ed. Elaine Treharne and Greg Walker (Oxford: Oxford University Press, 2010), 617–18.

privilege across disparate elite Mediterranean households reading and listening to medieval stories of encounter.

In this chapter, I propose that medieval narratives of encounter deploy an erotics of grief that rely on an emotional intertextuality with an elite, Mediterranean past in order to figure elite practices of power in an interwoven, Mediterranean present. I claim that the erotics of grief that course throughout medieval literature are a deeply Mediterranean, intertextual, and intercultural negotiation of status and community through emotion. As I will discuss in readings of affective encounter in Middle English travel narratives, Old French *romans antiques*, Mediterranean romances, and Arthurian myths, textual and codicological evidence suggests that for elite medieval audiences, the emotional boundaries of their community were delineated by feeling rules imparted by dialogue with Mediterranean literary and emotional traditions to figure power among interconnected elite medieval Mediterranean reading communities.

Literary Encounters and Mediterranean Exemplars

Like *Mandeville's Travels*, literature from across the Mediterranean imagines the self through affective encounters with the other, and though the *romans antiques* and chansons de geste have been analyzed through the lenses of translation and postcolonial studies, their figuring of *emotional* exemplarity, place, and power has been unexplored.[11] In texts like the *Le roman d'Alexandre*, *Le roman de Troies*, and the *Roman d'Enéas*, twelfth-century audiences learn that their nobility flows from the veins of Mediterranean forebearers; it is no stretch to read these texts as melding a medieval noble present to a mythicized, Mediterranean past. As R. Howard Bloch has noted in *Etymologies and Genealogies*, the twelfth century witnesses a rise in genealogically articulated claims to power; in the *romans antiques*, encounters with and defeat of the other construct, explain, and eventually reproduce genealogical claims to power.[12] However, the chansons de geste also imagine noble

---

11. For a sampling of the now extensive work on cross-culturalism within the *romans antiques* see Krijna Nelly Ciggaar, "Encore une fois Chrétien de Troyes et la 'Matière Byzantine': La révolution des femmes au palais de Constantinople," *Cahiers de Civilisation Médiévale* 38, no. 3 (1995): 267–74; Renate Blumenfeld-Kosinski, "Chrétien de Troyes as a Reader of the Romans Antiques," *Philological Quarterly* 64, no. 3 (1985 Summer 1985): 398–405; Raymond Cormier, "Virgil Re-purposed in the Old French *Roman d'Eneas*," *Carte Romanze* 3, no. 1 (2015): 87–105; Émilie Deschellette, "L'identité à l'épreuve du mythe: La fabrique des origines, d'Énéas à Brutus." *Questes: Revue pluridisciplinaire d'études médiévales* 24 (2012): 66–84.

12. R. Howard Bloch, *Etymologies and Genealogies: A Literary Anthropology of the French Middle Ages* (Chicago: University of Chicago Press, 1983).

CHAPTER 4

power as figurative, and they depict that power by translating and diffusing Mediterranean *emotional* models in both the thematic *and* codicological proliferation of the legends of Alexander, Aeneas, and the Troy story into multiple languages and versions.

In medieval retellings of the life of Alexander the Great, for example, the processes of *translatio imperii* are imagined through Mediterranean emotional exemplarity, tying emotion to the propagation of imperial power. One thirteenth-century retelling of Alexander by French chronicler Philippe Mousket stages the glory of French kings in relation to a Mediterranean affective past. Mousket's *Chronique* fits into a pattern in which narrative tools such as iteration and *amplificatio* relay emotional regimes, providing a model for translating practices of power through affective codes.[13]

In an introduction (lines 1–49) that feels familiar to readers of romance, Mousket, much like contemporaries Chrétien de Troyes and Benoît de Sainte-Maure, asserts his own prowess by denigrating contemporary morals and professing to reintroduce tales of a glorious, mythicized past.[14] Following convention, Mousket inserts his text into an established tradition positing *translatio* as a comparative endeavor in which work with Mediterranean sources articulates prowess, both his own and that of the noble genealogies he depicts. The translation of Mediterranean feeling models is powerful, not only for describing feeling rules indigenous to medieval nobles, but also for positing Mousket's own prowess as an author.

Mousket's description of his textual frame is layered, imagining his book not only as a performance, or his text as didactically addressing the nobility, but also as privilege in dialogue with other audiences, specifically here the poor. This juxtaposition echoes the contrasts he articulates several lines earlier when he deploys internal and end rhyme to contrast couplings such as *li menut / bas devenut* (the people / become low); *li povre niche / mauvais deviennent li rice* (the poor foolish / bad become the rich) (lines 24–27). Though reminiscent of other descriptions of Fortune's wheel, the introduction describes privilege through its relation to *not* privilege, by its lack, through social stratification. That is, the prologue predicts what the later scene of royal mourning

---

13. For more in this vein see Jeanette M. A. Beer and Kenneth Lloyd-Jones, eds., *Translation and the Transmission of Culture between 1300 and 1600* (Kalamazoo: Medieval Institute Publications, Western Michigan University, 1995); Blumenfeld-Kosinski, "Chrétien de Troyes as a Reader of the Romans Antiques"; Christopher Baswell, "Marvels of Translation and Crises of Transition in the Romances of Antiquity," in *The Cambridge Companion to Medieval Romance*, ed. Roberta Krueger (Cambridge: Cambridge University Press, 2000), 29–44.

14. Philippe Mouskés, *Chronique rimée*, ed. Frédéric Auguste Ferdinand Thomas de Reiffenberg (Brussels: M. Hayez, 1836), 1–4.

confirms: the poor help cement the contours of the communities of the privileged who are commanded to "oiez [s]on livre" (48).

Mousket imagines this emotional community to be anchored in specifically *Mediterranean* storytelling. He explicitly ties his lament about the degradation of love to the sea when he rhymes *la mer* with *par amors amer* (lines 30–31). His rhyme highlights how the Mediterranean serves not only as a textual node for the *romans antiques*, but also as a site for figuring the feeling codes of privilege. In Old French, the slippage is nearly total, with the sea (*la . . . mer*) aurally and visually replicating loving (*amer*); it is a fracturing dependent on the audience's talents in aural parsing and on the scribe's goodwill toward attentive spacing.[15] And when his prologue is completed, Mousket opens his chronicle of French-speaking power with the founding story of western literature, Paris's abduction of Helen, a decidedly Mediterranean depiction of love, death, and heroism.

Texts such as the *Chronique* participate in literary conversations about the origins of French-speaking authority, often through references to Mediterranean affective models. In the *Chronique*, for example, Mousket uses genealogy to trace royal power from rulers of antiquity; in particular, he repeatedly turns to scenes of mourning to depict a dead ruler's power. In one example, Mousket invokes the Alexander legend to exemplify the good rule and worth of a contemporary French king, Philip II (d. 1223, also known as Philip Augustus). He specifically invokes the mourning of Alexander to frame the mourning of Philip:

> Quant rois Alixandres fu mors
> Ne fu mie li dious si fors
> Des XII pers, com si barons
> Fisent et partout environ
> La pais, et li bas et li haut. (23847–51)

> When King Alexander died,
> the grief was not at all as strong
> as that of the twelve peers as well as that of the barons
> and everywhere around
> the kingdom, by the low and the high.

Mousket skillfully amplifies the mourning of Philip II through comparison with the mourning of Alexander, underlined in the Old French emphatic "ne fu *mie*," suggesting that exemplary emotional practices from a

---

15. Spacing distorted for emphasis.

Mediterranean past may help negotiate and articulate identity within a contemporary noble present. Widespread, eroticized public grief transforms the private, bedside sorrow of Alexander's men in a mythicized, Mediterranean past into a thirteenth-century public display of contemporary French-speaking power.

Initially consigning mourning to Philip's family, then widening it to his twelve peers, and finally strategically expanding it to include a broader community of grieving peasants, the *Chronique*'s retelling deploys hyperbolic amplification of the mourning for Alexander to construct thirteenth-century power. Specifically, Mousket expands on his characterization of grief as a performance of power by depicting grieving through social hierarchies:

> Et, se verté dire vous voel,
> la roïne fist trop grant duel,
> sa feme, qui Ruesele ot à non,
> qui moult estoit de grant renon.
> ausi fist ses fius Loéis, ...
> et, çou que vaut, trop en fu tristes
> hireciés li siens fius Felipes,
> Et Carles, ses fius, li senés,
> ki par sa mère ert d'Arras nés.
> et la feme al duc de Louveng,
> sa fille, se le voir n'en feng,
> quant la mort de son père sot,
> Grant dol en fist et bien droit ot.
> ausi fisent partot à plain
> clerc, chevalier, bourgois, vilain.
> çou fu partout c'on le plora,
> si com drois fu; et c'estora
> Diex, mort à mort, les vis à vis.
> que vaut çou que tant vos devis;
> s'il est mors tot ausi morrons,
> nous qui apriés lui demorons. (2.23885–905)

> And, if I want to tell you the truth,
> the queen, his wife, who was named Ruesele,
> who was very renowned,
> made too much grief.
> So did his son Louis, . . .
> And, what's more, both his own sons Philip
> and Carl, his son, the wise,

who was born by his mother of Arras.
And the wife of the Duke of Louveng,
his daughter, if they tell the truth,
when she found out about the death of her father,
she expressed great grief and she was right to do so.
Likewise, so did
clerics, knights, bourgeois, and commoners everywhere.
It was such that everywhere they were weeping for him,
as is right; and so God provided for it,
death to death, life to life.
What does it matter that they be so separated;
if he dies, so will we also die,
we who after him remain.

The narrative expands on the strategic, seemingly endless repetition through which martial prowess is articulated in battlefield combat in earlier chansons de geste and consigns the same, serial iterability to grief, enumerating mourner after mourner to portray sorrow as a performance of prowess. The transformation of grief from private, textual voyeurism into public, civic spectacle invokes and expands on the erotics of grief in twelfth-century romance (where we typified women's tears as narrating masculine glory), chanson de geste (where we witnessed men's tears eroticizing and validating men's sacrifices), and *romans antiques* (where the twin topoi of *translatio imperii* and *translatio studii* become tools for explaining the origins of French authority).

Yet here, the mourning of Philip II invites more consideration in a contrast between the questions "Who may grieve?" and "What is a grievable life?" Mousket is careful to expand upon and extol the grief of a series of individual nobles, and he imagines that noble grief as contextualized by and also differentiated from that of "clerc, chevalier, bourgois, vilain." Peasants may certainly grieve, but they are pointedly *not* its grievable subjects: they are the last on the list of mourners, and their mourning from the peripheries only further highlights the value assigned to the wails of Philip's *pers*. In particularizing the kinds of people who grieve for Philip II, the author not only imagines grief as essential to the performance of sovereignty and nobility, but also to community, in ways that resonate with what Patricia Ingham has identified as the work mourning does *for* a culture.[16] Mousket's text seems to invite us to go

---

16. Patricia Clare Ingham, "From Kinship to Kingship: Mourning, Gender, and Anglo-Saxon Community," in *Grief and Gender: 700–1700*, ed. Jennifer C. Vaught and Lynne Dickson Bruckner (New York: Palgrave Macmillan, 2003), 17–31.

further: in his account, that work is not only *for* the community, but it also constructs differences *within* communities, as revealed in his careful delineation of clerics, knights, bourgeois, and commoners.

Mousket's invocation of class terms to delineate groups of mourners and amplify Philip's worth recalls—and modifies—Judith Butler's formulation of a grievable life, in which the mourner is called into being through a relationship with the mourned, as when she queries of the mourner, "Who am *I* without *you*?"[17] Here, Mousket's formulation reverses Butler's: he seems to imply not only that *Philip himself* is reconstituted through the mourning, but also that mourning calls different groups into being relationally, here to the deceased king and, by extension, the Greek emperor. That is, Mousket's reformulation of Butler's question posed by the mourner might be, "Who are *you*, without *me*?" He imagines the mourner—or, here, the various groups of mourners—to constitute the mourned. And, in this scene of mourning, *all* are invited to constitute the mourned, to participate in forming the worth of the dead through the emotions of the living. Formerly private displays of grief among nobles are now deployed as part of a civic emotional code in which public mourning provides both validation of the dead and an aspirational script for onlookers. Essentially, communal, civic weeping becomes the apogee of noble worth, figuring power through an erotics of widespread, public grief. Mousket is careful to detail not only the weeping of people of power, but also the collective mourning of the masses—and in so doing, he associates mourning with community and aligns civic practices with feeling scripts, inverting Butler's question.

Read together, Butler and Mousket reveal the iterativity of mourning to have a double function: to construct not only the subjectivity of mourners, but also that of the mourned themselves. Iterating and reiterating Mediterranean models of public grief for an Old French elite reading public, eroticized grief becomes both feeling model and narrative script for emoting and constructing noble worth. It is in the very moment of stasis, amplification, and repetition that not only is the worth of the dead constructed by the erotics of onlookers' grief, but the living can interrogate who their beloved, lost leader might be without their mourning. Repetition is doubly effective at deploying affective practices to cement elite subjectivity as a performance in community. For, once the leader is dead, the only prowess left for him to inhabit is that of the renown created by the story of grief, which Mousket seems to

---

17. Judith Butler, *Precarious Life: The Powers of Mourning and Violence* (New York: Verso, 2006).

recognize when he imagines grief as the ultimate story of sovereignty, the climax of a *vita* he purports to relay better than anyone else.

When the chronicle turns to Roncesvalles, it expands on the intersection of place, power, and emotion in an extended examination of love-as-grief centered on Charlemagne's mourning of his dead vassals. The extended, comparative description of Charlemagne's grief recalls earlier scenes eroticizing men's grief for each other. Like in the *Roland*, in his chronicle Mousket describes a Charlemagne whose grief is overpowering; in several instances, he begs for death (8820, 8834). Charlemagne compares his own doleful plight to that of other great rulers, and he invokes the same sorts of genealogies of power that structure *translatio imperii* in contemporary *romans antiques*: he compares himself to Alexander, who did not have to mourn his own men ("ne vit pas sa gent soufrir / tel mort n'a traïson offrir"); to Arthur, who is lucky to have died at arms shortly after Gawain, and therefore his anguish was reduced ("Artus plainsist tos jors Gawain, Gawains Artu, non pas en vain / Ne jà la plainte ne fausist ... mais ma plainte ne faura jà; mal ait ki si m'adamagia"); and to a Priam whose family's annihilation perhaps brings relief, in their total *lack* of mourning and being mourned ("n'ot que plaindre ne que doloir / k'il fu destruis esrant avoec: / si ne fu plorés de nului / ne il ne plora pour autrui") (8839–928). In invoking these figures to amplify Charlemagne's distress, the text again imagines contemporary medieval grieving through intertextual references in part to a Mediterranean affective past; it imagines the crowds grieving the vassals in dialogue with those who grieved other famous men of ancient glory in extended, public scenes of weeping (8915–9190). Here, Mediterranean feeling rules become exemplary, informing contemporary depictions of medieval power through an erotics of grief.

Mediterranean sources about emotion codes are also integral to other texts' formulations of twelfth- and thirteenth-century genealogies of power.[18] Like the widespread public mourning of Alexander in the *Roman d'Alexandre* and that of Philip II in Mousket's *Chronique*, mourning at the Calabrian court in Hue de Rotelande's fictional twelfth-century Anglo-Norman *Ipomédon* deploys the Mediterranean as a site for staging public grief as elite power.[19] Through battlefield skirmishes and (sometimes comical) romantic

---

18. For more see Zrinka Stahuljak, *Bloodless Genealogies of the French Middle Ages: Translatio, Kinship, and Metaphor* (Gainesville: University Press of Florida, 2005).
19. Though interpretations of the text vary, its exploration of staging power remains at the center of many of the most recent studies. See, for example, Judith Weiss, "Ineffectual Monarchs: Portrayals of Regal and Imperial Power in *Ipomédon*, *Robert le Diable* and *Octavian*," in *Cultural Encounters in the Romance of Medieval England*, ed. Corinne Saunders (Woodbridge, UK: D. S. Brewer, 2005), 55–68; Carol M. Meale, "The Middle English Romance of Ipomedon: A Late Medieval 'Mirror' for

encounters taking place throughout the Mediterranean, the romance narrates Ipomédon's wooing of the Duchess of Calabria (nicknamed "La Fiere" or "the Proud") and his unwilling love triangle with the Queen of Sicily. Composed near Hereford, England, but set in what is now southern Italy, *Ipomédon* draws from elite feeling models stemming from the Mediterranean, evidence that Mediterranean affective models circulated well beyond the borders of the sea. The Mediterranean is thematically and emotionally omnipresent—in one episode, for example, the aggrieved duchess literally threatens to drown her sorrows and herself in the sea ("kar sun voil / En la *mer* se neiast de dol") (9956, emphasis mine).

Throughout *Ipomédon*, references to the Mediterranean eroticize grief as power. Beginning in the prologue, negotiations of textual authority and noble power are linked to shared Mediterranean affective practices. Whether or not, as some claim, the text draws from the *Roman de Troie*, the prologue of *Ipomédon* certainly imagines the staging of elite community to be in dialogue with Latinate sources, and here my interest lies in how it appropriates not only *thematic* but also *emotional* models from a Mediterranean textual community.[20] The text opens with a call to revisit and translate ancient models of *sens*:

> [Cil] qui bons countes voet entendre,
> Sovent il poet grans biens aprendre:
> Par escuter enveis[e]ures
> E(s)t retrere les aventures,
> K'avyndrent a l'ancien tens,
> Poet l'en oyr folie et sens.
> Ore lessums folie (la) ester,
> Kar de sens fet mult bien parler![21] (1–8)

Princes and Merchants," *Reading Medieval Studies* 10 (1984): 136–91; Paola Scarpini, "Locating the Audience(s) in Hue de Rotelande's *Ipomédon*," in *In Search of the Medieval Voice: Expressions of Identity in the Middle Ages*, ed. Lorna Bleach et al. (Newcastle upon Tyne: Cambridge Scholars, 2009), 90–108.

20. Hue de Rotelande's relation to other writers is varied, with some claiming Latin and Greek sources, and others focused on his contemporaries. See Robert W. Hanning, "Engin in Twelfth Century Romance: An Examination of the *Roman d'Enéas* and Hue de Rotelande's *Ipomédon*," *Yale French Studies* 51 (1974): 82–101; Lucy M. Gay, "Hue de Rotelande's *Ipomédon* and Chrétien de Troyes," *PMLA* 32, no. 3 (1917): 468–91; Paola Scarpini, "Quand les topoi ne sont plus les mêmes: *D'Ipomédon de Hue de Rotelande*," in *Stealing the Fire: Adaptation, Appropriation, Plagiarism, Hoax in French and Francophone Literature and Film*, ed. James Day (Amsterdam: Rodopi, 2010), 113–27; Neil Cartlidge, "Masters in the Art of Lying? The Literary Relationship between Hugh of Rhuddlan and Walter Map," *Modern Language Review* 106, no. 1 (January 1, 2011): 1–16.

21. Hue de Rotelande, *Hue de Rotelande's Ipomedon: Ein Französischer Abenteuerroman Des 12. Jahrhunderts*, ed. Eugen Kölbing (Breslau: Wilhelm Koebner, 1889).

> Whoever wants to hear a good story,
> Can often learn good things:
> In listening to the pleasures
> Retold in the adventures,
> That came about in ancient times,
> Whereby one can hear about folly and sense.
> Now let us leave aside folly
> Because it is better to speak about sense!

Here, Hue offers to imbue his listener with *sens* through his translation and reworking of the models provided in his Mediterranean exemplar. Like many medieval authors who deploy *translatio*, Hue imagines his project as exemplary, linking the Mediterranean *matière* with which he works to a didactic relation with his audience. I read Hue's prologue as forming not only a circuitry of textual authority, but also as making room for emotional exemplarity, linking *sens* to the practice of right emotions. Like other contemporary authors such as Chrétien de Troyes, Hue contrasts *sens* with *folie*—overtly, sense with folly, but, also, and in a more capacious translation, with madness, wantonness, and sexual ardor, all forms of emotional excess. *Sens* takes on the sense of emotional, as well as practical, wisdom. And this more capacious, emotional sense of *sens* is attested to in the epilogue, where Hue confirms that his words have indeed taught his audience how to love and be loved (10551–55).

In his reworking of Latinate sources for a contemporary present, Hue de Rotelande situates the emotional education of the medieval Anglo-Norman-speaking elite in dialogue with the textuality of the Mediterranean. In deploying Mediterranean texts—and their emotional exemplarity—to frame the translation, rewriting, and transmission of noble glory for what was likely an elite "English" audience, *Ipomédon* constructs *translatio studii* and *imperii* not only as devices of textual translation, but also of cultural transmission. *Translatio studii* and *imperii* become vehicles for expanding on and exploring how Mediterranean affective models could work within the plotlines of a romance composed for an elite audience far from its shores. That is, texts such as *Ipomédon* reveal that *translatio* is not only inherently about the translation, appropriation, and dissemination of *textual* exemplarity, but also about disseminating models of *emotional* exemplarity.

In one episode that deploys *amplificatio* to eroticize grief, for example, the extensive size and tenor of a Calabrian crowd's mourning amplifies a noble's worth:

> En la cité remeint meint murne
> E funt granz pleintes e granz dols,

> Plurent e tirent lur chevaus,
> Pasment plusurs e gisent freiz,
> Batent paumes, tortent lur deiz,
> Crient, huchent, guaimentent, braient,
> Pur lur dame forment s'esmaient
> E pur eus meisme reunt poür,
> Tut dis quident vivre a dolur;
> Unc mes tel dol ne fut mené
> Cum il en funt par la cité,
> Plurent burgeis e se dementent,
> Dames e puceles guaimentent. (9938–52)

> In the city remain many mourners,
> and they make great cries and great grief;
> they cry and pull out their hair,
> many fall faint and lie stone cold;
> they beat their palms, they wring their fingers;
> they cry, shout, lament, and bray.
> For their lady they are so dismayed,
> and for themselves they express fear.
> All of them say they will live in sadness;
> since then no grieving was done
> as extensively as they did in the city.
> The bourgeois cried and went crazy,
> ladies and maidens lament.

As in other texts in this study, iteration ties grief to *action in stasis*, to narrative generation in emotional stagnation: the citizens "tirent lur chevaus," "batent," "tortent," "crient, huchent, guaimentent, braient," "pasment," "gisent," "s'esmaient," "vivre a dolur," "plurent," and "se dementent" as a way of narrating their distress—language that recalls the earlier emotional work of a tournament for the hand of La Fiere (6162–67). Buried within this productive stasis are nouns that imagine subjectivity through a relation to grief: citizens are called into being as *meint murne*; likewise, public, mass mourning renders a leader a mournable subject, immortalized by the public's grief-as-approbation.[22] The text takes care to transform mourning from a homosocial moment shared by elite knights beside a private deathbed, to a public ritual including women and maidens, as well as a separate strata, the

---

22. Butler, *Precarious Life*.

bourgeois. Here, grief is reiterated and eroticized not only as an expression of *individual* identity, but also as a performance of *community*, conferred by and confirmed through collective, mass mourning.

More importantly, Hue's translation of Mediterranean mourning practices inverts easy assumptions about the gendering of mourning and the subjects it creates. Without more textual context, it would be easy to assume, in reading this passage of amplified, reiterated mourning, that the crowd mourns the loss of a male leader, for, as we have seen, some texts certainly suggest that men are the only grievable subjects of elite textual communities. Yet here, mourning reinforces a reading that elitism itself is the eroticized, grievable subject of medieval fiction. After all, it is not for a noble *man* that they mourn, but for a threat to their *lady's* life and honor, as an Indian outsider, Léonin, has arrived and threatens to abduct her. Even without an actual death to mourn or a body to grieve, this text deploys mourning as a way to describe the contours of community and the worth of one elite in particular, the Duchess of Calabria, "La Fiere." Here, the public's mourning of the *lady*—and not a king—suggests that not only do medieval texts reappropriate Mediterranean emotional codes, but they also transform them to imagine that, across a spectrum of gender positions and geographic locations, grief performs the story of noble worth, rendering elites the mournable subjects of both medieval crowds and medieval texts.

The crowd's collective, amplified, iterative grief underscores La Fiere as a grievable subject *in advance of her actual loss*, not only highlighting the relation between eroticized grieving and the construction of elite worth, but also interrogating the relation between grief and time. Even without a death or a body to grieve, the crowd can mourn the loss of their lady in advance of her actual death. The mourning happens in advance of the loss, untying the knot of temporality so dear to concerns about stasis in melancholia, which figure a problem of lethargy in the present as a contrast to imagined, idealized future productivity. That is, mourning takes the subject out of time, by continually reinscribing an individual's worth only in relation to others' presents.

Whereas Derrida's work suggests that iterativity and repetition destabilize the promise of mourning, reading with the medieval, in scenes like the not-death of La Fiere and the crowd's amplified mourning for her, we see that mourning can be a site of production and generation precisely because it exists in three times: through past, accretive experiences of what it means to lose someone; through present instantiations of sorrow; and through the future threat of final, absolute loss. Mourning works to resist all these times, and to render elite subjects simultaneously immortalized by and threatened with the eternal loss of commemoration. Mourning constructs the contours of the grievable elite subject in ways that resonate with the time of the promise, in Shoshana Felman's terms: here, death need not even happen for mourning to promise elite renown, to perform a lady's worth, and to construct a public's fears.[23] Thus through Hue de Rotelande, and with Felman, Butler, and Barthes but against Freud and Derrida, we could formulate the promise of the erotics of grief as such: we call you into being in the moment we mourn you; we are not without you, and you are not without us; the promise of our mourning writes your renown.

Misperforming the Emotions of Power

Some texts explore what happens to elite communities when grief is not properly or no longer eroticized—how a *misperformance* of emotion can also clarify the contours of community and reveal whose lives are grievable. In book 4 of Virgil's *Aeneid*, for example, Dido is described through her failed relation with lamentation, and Virgil depicts her as lapsing into a misperformance of elite desire when she betrays her vow to honor her dead husband in order to become Aeneas's lover. Eventually spurned by an Aeneas who heeds the call of duty and sets sail, Dido, repentant and suicidal, is summoned to death by cries emanating from Sychaeus's altar (4.460–65). The twelfth-century Old French *Roman d'Enéas* reworks material from Virgil's *Aeneid* to imagine what happens when Mediterranean feeling codes are *misperformed* for a contemporary elite medieval audience.

The prologue of the *Roman d'Enéas* stakes a claim to contemporary noble, French-speaking authority through genealogical and textual ties to a mythicized, Mediterranean past.[24] Within the text's articulation of genealogies of power in the transfer of imperium from Greece to Rome is a subtext about the emotional education of its protagonist, a shaping of Enéas from errant, single exile to founding father. And indeed, the epilogue aligns his success with his Mediterranean *education sentimentale*, specifically describing successful rulership through the successful performance of emotion. He is the epitome of careful rule predicated on regulation: "sans desroy, /

---

23. Shoshana Felman, *Le scandale du corps parlant: Don Juan avec Austin, ou, la séduction en deux langues* (Paris: Seuil, 1980).

24. See, for example, Christopher Baswell, "Marvels of Translation and Crises of Transition," 31–35, and "Men in the *Roman d'Enéas*: The Construction of Empire," in *Medieval Masculinities: Regarding Men in the Middle Ages*, ed. Clare E. Lees, Thelma Fenster, and Jo Ann McNamara (Minneapolis: University of Minnesota Press, 1994), 154; Stahuljak, *Bloodless Genealogies*.

amesurez, cortois et saiges" (without disorder / measured, courteous, and wise) (10314–15).[25]

Yet, as in Virgil, some of the text's most powerful scenes of emotion are *not* exemplary, as when Enéas falls for Dido and forgets his quest ("son afaire a mis en oubli") (1692). In an extended examination of their passionate courtship, the medieval text gladly imagines love across the border—the lovers' desire is not outlandish because it stems from some cross-cultural taboo or exotic exceptionalism. Rather, Enéas's desire for Dido removes him from an economy of heroism, pauses his quest toward a heroic identity, and undermines his reputation in ways that both draw on the emotions of the Latin exemplar and resonate with contemporary figures from romance, such as Chrétien's Erec or Yvain.[26] These heroes, the texts note, need an emotional education, and their excessive heterosexual desire must be abandoned in favor of emotional norms proper to the homosocial community of feudal masculinity. In aligning Enéas's misperformance of imperial identity with that of the unsuccessful characters of contemporary romance, the text aligns even the misperformances of elite emotions with power. Though all these men are eventually redeemed by learning to balance emotion and duty, the moments when they fail are as revelatory as the moments when they succeed.

Not only does the misperformance of desire temporarily render Enéas an antihero; it also leaves Dido reviled by her people, who claim that she has renounced governance in favor of making love. The text identifies her misperformance as problematic on several levels, thereby exposing the stakes of noble desire. From a civic and martial point of view, it interferes with maintaining the infrastructure that protects the city walls, rendering desire a civic force ("Amors li a fait oublïer / terre tenir et a garder") (1496–97). Her desire is economically and politically destabilizing, in that her people abandon their work (1505). Because Enéas is untitled, her desire also destabilizes boundaries of class (1670–71). Faithless to her vows toward her dead husband, Dido, in her desire, further undermines the felicity of the oath and reveals the instability of the relation between emotion, language, and truth (1590).

Most urgently, the text imagines Dido as infelicitous in desiring her dead husband, roundly condemning her new desire as *putaige* (1655), *fellonie* (1618, 1651), and *foloie* (1661), fricatives unsurprisingly aligned with *feme*. I contend

---

25. *Le roman d'Enéas*, ed. Michel Zink (Paris: Livre de Poche, 1997).
26. E. Jane Burns, *Bodytalk: When Women Speak in Old French Literature* (Philadelphia: University of Pennsylvania Press, 1993).

that the misperformance of *that* desire is the text's true anxiety, and it reveals a complex entwining of gender, power, and grief. Whereas the text spends hundreds of lines developing the moral and emotional education of its eponymous protagonist, and whereas it castigates Enéas when he chooses sexual desire over heroic quest, the true anxiety about desire in the *Roman d'Enéas* is that Dido abandons the mourning of her dead husband to make love with Aeneas, essentially *erasing the memory* of one of Carthage's most powerful and successful leaders.

Within the medieval text, several extended and often misogynous critiques of Dido's passion suggest that her misperformance of desire simultaneously misperforms her dead husband's power, and in one such passage, her vassals levy a juridical vocabulary to characterize her emotional misperformance as betrayal:

> Entr'euz le dient, si ont droit,
> Que moult est folz qui feme croit:
> Ne se tient preu en sa parolle,
> Tel tient on a saje qui est folle.
> Elle dissoit qu'a son seigneur,
> Qui mors estoit, proumis s'amor,
> Ne li toudroit a son vivant:
> Or en fait autre son talent,
> Or est mentie la fiance,
> Trespassee est la couvenance
> Qu'a son seignor avoir plevie.
> Ffolz est qui en feme se fie,
> Moult a le mort tost oublïé,
> Ja ne l'avra si bien amé,
> Puis fait du vif tout son deport,
> En nonchaloir a mis le mort. (1672–87)

> Between them, [the vassals] say it, and they are correct,
> that he who believes a woman is foolish:
> very little worth can be accorded to their words,
> and she who is foolish is often taken for wise.
> She said that to her lord
> who had died she had promised her love,
> and she would not be deterred [from it] while living:
> now she has fallen for another,
> now she has lied about her trust,
> and the covenant that she had sworn

to her lord has been violated.
Foolish is he who trusts in a woman,
who forgets the dead right away,
having not really ever properly loved him,
and then turns all her attention to the living,
and consigns the dead to forgetting.

The vassals describe Dido's betrayal using the terminology of a feudal legal system organized around the oath with words like *droit, parolle, proumis, mentie, fiance, couvenance, plevie,* and *fie*. They describe her relation to her husband through the same lexicon, insisting not on relations of love (using Old French descriptors like *ami* or *mari*) but instead on those of feudal power (using *seignor*). The vassals' condemnation of the new love affair exposes the liaison as jeopardizing the status of the feudal system, not only in betraying the juridical and sign system of meaning through which loyalty is guaranteed, but also in betraying what that guarantee is designed to bring: value to potential sacrifice, through remembrance. It is no coincidence that *plevie, fie,* and *oublïé* are all juxtaposed through the narrator's clever rhyme scheme. Indeed, he, too, participates in the misogynistic condemnation of Dido and deploys the same juridical vocabulary to seal his approval in the salvo "si ont droit." Though the Latin original focuses on aligning personal emotion with civic duty, the twelfth-century Old French rewriting uses a feudal legal lexicon particular to the Middle Ages to depict the (mis)performance of emotions as a (mis)performance of language about elite identity before the law in ways that resonate with Chrétien's recontextualization of Latinate models of emotion for a twelfth-century feudal system in *Philomena*, as we saw in chapter 1.

Whereas Virgil concludes from Dido's misperformance of desire that "varium et mutabile semper / femina" (4.569–70), our medieval text shifts the interpretation, advising "moult est folz qui feme croit." Virgil's conclusion aligns the feminine with mutability; the medieval text criticizes the relation between emotion and gender, by criticizing the sense of men who would believe women and their mutability. In a variation repeated throughout the passage, the problem with Dido—and all women, we are told—is not only that they are mutable, but that their emotional mutability has political and social consequences. Specifically, if grief is no longer eroticized, a dead man's memory is effaced: "mors estoit, proumis s'amor" and "moult a le mort tost oublïé." In my reading, this shift in the medieval text is purposeful, underlining not only how affective mutability threatens the performative felicity of speech and its ability to enact trust, but also the felicity of a feudal system designed to commemorate sacrifice through an erotics of grief.

Yet this passage also imagines that grief generates timeless remembrance, in the same time frame as the grieving of the not-dead La Fiere in *Ipomédon*: as soon as the lady stops grieving, the story of her dead husband's worth is effaced. The anxieties expressed here are not only about the mutability of a woman's sexuality and emotions, but also about the power of emotions to *misperform* identity: Dido misperforms her dead husband—and, by extension, the worth of his men—by falling in love with someone new. She demotes him from beloved, cherished, and mourned to forgotten, effaced, and obliterated. The mutability of Dido's grief reveals the precariousness of elite power constituted through the emotional community of the other, for if feelings are mutable, so are the meaning and memory accorded to elite sacrifice.

Moreover, the men's concerns reveal another critical piece in the puzzle about the relation between the promise of emotions, narration, and time: because Sychaeus deserves to be eternally remembered, so the logic of his men goes, Dido may never stop mourning. Mourning is eternal, timeless, and necessarily always in the present (attested to in the repetitive "or" of the passage); it is a constant fight to reiterate the memory of the dead and the status of the living, a constant threat of failure should emotions change. The passage's attention to tense and mood enunciates a critique of Dido's (perceived) emotional instability: in repeatedly contrasting what she promised and said with her current actions through contrasts in the imperfect and present indicative, the text underlines that what she *said she felt* about her dead husband did not turn out to be true. The promise of her continued grief was infelicitous and went unfulfilled, destabilizing the fabric of her community and interrogating the promise of renown implicit in the erotics of grief.

If the first critique is leveled internally by her men and externally by the narrator, it is most poignantly Dido herself who invokes the same feudal legal lexicon to query why she abandoned the faith that she had pledged to her lord ("Pour quoy trespassay je la foy / Que je plevis a mon seignor?") (2073–79). Dido's use of a legal lexicon based on the feudal oath (*foy, plevis, seignor, trespassay, fiance, mentie*) to describe her misperformance of desire reinforces the connection begun by her men between emotions, language, and noble feudal power rooted in the felicity of the oath of loyalty.

It would be easy to read these two passages as part of a larger medieval tradition of gendered condemnation of women's desire and speech, but both sides of the couple—and even the neglected, dead husband—together reify a system in which noble status is in part performed through an erotics of grief tightly tied to narration and commemoration. The passages suggest that in this system, noble women's commitment to a vow of marriage is also a commitment to performing an eternal narrative of commemoration, long after death. While we may certainly critique the misogyny of this passage, we can simultaneously identify it as redeploying Mediterranean exemplars to depict a spectrum of gendered elite subject positions in which even emotional misperformances reinforce the communal boundaries of a system that rewards loss with commemoration.

Medieval Mediterranean Affective Cultures

As we have seen here, literary accounts from genera as diverse as travel narratives, chronicles, romance, and the *romans antiques* invoke classical Mediterranean feeling rules to negotiate the staging of medieval power. In referencing an erotics of grief tied to the affective structure of ancient and classical texts, the medieval authors imagine medieval communities of privilege through a dialogue with classical Mediterranean exemplars for a medieval present. Yet, and as I argue, the erotics of grief that structure communities of privilege across these texts are not only anchored in feeling models from antiquity but also describe shared and often contested *contemporary, medieval* Mediterranean practices.

The erotics of grief permeating medieval texts describe a shared set of affective practices integral to the communities of privilege invoked, negotiated, and described within our texts. These feeling rules appear in texts written for elites throughout the medieval Mediterranean, suggesting commonalities in the ways elite medieval communities deployed Mediterranean feeling models to imagine and negotiate shared practices of power articulated through forms of emotional exceptionalism, such as the erotics of grief available only to the privileged subjects of mourning imagined in these story lines. Together, these texts suggest that one of the ways elites across the Mediterranean represented their power was through their practices of emotions: even as these texts describe nobles in constant competition with one another, they also recognize a common, Mediterranean language of emotions.

Once identified, commonalities among the emotional practices depicted within texts commissioned by, performed for, and read by medieval elites across the Mediterranean appear ubiquitous. For example, the multiple translations and reiterations of the *Apollonius of Tyr* story seem an obvious candidate for narrating eroticism and exploring emotional alterity in a tale about incest in *outremer*. Likewise, the cross-confessional love affairs depicted in the twelfth-century Old French romances *Floire et Blancheflor* and

Aucassin et Nicolette are widely translated, and they imagine love as a negotiation not only of ethnicity and religion, but also status. The manuscript evidence attests to the popularity of stories negotiating elite, multiethnic love through the Mediterranean: *Floire et Blancheflor*, for example, is translated and reworked into Middle High German, Middle English, Swedish, Danish, Norwegian, Castilian, Flemish, Italian, Latin, and Medieval Greek, and it has resonances with the *Arabian Nights* story of Neema and Noam.[27] The romance narrates the love affair between Floire, Muslim heir to the Al-Andulusian throne, and Blancheflor, a Christian knight's daughter born in captivity in Floire's household in Naples after her pregnant mother is seized by Floire's father. Once the children reach puberty, they fall in love, and, fearing that her Muslim son will fall for the "pagan" Blancheflor, Floire's mother devises a plot to separate them. She sells Blancheflor to merchants en route to Cairo and informs her son that his lover has died; Floire mourns her excessively, which his parents qualify as unbecomingly suicidal (795–895), until he discovers the ruse and rushes off across the Mediterranean to track the merchants and rescue her.[28]

When the lovers are finally reunited, they plot unsuccessfully to trick the emir, who in turn plans to kill them when he discovers this second ruse. The emir accuses Floire of a crime of property, claiming that he bought Blancheflor mere months before (2717) and that he paid seven times her weight in gold (2718). However, more tellingly, the emir's accusation reveals what is so valuable about Blancheflor's erotic potential: he declares that it is not only her beauty but also her *nobility* that make her an attractive captive, announcing "por çou qu'ele ert et bele et *gente* / avoie en li mise m'entente" (because she was beautiful and *noble* / I had placed in her my desire/design) (2727–28, emphasis mine). Blancheflor's status is part of what makes her desirable. The story line clearly borrows from the *Arabian Nights* to recharacterize the emir's threat of eroticism as the transgression of an emotional compact between elites—here, the threat is of an elite raping and killing a white, Christian captive (named, literally, a "white flower"), whom the emir acknowledges as similarly *gente* and whose very worth is tied to the ways an erotics of grief intersect with her privilege. Eroticized grief serves as both a common vocabulary for elite affective community and the tool through which power is negotiated and articulated as violation: it is through the threat of raping and killing another elite that the emir both

---

27. For a longer examination of cross-cultural marriage, codicology, and what I call an elite economy of exoticism see my discussion of *Floire et Blancheflor* in *Exchanges in Exoticism*.

28. *Floire et Blancheflor*, ed. Jean-Luc Leclanche (Paris: Champion, 1980).

acknowledges and eschews overlap in their communities of privilege to articulate his own personal power.

Floire et Blancheflor is a quintessentially Mediterranean text, then, with thematic and manuscript history that imagines the performance of emotion as a vehicle through which elite relationships can be established, negotiated, and reformulated across differences of confession, language, and geography. Yet it is not only in Old French or Middle English exemplars that the erotics of grief negotiate elite community—indeed, this eroticism is not a monodirectional, voyeuristic tool redolent of some kind of medieval Orientalism. Examples abound elsewhere in texts from across the Mediterranean. As I have written elsewhere, Medieval Greek texts invite us to rethink how the feeling rules we may identify as integral to "western" performances of power may be better characterized as articulated through a shared Mediterranean culture of exceptionalism and privilege.[29] The Satalian episode described in John of Mandeville and present in Templar trials, for example, has links with the association of death and desire present in both ancient Greek and Medieval Greek texts.[30] In book 5 of Xenophon's ancient Greek *Ephesian Tale*, the hero, Abrokomes, arrives in Sicily in a search for his lover, and instead he comes across an elderly fisherman named Aegialeus. In his youth, Aegialeus had eloped from his highborn position in Sparta with his lover Thelxinoe. She has died, but rather than bury her, he continues to have intercourse with her, claiming that "the way you see her now is not the way I see her. My boy, I think of her as she was in Laconia, as she was when we eloped" (327).[31]

Yet the erotics of grief is not merely an ancient world motif deployed to articulate elite worth. Like many lovers in romance, in Niketas Eugenianos's twelfth-century *Drosilla and Charikles*, the protagonists are repeatedly separated and reunited on an adventure that serves not only as a chastity test for Drosilla but also as a meditation on the nature of love. In passage after passage, lovers express affection through an erotics of grief: Kleinias expresses his love as "dying . . . before time" (4.305); Kallidemos wishes to take the unwilling Drosilla to be his "beloved as a tomb-companion" (6.478); love is perfected in the deaths of Daphnis and Chloë (6.440) and Hero and

---

29. Moore, "Romance and the Love of Death in the Medieval Mediterranean."
30. Roderick Beaton discusses examples of love-as-death in Makrembolites's *Hysmine and Hysminias*, *Drosilla and Charikles* (*The Medieval Greek Romance*, 60–62); and Adam Goldwyn examines Gobryas's assault of Rhodanthe in his *Byzantine Ecocriticism: Women, Nature, and Power in the Medieval Greek Romance* (New York: Palgrave Macmillan, 2018), 98–99.
31. Longus, and Xenophon of Ephesus, *Daphnis and Chloe; Anthia and Habrocomes*, ed. and trans. Jeffrey Henderson (Cambridge, MA: Harvard University Press, 2009).

Leander (6.489); and even Philomela and Itys reappear as noisy birds breaking the dawn of a sleepless unrequited lover's night, the "worst species of wicked birds" whose squawking upends the kingdom (7.645–55).[32] Not only is love repeatedly linked to mourning by all those in the medieval text, but the emotional language of the text is articulated through a communal language negotiating elite emotion through ancient Mediterranean myth.

Another twelfth-century Greek romance, *Belthandros and Chrysandza*, stages the erotic education of a young nobleman in ways that resonate with contemporary Old French texts such as the *Enéas*, *Erec et Enide*, *Floire et Blancheflor*, and *Aucassin et Nicolette*. In this romance, the eponymous protagonist is exiled from his father's lands until he learns how to love correctly in order to rule. Like other texts in this chapter, *Belthandros* imagines an erotic education as foundational to articulating the self in community. By focusing on Love's conquest of the obdurate Belthandros and his subsequent transformation from stoic to lover, the text recognizes private emotions as having a kind of social performativity; here, they help build and regulate communities in power. The performance of love permits a performance of kingship—and, when read within a Mediterranean textual community, eroticism becomes a site for the negotiation of shared power within a broader elite, Mediterranean emotional community.

Like Belthandros—and perhaps like the narrator in Mandeville—the Latin traveler whose tale is told at the outset of another medieval Greek romance, *Livistros and Rhodamni*, is a man whose nobility is incomplete, though he has all the worldly goods one could desire. The narrator, Klitovon, recounts coming across an aggrieved Latin nobleman, Livistros, and hearing his story of love's afflictions: "Amid so much joy, amid so many pleasures, amid all my wealth and prosperity, amid the many luxuries and delights which I possessed and had at my command and in which I took pleasure, no concern for love ever came to me," bemoans Livistros to his new companion.[33] Though the Latin traveler, Livistros, has all the requisite material goods (emphasized here as "amid" and reinforced by the anaphoric repetition in the Greek of variations on the sounds of $\mu\grave{\epsilon}$), without an education in love, his performance of elite masculinity is infelicitous.

After Livistros is finally consumed by Eros's afflictions, he seeks out his fated Rhodamni, and they begin a love affair through letters, which, as Panagiotis Agapitos notes, represents a break from Latinate traditions and offers

---

32. Niketas Eugenianos, *Drosilla and Charikles: A Byzantine Novel*, trans. Joan B. Burton (Mundelein, IL: Bolchazy-Carducci, 2004).

33. Gavin Betts, *Three Medieval Greek Romances* (New York: Garland, 1995), 97.

insight into how emotional practices are both shared within and negotiate elite community in the Mediterranean.[34] Love is an epistolary volley, letters lobbing emotions into being, creating and sculpting responses even as the feelings themselves are beyond control and processing. The lady, Rhodamni, is advised by her eunuch to avoid passion's deadly invitations in wording that further underscores Eros's chthonic register: its depths, it fiery furnace, its invitation to drown in a sea of longing (125). Livistros implores his paramour, "if you have been reared by Desire . . . share my woes, pity what I suffer" (129). Livistros pointedly allies desire with death, lamenting that he saw "a letter of love become a man's grave and words of affection my soul's death" (133), while in another letter he more concretely describes Love as a mixture of grief and joy, exclaiming, "suddenly I again find joy in my grief and woes" (139). In *Livistros*, the vocabulary of love is a vocabulary of death; the edges of noble love are also the edges of existence.

In *Livistros*, Eros is not merely an embodied performance of the erotics of grief; it is also a performance of community—a noble, privileged, and *Mediterranean* community. The text takes care to describe the love affair in terms of *status* (pointedly, in terms of nobility) as well as in terms of *geography*—this is a love affair between a Byzantine woman and a Latin nobleman, staged as a frame narrative conversation between a Latin traveler and a Byzantine wanderer. The other metanarratives within the story also imagine crosscultural love between Armenians, Syrians, Litavians, and Byzantines; part of Livistros's and Klitovon's journey to recover Rodamni takes them to Egypt, where the king himself has fallen in love with her. The love affair imagined here is literally predicated on a shared, Mediterranean sense of emotion, and it imagines a community of possible lovers (the Mediterranean nobility) as sharing an understanding not only of love, but also of the erotics of grief that structure their negotiations of power through its performances.

I agree with Agapitos's assessment of *Livistros*'s multiculturalism, which I see as bearing witness to how community and class entwine in a Byzantine text exploring the erotics of grief within "a contemporary aristocratic setting; a set of characters whose ethnic origins are Latin (i.e., French and Italian), Armenian and Saracen but not Byzantine; elements of 'Latin' chivalric practice (oath of vassalage, jousting, hawk hunting, dress); and the presence of allegorical characters."[35] That is, the Byzantine text invokes elite

---

34. "'Words Filled with Tears': Amorous Discourse as Lamentation in the Palaiologan Romances," in *Greek Laughter and Tears*, ed. Margaret Alexiou and Douglas Cairns (Edinburgh: Edinburgh University Press, 2017), 357–58.

35. Ibid., 357.

Latinate cultural practices from across the Mediterranean to imagine the elite, Byzantine self. The text imagines the Byzantine self in dialogue with Latinate and Mediterranean feeling models, and it uses an erotics of grief to negotiate and construct subjectivity within a larger discourse of Mediterranean performances of power.

That there could be a shared erotics of grief across boundaries of "nation" or "culture" in cross-cultural love affairs in Palaiologan romance suggests that elite love performs and is shaped by Mediterranean communities of privilege. As in Mousket's *Chronique*, in *Ipomédon*, in *Floire et Blancheflor*, or the *Alexandre*, *Enéas*, and *Troie*, the emotional community of these medieval Greek protagonists is constituted through intertextuality with an elite Mediterranean emotional community that eroticizes loss. From medieval Greek romance to Old French travel narrative, from chansons de geste to the *romans antique*, medieval texts describing privilege forge a connection between affective exemplarity and Mediterranean models of privilege. As we have seen, texts from a variety of generic, linguistic, and cultural standpoints depict elite identity in dialogue with an erotics of grief, and I claim they do so by depicting contemporary Mediterranean emotional practices as a way of negotiating, translating, and disseminating elite community among competing communities of power in the medieval present.

Codicology and Elite Mediterranean Feeling Communities

The elite emotional communities depicted in the fictional texts within this study are also attested to by medieval Mediterranean objects themselves. If we accept medieval books not only as markers of ideas through words on the page, but also as things whose design, function, and use offer evidence about medieval culture, we can then question how books interact with their communities. That these stories we have explored have survived in so many manuscripts and have been so widely translated and reproduced is a testament to their popularity; that they are so often included in codices with documented noble readership underscores the relation between the kinds of communities imagined within the texts and the function of the books as objects in—and constructing—community themselves.[36]

---

36. Beyond BNF Fr. 2810, for example, there is documentation that Charles V had a copy of the *Travels* in his library; the codex is hardly a luxury product, but it has evidence of his use and contains his signature. Other codices contain royal letters and diplomatic documents, as well as the more traditional *vitae*, prayers, and romances we typically see bound together in medieval codices.

In their cost and exclusivity, illuminated manuscripts are objects that figure power. Commissioned by and produced for the nobility they often represent, they are objects with a multitude of valences that perform medieval privilege as much as they transmit a story. I agree with Gerald Guest when he asserts that "medieval illuminated manuscripts created meaning for their historical readers . . . [that is] bound up with the subjectivity of a book's reader; indeed, we could say that meaning here exists as the by-product of the encounter between individual and object."[37] One such object, BNF Fr. 2810, offers 265 illuminations depicting encounters in a compendium known as the *Livre des merveilles et autres récits de voyages et de textes sur l'Orient*, including more specifically Mandeville's *Travels*, the source of our Satalian episode.[38] Created and assembled for Jean sans Peur, the Duke of Burgundy, as a gift for his uncle and opponent in the Hundred Years' War, the Duke of Berry, in January 1413,[39] BNF Fr. 2810 is widely considered "a prime example of the culture of the book as a luxury and privilege for the European elite in the Middle Ages."[40] Illuminated within the school of the Boucicaut master, this luxury codex was produced later than the twelfth- and thirteenth-century texts under consideration in chapters 2 and 3, yet its interest in the foreign suggests that the same dynamics of eroticism, taboo, and transgression functioning in the *Travels* still hold resonance in later visual representations.[41]

With its history of transmission as a gift for Jean de Berry and its documented use within the houses of Burgundy and Armagnac, BNF Fr. 2810 is not only a luxurious depiction of the other, but it is also a way of creating

---

37. Gerald B. Guest, "Illuminated Manuscripts as Machines," *Manuscripta* 55, no. 2 (2011): 139. Through an extended exploration of the relation between medieval reader and object in terms of Deleuze and Guattari's idea of "desiring machines," Guest elaborates that medieval manuscripts are "inflected by concerns that might be described variously as ideological, aesthetic, spiritual, and libidinal (to name just a few areas open to scholarly investigation). In seeking to tease out these flows of desire and to consider them historically, manuscripts should be seen as embodying or encoding the residual traces of past desires as well as being the partial producers of new desires" (143).

38. BNF Fr. 2810 also includes Marco Polo's *Devisement du monde*; the *Travels*; Hayton's *Fleur des estoires de la terre d'Orient*; and several texts translated by Jean le Long, including Odoric de Pordenone's *Itinerarium de mirabilibus orientalium Tartarorum*, Guillaume de Boldensele's *Liber de quibusdam ultramarinis partibus et praecipue de Terra sancta, de l'estat et du gouvernement du grant Kaan de Cathay, empereur des Tartares*, and Ricoldo da Monte Croce's *Liber peregrinationis*.

39. Margaret Kim, "The Material Culture of Princely Power and the Art of the Exotic East: The Miniatures of MS Français 2810 of the Bibliothèque Nationale de France," *Sun Yat-Sen Journal of Humanities* 43 (July 7, 2017): 27.

40. Ibid., 26.

41. See, for example, Paul Zumthor's contention that the codicological popularity of Marco Polo's *Travels* reveals the extent to which the sponsoring nobility had an appetite for such works in "Medieval Travel Narrative," 809.

a community to receive the performance of the noble French self. Margaret Kim writes that the Duke of Berry's "political uses and enjoyment of magnificent illuminated books, exotic objects, and rare animals bespeak the extravagant way of life that was considered the exclusive privilege of the ruling elite of Europe. Exotica and prized art displayed conspicuously the power of a prince and they served as a means for the prince to establish and maintain personal correspondence and political relations with other princes in the world. . . . The prestige associated with them, therefore, was exclusively for the nobility."[42]

Though the recent scholarship on the illuminations of BNF Fr. 2810 has explored how they figure royal power and debated whether they figure a pejorative exoticism, I am interested in how this codex creates a circuit of meaning with its elite readers through representations of affective encounter—how it creates emotional community with and for its readers.[43] If we follow recent thinking in which manuscripts might be considered what Gerald Guest calls "desiring machines" assembled through object and reader, BNF Fr. 2810 becomes part of a circuit, depending on transmissions between giver, receiver, illuminator, author, and scribe to create a meaningful community of interpretation. This circuit shapes shared practices. Here, I claim that one of the codex's circuits created a community of readers through its staging of elite feeling rules that transcend geographic boundaries. The circuit supposed by BNF Fr. 2810 delineates the affective boundaries of medieval privilege through literary (fictional) and literal (visual) depictions of Mediterranean desire.[44]

With its placement and use within a circuit between the Dukes of Burgundy and Berry, then, the depiction of the Satalian episode on BNF Fr. 2810, folio 147, invites further attention. The illuminator's choices form part

---

42. Kim, "Material Culture," 29.
43. Christine Bousquet-Labouérie, "Un espace révelé: Les miniatures du livre de Jean de Mandeville ms fr 2810," *Cahiers de recherches médiévales (XIIIᵉ–XVᵉ siècles)* 3 (1997): 71–78; Philippe Ménard, "L'illustration du 'Devisement du Monde' de Marco Polo," *Bulletin de la Société nationale des antiquaires de France* (1987): 85–91; Christine Gadrat-Ouerfelli, "La diffusion et la circulation manuscrite d'un texte médiéval: L'exemple du *Devisement du monde* de Marco Polo," in *Les échanges en Méditerranée médiévale. Marqueurs, réseaux, circulations, contacts*, ed. Elisabeth Malamut and Mohamed Ouerfelli (Aix-en-Provence: Presses Universitaires de Provence, 2012), 273–88.
44. See the description of the manuscript primarily in François Avril and Nicole Reynaud, *Les manuscrits à peintures en France: 1440–1520* (Paris: Flammarion; Bibliothèque nationale, 1993); Partha Mitter, *Much Maligned Monsters: A History of European Reactions to Indian Art* (Chicago: University of Chicago Press, 1977); Christiane Deluz, *Le livre de Jehan de Mandeville: Une "géographie" au XIVᵉ siècle* (Louvain: Institut d'études médiévales de l'Université Catholique de Louvain, 1988). See also the detailed notice and provenance notes in the BNF catalog entry at MS Fr. 2810.

FIGURE 4.1. The Satalian episode of Mandeville's *Travels*, depicted in the *Livre des merveilles* (BNF Fr. 2810, fol. 147)

of the circuit, revealing more about one way of reading the story: neither the fantastic gorgon-headed serpent nor the roiling seas that result from its disposal in a nearby strait are depicted, though they are arguably the most interesting markers of geo-cultural alterity in the passage. Rather, the image depicts necrophilia. A traditional interpretation might focus on the depiction of corrupted practices of kingship, in keeping with the codex's interest in the practice of power, serving, as some have claimed, as a kind of utopian mirror for princes.[45] Instead, I focus on the illumination as an *emotional* lesson about the self, a representation of desire that resonates with the codex's widely acknowledged interest in figuring noble exceptionalism.

While the scholarship is divided over how to characterize the text's exploration of royal power, I agree with Gérard Veyssière that its illuminations are *not* exotic.[46] As in the narrative itself, the distance the illustration supposedly reifies—that is, the horror of eastern desire—is only rendered more unstable by its *rapprochement* with visual traditions of the French-speaking west.

---

45. See, for example, Karma Lochrie, "Provincializing Medieval Europe: Mandeville's Cosmopolitan Utopia," *PMLA* 124, no. 2 (2009): 598.
46. Gérard Veyssière, "Les illustrations du *Livre des merveilles* sont-elles exotiques?," in *L'exotisme*, ed. Alain Buisine and Norbert Dodille (Paris: Didier-Érudition, 1988), 172.

Indeed, neither the king nor his dead queen bear any particular markings of the "other": both are dressed in keeping with the sartorial markings of French royalty, with the king in a vivid royal blue that clearly places him at the center of the miniature. The queen is a faded, earthly gray, the same color as the walls that have been breached to violate her corpse; though nude, she is nonetheless marked as powerful, buried in crown and veil.[47]

Whereas other contemporary accounts imagine religious complexes as a place of refuge and welcome, instead, our image depicts a sterile, deserted landscape devoid of the pilgrims, travelers, or traders whose work brought them through one of the most important centers in the eastern Mediterranean.[48] Indeed, aside from the palm tree, little evokes the bustling crossroads described by contemporary traveler Ibn Battuta and supposedly depicted here.[49] In the image, the locus of desire is a nonspecific garden of death, and nothing evokes the splendors of Antalya's booming port or its caravansarys, where, according to Battuta, privilege and welcome were indicated

---

47. Charlotte Stanford suggests that in thirteenth-century France, elite bodies were displayed with headdresses indicating their status. See "The Body at the Funeral: Imagery and Commemoration at Notre-Dame, Paris, about 1304–18," *Art Bulletin* 89, no. 4 (2007): 660. See also Christopher Daniel, *Death and Burial in Medieval England, 1066–1550* (New York: Routledge, 1998), 44. See also the extended descriptions of Edward II's burial preparations in 1327 detailed in Chris Given-Wilson, "The Exequies of Edward III and the Royal Funeral Ceremony in Late Medieval England," *English Historical Review* 124, no. 507 (2009): 265.

48. In discussing Karatay Han, a notable regional caravansary, for example, Pancaroğlu notes that the documents surrounding its *waqf* stipulate for

> the numerous provisions which were to be made available free to travelers, including lodging, meals, medical care, bathing, and shoe repair, in addition to the feeding and looking after of animals. According to the document, the caravanserai was also provided with an imam to lead the guests in prayer and a muezzin to perform the call to prayer five times a day. The prayers would have been held in the masjid mentioned in the endowment which is a domed chamber at the end of the entrance vestibule of the building. The inclusion of this masjid required the entire caravanserai to be oriented towards the qibla and the same situation can be observed in other caravanserais that incorporate a prayer hall. ("Devotion, Hospitality and Architecture in Medieval Anatolia," *Studia Islamica* 108, no. 1 [2013]: 53)

49. Battuta writes of his visit to Antalya in 1335–1340,

> Nowhere in the world will you find men so eager to welcome strangers, so prompt to serve food and to satisfy the wants of others, and so ready to suppress injustice and to kill [tyrannical] agents of police and the miscreants who join with them. . . . The leader builds a hospice and furnishes it with rugs, lamps, and other necessary appliances. The members of his community work during the day to gain their livelihood, and bring him what they have earned in the late afternoon. With this they buy fruit, food, and the other things which the hospice requires for their use. If a traveler comes to town that day they lodge him in their hospice; these provisions serve for his entertainment as their guest, and he stays with them until he goes away. (Ibn Battuta, *Travels in Asia and Africa, 1325–1354*, ed. and trans. H. A. R. Gibb [London: Routledge, 1929], 123–25)

by luxurious displays of goods to trade—fruits, carpets, and other accoutrements markedly absent from this illumination. Such contextual cues are pointedly on display in other illuminations within this codex.

Oya Pancaroğlu explains that Antalyan complexes of religious worship would have been bustling centers of trade and hospitality, filled with objects and architectural features used to advertise their function to weary travelers.[50] Pancaroğlu's observations about architecture and community are of interest in reading our image because they ground contemporary Antalyan practices of welcome in a specifically Anatolian visual landscape. There is a link between visual representation and cultural practice, and it is coded onto a specifically Muslim kind of architecture, here advertised to travelers through the *masjid*, or domed chamber, conspicuously absent from our image.[51]

Contemporary charters, traveler accounts, and historians all read religious architecture as advertising a particular kind of refuge; in BNF Fr. 2810, however, the depiction of an Anatolian place of worship—the very site of deviancy imagined and invoked by the text—is devoid of any of these legible signs. None of the imagery associated with the "church" in the miniature actually resonates with the ample descriptions of Anatolian religious communities and their buildings found in contemporaries like Ibn Battuta or the accounts of Johannes Schiltberger, a German-speaking prisoner of war in Anatolia. Schiltberger elaborates on these all-purpose, architecturally advertised gathering centers as centralized spaces for displaying success when he observes that, as for the *imārets*, "'kings and aristocrats are buried in them. Whether Jew, Christian, or Muslim, the needy may lodge in them.'"[52] This account from early fifteenth-century Anatolia suggests that not only were religious establishments known through the social frameworks their architecture facilitated, but that they were also known to codify centralized cultural rituals of power, including indoor burial in the case of royalty.[53]

---

50. As Oya Pancaroğlu notes, "[Battuta's] testimony to the profuse nature of akhī generosity in Anatolia illuminates the nature of burgeoning social configurations in Anatolia which were articulated by elaborate displays of hospitality combined with rituals of devotion." "Devotion, Hospitality and Architecture," 49.

51. Later, when the Ottomans invaded, Pancaroğlu notes, they continued to see the value of these rural hospitality centers and continued to build and use them to house travelers, pilgrims, and traders; diplomacy was also conducted in them. So, whether or not the *Travels* were composed while Satalia was under Seljuk or Ottoman control, these sorts of religious edifices and the richly mixed communities they welcomed were some of the most visible markers of faith.

52. Johannes Schiltberger, *Als Sklave im osmanischen Reich und bei den Tataren, 1394–1427*, ed. Ulrich Schlemmer (Stuttgart, 1983), 174. Quoted in Pancaroğlu, "Devotion, Hospitality and Architecture," 81.

53. And, if the Satalia image is supposed to evoke an imaginary "Byzantium," the Byzantines, too, interred their elite within consecrated buildings. As Vasileios Marinis points out in his study of fourteenth-century burial practices in Byzantium, burying the dead in places of worship directly

Our painting invokes a purposefully deserted and culturally ambiguous religious edifice, a vacated space where nighttime indiscretions could be permitted, and royal bodies could be exhumed from simple wooden coffins. In our image, neither the imagined emptiness, the roofline, nor the burial scene seem in keeping with the practices of the Seljuks, whose *waqf* were the site of nighttime gatherings of travelers, and who used mausoleums with square bases and conical roofs to house their royalty (those who were not interred elsewhere) inside the buildings of the compound.[54]

In contrast, in BNF Fr. 2810, the queen is depicted as buried outdoors in a wooden coffin, atypical for both her status and contemporary interment practices in medieval England, France, and fourteenth-century Antalya. When the text was composed, royal burials were moving away from churchyard cemeteries and into the interior spaces of churches; in early fifteenth-century Antalya, as Schiltberger's account suggests, royals were for the most part buried indoors. By the fourteenth century in England, burials were carefully codified, and embalming and preservation methods followed in order to facilitate increasingly elaborate grieving processes, many of which assumed the body would be around for quite some time.[55] Royal and noble bodies were increasingly buried within the ecclesiastical spaces they patronized; most queens were no longer buried in churchyards when this copy of the *Travels* was illuminated, rendering the disjuncture between text, rubrication, and illumination that much more puzzling. Our image of Satalia purposefully blurs the boundaries between western nobility and a supposedly eastern, deviant eroticism through misleading architectural and anthropological imagery. Why the insistence not only on the image as (mis)interpretive apparatus about contemporary Muslim architectural-cultural spaces or sexual practices, but also on wildly incorrect burial practices?

---

contradicted earlier proscriptions by Gratian, Valentinian, and Theodosius I, who were vehemently opposed. However, the elite had almost never conformed to the prohibition, and as he notes, "the widespread contradictions in Byzantine church burial have often been dismissed as yet another example of the disparity between official legislation and everyday practice. Burying important persons inside a church (and indeed intra urbem) had a very old precedent: emperors, members of the imperial family, and bishops were buried inside the church of the Holy Apostles." Marinis's work thus makes another link between elite status, grieving practices, and exceptionalism, in burial locations. "Tombs and Burials in the Monastery Tou Libos in Constantinople," *Dumbarton Oaks Papers* 63 (2009): 150–51.

54. Patricia Blessing, *Architecture and Landscape in Medieval Anatolia, 1100–1500* (Edinburgh: Edinburgh University Press, 2017), 207.

55. Anna Maria Duch, "The Royal Funerary and Burial Ceremonies of Medieval English Kings, 1216–1509" (PhD diss., University of York, 2016).

Additionally—and of great interest to us—the visual program takes liberty with the text's precision: whereas the textual underpinning of the Satalian episode describes a sexual encounter between a young, *not specifically noble* man and his dead wife, both the rubricator and the illuminator recast the story as one of *royal* desire and transgression. That is, whereas the text specifies it is a young *man* who makes love to his dead wife, here, in BNF Fr. 2810, the rubricator explicitly insists that it is a *king* who feels deviant desire, and the illuminator employs textiles (in the form of blue-hued luxury fabrics) and objects (gilded crowns) to depict royal deviancy. If we assume that both as a particular text and as a codex, the *Livre des merveilles* is invested in (re)constructing a circuit of noble power between the Dukes of Burgundy and Berry, then why does this lone miniature re-ascribe foreign desire for the dead specifically to nobility, to *western* nobility for its elite readers?

The answer may lie in following the circuitry of meaning created by this image, this codex, and its readership within a broader context of elite storytelling, through intertextuality. Not only does the story participate in a circuitry about travel, privilege, and Mediterranean feeling rules, but here the text is supplemented by the codex's participation in a larger circuitry of elitism, this time through intertexts with the privileged community of romance. That is, the codex—and this illumination—participate not only in meaning-making within the ethos of the medieval Mediterranean travel narrative, but also in intertextuality between Arthurian courts and Mediterranean feeling models.

In particular, Arthurian romance may supplement how this episode functions to reveal grief as both eroticized and integral to performing noble privilege in late thirteenth- and early fourteenth-century artifacts, in the locus of myth, sacrifice, and storytelling. If the Satalian episode within Mandeville attempts to recast the erotics of grief as a performance of privilege, its Arthurian circuit further connects privilege to storytelling. In an extended, twenty-page episode known as the *Laide semblance*, or the "Ugly Appearance," in the thirteenth-century Old French prose *Livre d'Artus*, a beautiful demoiselle presents Arthur and his court with a challenge to release her land of the scourge brought by the ugliest creature ever seen. She describes the demon-child's exterior physical ugliness in terms of her interior, moral deformity: "ce est uns cors formez petit aus[s]i come uns enfes de trois anz, qui fu engendrez d'un cheualier en une femme morte quil amoit par amors, et est en semblance de fame"[56] (it is a body formed as small as a child of three years, that was conceived by a knight and a dead woman

---

56. *The Vulgate Version of the Arthurian Romances*, ed. Heinrich Oskar Sommer (Washington, DC: Carnegie Institution, 1913), 149–50.

with whom he was in love, and it is in the form of a woman). The demoiselle reveals that the adventure is founded upon an erotics of grief, here cast as a *misperformance* of desire for the dead, one that results in catastrophic ugliness. Indeed, when he reaches her land, Arthur's knight is so terrified by the dark thing he sees that he flees and is unable to complete the challenge (lines 15–20, p. 152). As in Mandeville, the aberrant creature is linked to *outremer*—here, specifically, to the island of Cyprus. Like in Mandeville, the Arthurian *outremer* does little to invoke realistic religious or geo-cultural contextual cues of the other.

After the *Laide semblance* has been defeated, Arthur specifically demands narration as the vehicle for propagating renown, commanding,

> Grex or nos contez quex cele Laide Semblance est & coment uos leustes. Et il dit quil lot par la Sage Dame non mie por proesce que il eust. Lors li conta coment il i failli auant & coment il dut estre morz & coment sa dame le gairi & coment il lot la Semblance par son enchantement. Et li rois refist metre en escrit toutes iceles auentures. Et lors recomenca la ioie. (7.162)

> "Greus now tell us all about what the Laide Semblance is and how you obtained it." And he says that he got it through the Wise Lady not at all through [chivalric] prowess that he had. Then he recounted how he failed at his first attempt and how he should have been dead and how his lady healed him and how he achieved the Semblance by his enchantment. And the king had all of these adventures put down into writing, and then the joy began again.

After his men listen to this second, aural reiteration of the defeat of the monstrous *Laide semblance*, Arthur commands that the whole episode be transcribed and reiterated into a third, *written* version. Although the Old French text specifies *refist* as the action of having something written down, the English translation "rendered" or "put down into writing" lacks. *Refist* imagines, through an iterative version of the verb *faire* (to do, to make) that something can be re-rendered in writing, that there is a space for supplemental meaning in the space of translation from event, to oral recounting, to written documentation. Arthur's decision to supplement the success of the episode *and* its retelling with a written account—his decision to add on or remake—*refist*—imagines storytelling as a necessary supplement to noble renown. Here, then, the erotics of grief that produce the *Laide semblance* episode *fist* and *refist* the story of noble exceptionalism, through repetition engendering narration.

Arthur's command also links commemoration, narration, and *joie*. Though *joie* here certainly connotes "joy," in the sense of amusement, in several Old French romances *joie* is also the desired object of the adventure, as in the "Joie de la cour" episode within Chrétien's earlier romance, *Erec et Enide*. There, the joy functions as a quest-object, the desired "joy" of victory. In that episode, as in ours, *joie* might also have a third semantic layer, where *joie* figures the *jouissance* of eroticism, as part of that *joie* is the stymied threat of Erec's own death. That Arthur is always in search of the "joy" of a good story about chivalric exceptionalism—and that here, that story is the erotics of grief—seems no coincidence.

The connection between privilege, storytelling, and eroticized grief is further elaborated within the thirteenth-century vulgate *Merlin*, where the *Laide semblance* is explicitly cited as the basis for *all* the storied adventures of Logres, linking the narration of Arthurian romance to the (supposed, necessary) alterity of necrophilia.[57] We learn from Arthur's opponent, Rion, that the successful resolution of the monstrous necrophilia threatens to end the adventures of Logres when he warns Arthur,

> Ore saces de uerite que iou ai non rions & sui rois dierlande. Si tieng toute la terre iusquen la terre des pastures & outre fust ele encore moie son i peust passer mais on ni passera iamais tant comme la laide samblance en sera ostee & cest vne bone que iudas i geta & ce fu ensenge quil auoit la terre toute iusques la conquise & li anchien dient que ia si tost ne sera cele figure ostee que les auentures del roialme de logres ne commencheront a finer. (2.231)

> Now you must truly know that I am named Rion and I am King of Ireland. Thus I hold all of the land up to the land of pastures and beyond it would also be mine if anyone could pass through there but no one will be able to pass through until the Laide Semblance will be defeated. And it is a thing which Judas threw there and it was taught that he had conquered all the lands up to there and the ancients say that as soon as this face [the Laide Semblance] will be defeated that the adventures of the kingdom of Logres will begin to finish.

Here, Rion claims that the very basis for Arthurian narration is both a story of Mediterranean resistance (encoded by *iudas*, and, possibly, *li anchien*) and one defined by the erotics of grief. Judas Maccabeus, who repelled Greek

---

57. For more see Sommer's note 3 in 7.156, where he discusses intertextual influences within the Arthurian cycles and argues for placing the Satalian episode within the Medusa tradition.

invasion, is a decidedly Mediterranean hero whose story is framed by cross-cultural warfare and colonialism, cross-confessional struggle, and sea travel. In Rion's mythicized origin story, Judas's throwing of the grief-conceived monster into the gulf guarantees iterative, episodic tests of Arthur and his men, generating and securing their fame through storytelling about their chivalric exploits. Rion's story thus creates a genealogical claim to noble power articulated by linking Mediterranean privilege, Arthurian storytelling, and an erotics of grief embodied in the monster conceived through necrophilia.

This gorgon motif spreads throughout the literary imagination, as it appears not only in the *Livre d'Artus* and the prose *Merlin*, as we have seen, but also in the Old French *Guillaume d'Orange* and in the *Bataille Loquifer*. If, as Keith Busby contends, we should take the Arthurian corpus as a set of intertexts, then the figuring of desire, taboo, and death in the *Laide semblance* episodes constructs an erotics of grief as integral not only to the adventures of Logres, but also to the functioning of the genre itself, perhaps even predicting its incestuous downward death spiral in *La mort le roi Artu*.[58] Here, then, what seems to be foreign and "othered" instead becomes integral to Arthurian community, a cornerstone of Arthurian romance.[59] Eliminating the erotics of grief would mean ending Arthurian narration of renown; the *Laide semblance* suggests eroticized grief and the performance of privilege go hand in hand with the Mediterranean.

In explaining the link between emotional and geographic alterity, the erotics of grief, and the genre of romance, the *Laide semblance* helps us respond to our queries about the BNF Fr. 2810 miniature, where a narrative originally about a man's love for his dead partner in *outremer* is recast as a king's desire for his dead queen. The visual recentering of the story from an erotics of transgression to an erotics of privilege reveals an interest in positing an alternate set of feeling rules specifically for the elite community of BNF Fr. 2810. What was once forbidden and monstrous—transgression and the

---

58. Keith Busby, "L'intertextualité du *Livre d'Artus*," in *Arturs Rex, II: Acta Conventa Louvanensis 1987*, ed. W. van Hoecke, G. Tournoy, and W. Verbeke (Leuven: Leuven University Press, 1991), 316.

59. In this vein, Marie Blaise argues that the disappearance of the Satalian curse causes the end of the communal adventure and the end of all Arthurian narration. She argues that "si l'épreuve de la Laide Semblance, revers de celle du Graal, était menée à bien, l'ordre serait rétabli et les aventures chevaleresques trouveraient ainsi leur fin, non dans un grand désastre, comme on l'entend en général, mais dans la fin du désastre qui les a initiées, désastre dont tous les textes, depuis les romans d'Antiquité, en passant par l'oeuvre de Chrétien et de ses continuateurs, jusqu'à la grande somme romanesque en prose, se font tous l'écho." Marie Blaise, *Terres gastes. Fictions d'autorité et mélancolie* (Montpellier: Presses Universitaires de la Méditerranée, 2005), 145.

erotics of grief—becomes a site of privilege in a manuscript commissioned by and destined for elite consumers, posing fundamental questions about the circuitry of privilege in the medieval period: Who has the power to transgress? Who can articulate an "I" by practicing desire outside the boundaries of community?

Reading the *Laide semblance* with Mandeville's *Travels* links the staying power of romance—its power to perform and reproduce the privilege of elite community through storytelling—to the horror of the Satalian gorgon. The narrating force of romance is thus at least partly linked to the (re)productive productivity of coupling love with grief. Here, the motif is no longer about a geographic other, but rather it is imagined as tracing the boundaries of the emotional communities of romance, underscoring romance's articulation of privilege through its negotiation of a shared erotics of grief. The erotics of grief become a way of binding the elite self to a Mediterranean community of privilege articulated through a circuitry of shared exceptional emotional practices made most explicit in the Satalian miniature of BNF Fr. 2810.

The affective intertextuality with Mediterranean feeling rules pointed to within the *Travels* and coursing throughout representations of medieval elite emotional communities in genres as diverse as romance and the *romans antiques* suggests that the path of affective voyage is not bounded by religion, geography, or language; rather, it is a path trod by the elite who imagined travel, Crusade, and cross-cultural marriage as integral to figuring the community of the self. Reading affective travel invites us to consider not only the place of emotion in formulating and defining the contours of elite community, but also how texts designed for elite emotional communities imagine shared, Mediterranean emotional models as integral to describing and negotiating elite power.

Conclusion
The Erotics of Grief and the Stakes of Community

> I say the unique and supreme pleasure of love lies in the certainty of doing evil. And men and women know from birth that all pleasure is to be found in evil.
>
> —Baudelaire, *Fusées*

Having studied the function of grief and desire in texts and artifacts as diverse as *Philomena*; Philippe de Mousket's *Chronique*; *La chanson de Roland*; the *romans antiques*; Old French, Medieval Greek, and Middle English romances; Arthurian myth; and medieval Anatolia, where Mandeville described his strangely transformed Satalian miniature, it seems logical to turn to the most famous of medieval reflections on the nature of desire, the thirteenth-century Old French masterpiece by Jean de Meun and Guillaume de Lorris, *Le roman de la Rose*. Readers of the *Rose* might reasonably wonder why medieval love is so relentlessly associated with pain, violence, death, and grief; of course this conclusion can only provide more queries to guide further study. Provoked by Cupid, educated by Love and Reason, the lover of the *Rose* is urged to war against his beloved. It is a war with vicious consequences for the fictional girl and for the place of women in contemporary debates on medieval misogyny in the ensuing philosophical and literary *querelle*. After hundreds of folios spent explaining, educating, and rationalizing, the lover finally takes his prize in a scene read either as a violent rape or barely consensual sex. Consent seeming, even in the medieval period, most unlikely from a barely pubescent girl, we are left to puzzle over the violence of sex as a battlefield, death the barely whispered threat posed by men's desire. As Christine de Pizan wondered, here in the tale of love most popular in the Middle Ages, why must sex be an erotics of pain,

FIGURE C.1. Cupid aiming at lovers, from the *Roman des fables Ovide le Grant* (BNF Arsenal Ms-5069, fol. 3v)

of grief? Or, in consonance with this study, how can the *Rose*'s insistence on gazing upon, witnessing, and even celebrating the highly eroticized violation be interrogated or informed by our readings attesting to a more generalized erotics of grief in medieval culture?

Perhaps our eroticized grief can offer a few, initial thoughts for further consideration. From the wounds of Love's first assault (shown here in figure C.1, one of hundreds of similar illuminations); to Cupid's arrows destined to strike the uninitiated lover; to the violent, deathlike deflowering of his virginal "rose," the text is replete with images of love deeply studded with a threat of death and an erotics of grief.

Specifically, though many have studied the *Rose*, and though its codicological and literary influence remains uncontested, few have sought to unravel why *douleur* and *amors* elide in this text, inviting a reconsideration of the text's deployment of love and the emotional communities it strives to create.

I am not, of course, the first to have identified the violence inherent in the *Rose*; many scholars from divergent theoretical approaches have been attentive to what we typically identify as a fundamental disjuncture in the lover in question, perhaps most notably medieval contemporary Christine de Pizan and her *querelle*.[1] Yet I contend that the erotics of grief I have developed in this book invite a rereading of the *Roman de la Rose*, perhaps even one that situates it as a representation of medieval desire par excellence. However repugnant the taboo and its transgression are, the erotics of the *Rose* resonate directly with the kinds of repulsion evoked in the love, rape, infanticide, incest, and cannibalism in *Philomena*; with the near-rape of widows on their dead husband's corpses represented in romance and fabliau in order to narrate men's worth; with the eroticization of the power made transparent in the bond between king and warrior in epic; and with the odd, Mediterranean erotics of the love affair with the dead that produced that Satalian gorgon in Mandeville's *Travels*, the *Livre d'Artus*, and the prose *Merlin*.[2]

In this kind of reading, *Le roman de la Rose* becomes a natural extension of a culture dedicated to celebrating socially stratified power through an expression of emotional exceptionalism, eliding pain, desire, and power in an erotics of grief. We have already witnessed this enunciation of status by eroticizing grief in diverse generic representations from the twelfth and thirteenth centuries. The chansons de geste, for example, celebrate sacrifice through the onlooker's gaze, where men witness and eroticize Charlemagne's tears for his vassals, immortalizing their sacrifice in the narrative made legible through his weeping. Likewise, romance imagines women's grief as desirable, sexualized by onlooking men as an attestation of and witness to dead men's power. The Satalian image imagines noble exceptionalism as a right; in that image, and in particular in the circuitry of the BNF Fr. 2810 codex, the erotics of grief participate in the articulation of power as the rape of a corpse, the defiling of a woman whose subjectivity is neither preserved nor protected in death, but rather violated in service of modeling noble exceptionalism. Whereas the Satalian episode pretends to mythify the episode as indicative of "othered" Mediterranean emotional practices, the

---

1. E. Jane Burns, "Raping Men: What's Motherhood Got to Do with It?," in *Representing Rape in Medieval and Early Modern Literature*, ed. Elizabeth Robertson and Christine M. Rose (New York: Palgrave, 2001), 127–60; David F. Hult, "The *Roman de la Rose*, Christine de Pizan, and the *Querelle des femmes*," in *The Cambridge Companion to Medieval Women's Writing*, ed. Carolyn Dinshaw and David Wallace (Cambridge: Cambridge University Press, 2003), 184–94; Sarah Kay, "Women's Body of Knowledge: Epistemology and Misogyny in the *Romance of the Rose*," in *Framing Medieval Bodies*, ed. Sarah Kay and Miri Rubin (Manchester: Manchester University Press, 1994), 211–35.

2. Indeed, the relation between Medusa and the *Rose* has already been explored in Francis Gingras, "La chevelure de Méduse au miroir du roman d'après une interpolation du *Roman de la Rose*," in *La chevelure dans la littérature et l'art du Moyen Âge*, ed. Chantal Connochie-Bourgne (Aix-en-Provence: Presses Universitaires de Provence, 2014), 167–79.

Rose abandons the conceit of the artistic redactions of status within the folio 147 miniature, insisting instead that Old French–speaking exceptionalism is power expressed through transgressive emotional regimes, regularizing the erotics of grief as describing the boundaries of power.

The *Rose* is a flagship case, then, for all the elements teased out in our erotics of grief: taboo and its transgression, which we identified in *Philomena*, where love is articulated through force and pain, in the rape and subsequent mutilation; the *education sentimentale* of warrior-lovers such as Erec, Yvain, Enéas, and Belthandros, whose renown is articulated through an erotics of grief; the communal valorization of sacrifice by grieving kings and emperors in medieval chansons de geste and chronicles; and the deployment of a common, Mediterranean language of elite emotional exceptionalism stemming from classical representations of the embodied gods of Love and Death in ancient Mediterranean texts, visually invoked in our *Rose* miniature through wounds inflicted by personified Cupid, Reason, and Love.

In the context of the erotics of grief, the *Rose* reads like a hymn to love and pain. Indeed, its opening folio often frames the dreamer's bed with birds—specifically, nightingales—whose warbles are imbued with the song of Philomena's suffering:

> Li oissel qui se sont teü
> Tant qu'il ont le froit eü
> Et lou tens d'yver et frerin,
> Sont en may pour le tens serin
> Si lié qu'il mostrent en chantant
> Qu'an lor cuers a de joie tant,
> Qu'il lor estuet chanter par force.
> Li rossignous lors se reforce
> De chanter et de faire noise. (BNF Français 1565, fol. 1, transcription mine)

> The birds that have become silent
> since they have become cold
> and winter and frost have arrived
> are in May by sweet weather
> so joyful that they show by singing
> that they have so much joy in their hearts
> that they are forced to sing out.
> The nightingale then forces itself to sing and make noise.

By the fourteenth century, the nightingale is both visually and textually bound to both love and pain within the first folio of the *Rose*, highlighted

160   CONCLUSION

FIGURE C.2. Nightingales frame the love story in *Le roman de la Rose* (BNF Fr. 1565, fol. 1r)

here by words such as *lié, estuet, force,* and *reforce* used to describe a dream of love while concomitantly connoting coercion. Of the 320 extant manuscripts of the *Rose*, a large percentage feature the dreamer with the nightingale, as in figure C.2.[3]

---

3. See, for example, Fondation Martin Bodmer, Bodmer 79, fol. 1r; BNF français 1560, fol. 3r; Bibliothèque de l'Arsenal 3339, fol. 1r; Bodleian Library, MS Selden Supra 57, fol. 1r; J. Paul Getty Museum, Ludwig XV 7, fol. 1r; Bodleian Douce 332, fol. 1r; Bodleian Library, MS Douce 195, fol. 1v; Walters Art Museum, W. 143, fol. 1r; Bibliothèque de l'Arsenal, 5209, fol. 1r. Nightingales also appear in the first folio's marginal illuminations in the Ferrell Collection, Ferrell Rose, fol. 1r; Library of Congress, Rosenwald 396, fol. A2r; BNF Français 12595, fol. 1r; Bibliothèque municipale de Châlons-en-Champagne, 270, fol. 1r. Notably, the birds do *not* appear in the opening folios of the dreamer

Our exploration of the nexus of love and death explains the emotional, narratological, and visual framing of the *Rose* within a garden full of nightingales as a way of contextualizing its attention to power, violation, and suffering. These same nightingales also presage the violence to come, creating an eroticism particular to the domination and pain of young girls, power couched in the beauty of a flower, perhaps truly a *fleur du mal*.

Reading with an erotics of grief suggests it could be profitable to situate the *Rose*'s discussion of emotion within a broader dialogue about the nature of elite love and privilege, both intellectual and literary.[4] I hope that this study invites further research in considering how emotions and community intersect in medieval literature, perhaps most notably and visibly in the ways that medieval elite communities deploy emotions to create, maintain, and police their privilege. As I suggested in the last chapter, with its long history of violent warfare, conquest, rape, and death, the Mediterranean provides a backdrop for negotiating medieval elite communities, often in ways that elide death and love, grief and glory, remembrance and honor. As such, there is space for more focus in medieval studies on how emotional practices help navigate diverse communities across the Mediterranean.

While this study of the erotics of grief has focused on elite medieval communities, these erotics may play out differently in other communities. Medieval literary culture—often commissioned by and for elites—most often also reflected the emotional culture of that social milieu; with the limited sources we have, this study is anchored in exploring the particulars of desire and grief within that community attested to within elite codices. Yet even in its limitations, this is perhaps not a flaw of this study, but a strength: it prompts us to be attentive to the community we *can* study, and as such, it invites attentiveness to the kinds of communities we *cannot*. Here, I have focused on how elite material culture deployed elite, implicitly Christian, emotional regimes to maintain and propagate its power; other studies could and should explore how different materials attest to and construct alternate emotional communities, hopefully attentive to communities disenfranchised by the nobility.

---

in Arsenal 3338, fol. 1r; BNF Français 380, fol. 1r; BNF Français 805, fol. 1r; University of Chicago Library, MS 1380, fol. 1r; BNF Français 1665, fol. 1r.

4. And, as Masha Raskolnikov points out in a reflection on the romantic—if not sexual—relationship between mourning, eroticism, and elite intellectual communities in work on Guillaume de Dole and Jean de Meun and Jacques Derrida and Paul de Man, "this mourning takes on the challenge of internalizing the *work*, rather than the *being* of the lost other, mourning without introjecting what is mourned by leaving it intact in its alterity." Raskolnikov, "Between Men, Mourning: Authorship, Love, and the Gift in the *Roman de la Rose*," *GLQ* 10, no. 1 (2003): 47.

CONCLUSION

As clearly as our elite literature figures its own elite emotional community, the philosopher with whom this work most energetically engages, Georges Bataille, is conversely mute about how community and class structure the creation of eroticism. We might ask, pointedly, of both Bataille and the Sade he reads: where is class in this model of power, of eroticism? So integral to our consideration of medieval erotics, which my readings have suggested are invested in a culture of privilege interested in renown, reputation, and glorification, class is conspicuously absent in the philosophy of the erotic in Bataille, as in when his analysis of language precludes the concept of community: "Lynch law belongs to men who rate themselves as among the most highly civilized of our age. If language is to be extricated from this impasse, we must declare that violence belongs to humanity as a whole and is speechless, and that thus humanity as a whole lies by omission and language itself is founded upon this lie. . . . It is a language which repudiates any relationship between speaker and audience. In true solitude there could be no semblance even of solidarity."[5] While Bataille's concern here is coming into being through language, he nevertheless conflates his erotic with total individualism, precluding the consideration of the "other" as in any way defining "self," obfuscating the relation between community and emotion. With their intense focus on how eroticism articulates the privileged communities of feudalism, our medieval texts insist on the relationship between emotion, language, and community in ways that highlight differences between medieval and modern theoretical approaches to affect. Here, the medieval interrogates the felicity of the modern, particularly in a poststructuralist analysis of subjectivity committed to intersectionality.

If a consideration of privilege seems absent from Bataille's exploration of how erotism is experienced by some at the expense of others, gender also seems to disinterest him, as when he asserts, "Women . . . are no more desirable [than men], but they lay themselves open to be desired. They put themselves forward as objects for the aggressive desire of men. Not every woman is a prostitute, but prostitution is the logical consequence of the feminine attitude."[6] Our medieval texts suggest that, across the gender spectrum, medieval elites eroticized grief in service of power; the emotions surrounding death helped to buoy the worth of feudal sacrifice and became an erotics of commemoration and narratological immortality. Yet Bataille starkly differentiates between the ways that women participated in

---

5. Georges Bataille, *Erotism: Death and Sensuality*, trans. Mary Dalwood (San Francisco: City Lights Books, 1962), 186–89.
6. Ibid., 131.

eroticism, implicitly gendering the erotic as male. In aligning the feminine with objectification, Bataille offers little room for either gender negotiation or a more considered formulation of the kinds of emotional communities created and policed in our medieval texts. Absent is the homosocial—and perhaps homoerotic—desire of men *for* other men and their approbation; absent is the work of women's eroticism *for* maintaining their own privilege in feudal culture; absent is the work of a feminine erotic *for* the lovers whom their grief narrates and immortalizes. In short, absent is much of the work that reading with the medieval imagines is made possible by the erotic.

My medieval readings are not only informed by a plethora of models—from ancient Greek philosophical and elite cultural texts to postmodern readings of Sade, Bataille, Barthes, Derrida, and Butler—but they also suggest that in some ways moderns may do well to look to the educational and disciplinary functions of medieval emotional communities. The kinds of medieval communities we have seen depicted in the texts in this study not only resonate with many modern expressions of passion-as-death (think of the variety of communities swooning for the erotics of *Fifty Shades of Grey*), but their attention to community should also inform modern scholarly considerations of how different groups of people experience emotion, and by whom and for whom their emotions are constructed. In the end, both the medieval and the modern invite us to interrogate the felicity of Bataille's assertion that "the fundamental violence that makes us lose control always tends to disturb a relationship of tenderness—to make us find in that relationship that death is near, and death is the symbol of all sensuality."[7] Or, to put it more colloquially, our medieval texts might help us think along with Paulo Coelho about how we create and negotiate community, privilege, and remembrance through emotion when "at every moment of our lives, we all have one foot in a fairy tale and the other in the abyss."[8]

---

7. Ibid., 242.
8. Paulo Coelho, *Eleven Minutes* (New York: HarperCollins, 2009).

Appendix 1

Selected Illuminations of Knights Being Grieved

From the Bibliothèque Nationale de France

Français 52, fol. 7v, Charlemagne trouvant Roland mort
Français 60, fol. 97, Lamentations sur Hector
Français 97, fol. 23, Tristan et demoiselle se lamentant
Français 97, fol. 328v, Faran de la Tour pleuré par son amie
Français 100, fol. 36, Lamentations sur Meliadus
Français 102, fol. 247v, Tristan et demoiselle se lamentant
Français 112 (3), fol. 111v, Mort d'Erec
Français 112 (3), fol. 113v, Arthur pleurant Erec
Français 112 (3), fol. 206, Gauvain pleurant ses frères
Français 119, fol. 369v, Agravain au Tertre as Caitis
Français 123, fol. 244v, Arthur pleurant ses neveux
Français 310, fol. 370v, Charlemagne pleurant Roland
Français 334, fol. 294, Tristan et demoiselle se lamentant
Français 344, fol. 319v, Lamentations devant le lit de Lancelot
Français 364, fol. 89F, Pyrrhos I pleurant les morts
Français 364, fol. 105v, Pyrrhos I pleurant les morts
Français 750, fol. 311v, Tristan et demoiselle se lamentant
Français 782, fol. 183v, Lamentation sur Ajax
Français 6465, fol. 113, Mort de Roland

Français 1433, fol. 69v, Lamentations sur Esclados
Français 2820, fol. 133v, Charlemagne pleurant Roland
Français 22554, fol. 141, Achille pleurant les morts
Français 24364, fol. 35, Alexandre pleurant les morts
Grec 2878, fol. 195v, Lamentations sur Pâris
Latin 4915, fol. 97v, Mort d'Alexandre
N.A. Français 24920, fol. 34v, Polyxène pleurant Achille
N.A. Français 886, fol. 12v, Lamentations sur Barkiyâruq
Smith-Lesouëf (oriental) 244, fol. 6, Lamentations sur Suhrâb
Supplément persan 489, fol. 436v, Ram Burzîn devant le corps de Nûshzâd
Supplément persan 581, fol. 105, Lamentations sur Husraw II

From the British Library

BL Royal MS 16 G VI, fol. 180v, Charlemagne mourning Roland
BL Royal MS 20 D IV, fol. 168v, A woman mourning in a tent as Agravain rides up

From the Getty Museum

MS 63, fol. 41, Suicide of Dido

From the Koninklijke Bibliotheek

The Hague, KB, 78 D 47, fol. 90v, Mourning for Brutus: the dead body is brought to Rome
The Hague, KB, 134 C 19, fol. 92v, Mourning the dead Strabo
The Hague, KB, 134 C 19, fol. 242r, Cornelia with her company mourning Pompey and weighing anchor to flee

Appendix 2

Selected Illuminations of Lovers in Death

From Arsenal

Arsenal 5069, fol. 159, Alcyonè metamorphosé embrassant le cadaver de Céyx

From the Bibliothèque Nationale

Français 239, fol. 273, Gentil Carisendi exhumant Catalina
Français 598, fol. 20v, Suicide de Thisbè
Français 606, fol. 18v, Suicide de Thisbè
Français 874, fol. 40, Didon se lamentant
Français 2810, fol. 149, Roi profanant le corps de son amie
Grec 2736, fol. 40v, Vengeance de Médée

From the British National Library

Harley 4867, fol. 51, Dido

From the Getty

MS 63, fol. 41, Suicide of Dido
MS Ludwig XV 7, fol. 29v, Love instructing the Lover in the *Roman de la Rose*

From the Pierpont Morgan

Morgan Library M. 126, Thisbe in the *Confessio amantis*

Bibliography

Primary Sources and Translations

Aquinas, Thomas. *Summa Theologiae*. Edited by Petrus Caramello. Turin: Marietti, 1952.
Bédier, Joseph. *Les légendes épiques*. Vol. 3. Paris: H. Champion, 1929.
Betts, Gavin. *Three Medieval Greek Romances*. New York: Garland, 1995.
Capellanus, Andreas. *Andreas Capellanus on Love*. Translated by P. G. Walsh. London: Duckworth, 1982.
Chrétien de Troyes. *Philomena, conte raconté d'après Ovide*. Edited by Cornelius De Boer. Geneva: Slatkine, 1974.
———. *Erec et Enide*. Edited by Jean-Marie Fritz. Paris: Livre de Poche, 1992.
———. *Yvain ou le chevalier au lion*. Paris: Librairie Générale Française, 1994.
Christine de Pizan. *Le livre du chemin de lonc estude*. Paris: Librairie Générale Française, 2000.
Claris et Laris. Edited by Corinne de Pierreville. Paris: Champion, 2008.
Eugenianos, Niketas. *Drosilla and Charikles: A Byzantine Novel*. Translated by Joan B. Burton. Mundelein, IL: Bolchazy-Carducci, 2004.
Euripides. *Phoenissae*. Edited by Donald J. Mastronarde. Cambridge: Cambridge University Press, 1994.
Floire et Blancheflor. Edited by Jean-Luc Leclanche. Paris: Champion, 1980.
Gratian. *Gratiani Decretum: La traduction en ancien français du décret de Gratien*. Helsinki: Societas Scientiarum Fennica, 1992.
Guillaume d'Orange: Four Twelfth-Century Epics. Translated by Joan Ferrante. New York: Columbia University Press, 2001.
Homer. *The Iliad*. Translated by Robert Fagles. London: Penguin Books, 1990.
Hue de Rotelande. *Hue de Rotelande's Ipomédon: Ein Französischer Abenteuerroman Des 12. Jahrhunderts*. Edited by Eugen Kölbing. Breslau: Wilhelm Koebner, 1889.
Ibn Battuta. *Travels in Asia and Africa, 1325–1354*. Edited and translated by H. A. R. Gibb. London: Routledge, 1929.
Isidore of Seville. *The Etymologies of Isidore of Seville*. Edited by Stephen A. Barney et al. New York: Cambridge University Press, 2010.
John of Mandeville. *The Travels of Sir John Mandeville*, trans. C. W. R. D. Moseley. London: Penguin, 2005.
La chanson de Roland. Edited and translated by Ian Short. 2nd ed. Paris: Livre de Poche, 1990.
La mort le roi Artu: Roman du XIIIe siècle. Edited by Jean Frappier. Geneva: Droz, 1996.
Le cycle de Guillaume d'Orange. Edited and translated by Michel Zink. Paris: Livre de Poche, 1996.

Le mesnagier de Paris. Paris: Livre de Poche, 1994.
Le roman d'Enéas. Edited by Michel Zink. Paris: Livre de Poche, 1997.
Le roman de Tristan / par Thomas. Edited by Félix Lecoy. Paris: Champion, 1991.
Li chevaliers as deus espees. Edited by Wendelin Foerster. Halle: Max Niemeyer, 1877.
Longus, and Xenophon of Ephesus. *Daphnis and Chloe; Anthia and Habrocomes.* Edited and translated by Jeffrey Henderson. Cambridge, MA: Harvard University Press, 2009.
Marie de France. *Lais de Marie de France.* Edited by Laurence Harf-Lancner. Paris: Livre de Poche, 1990.
Ovid. *Metamorphoses, Books I–VIII.* Edited by Frank Justus Miller. 3rd ed. Cambridge, MA: Harvard University Press, 1984.
———. *The Metamorphoses of Ovid.* Translated by Allen Mandelbaum. San Diego: Harcourt Brace, 1995.
Paris, Gaston. *Histoire poétique de Charlemagne par Gaston Paris.* Paris: Franck, 1865.
Philippe Mouskés. *Chronique rimée.* Edited by Frédéric Auguste Ferdinand Thomas de Reiffenberg. Brussels: M. Hayez, 1836.
Pyrame et Thisbe, Narcisse, Philoména. Edited by Emmanuèle Baumgartner. Paris: Folio, 2000.
Raoul de Cambrai. Edited and translated by William Kibler and Sarah Kay. Paris: Livre de Poche, 1996.
Renaud de Beaujeu. *Le Bel Inconnu: Roman d'aventures.* Edited by Gwladys Perrie Williams. Paris: H. Champion, 1929.
Robert d'Orbigny. *Le conte de Floire et Blancheflor.* Edited and translated by Jean-Luc Leclanche. Paris: Honoré Champion, 2003.
Sade, Marquis de. *Oeuvres.* Edited by Michel Delon. Vol. 2. Paris: Gallimard, 1995.
Sappho et Alcaeus. *Fragmenta.* Edited by Eva-Marie Voigt. Amsterdam: Athenaeum, 1971.
The Song of Roland and Other Poems of Charlemagne. Translated by Simon Gaunt and Karen Pratt. Oxford: Oxford University Press, 2016.
Tristan et Yseut. Edited by Christianne Marchello-Nizia. Paris: Gallimard, 1995.
The Vulgate Version of the Arthurian Romances. Edited by Heinrich Oskar Sommer. Washington, DC: Carnegie Institution, 1913.
Wace. *Le roman de Brut. Tome 2 / par Wace, poète du XIIe siècle; Publié pour la première fois d'après les manuscrits des bibliothèques de Paris, avec un commentaire et des notes par Le Roux de Lincy.* Rouen: É. Frère, 1836.

Secondary Sources

Abu-Asab, Mones, Hakima Amri, and Marc S. Micozzi. *Avicenna's Medicine: A New Translation of the 11th-Century Canon with Practical Applications for Integrative Health Care.* Rochester, VT: Healing Arts, 2013.
Agapitos, Panagiotis. "'Words Filled with Tears': Amorous Discourse as Lamentation in the Palaiologan Romances." In *Greek Laughter and Tears*, edited by Margaret Alexiou and Douglas Cairns, 353–74. Edinburgh: Edinburgh University Press, 2017.
Ahmed, Sara. *The Cultural Politics of Emotion.* 2nd ed. New York: Routledge, 2014.

BIBLIOGRAPHY

Allison, David B., Mark S. Roberts, and Allen S. Weiss, eds. *Sade and the Narrative of Transgression*. Cambridge: Cambridge University Press, 1995.

Archibald, Elizabeth. "Gold in the Dungheap: Incest Stories and Family Values in the Middle Ages." *Journal of Family History* 22, no. 2 (1997): 133–49.

———. *Incest and the Medieval Imagination*. Oxford: Oxford University Press, 2001.

Austin, J. L. *How to Do Things with Words*. Oxford: Clarendon, 1975.

Avril, François, and Nicole Reynaud. *Les manuscrits à peintures en France: 1440–1520*. Paris: Flammarion; Bibliothèque Nationale, 1993.

Barber, Malcolm. *The Trial of the Templars*. Cambridge: Cambridge University Press, 2012.

Barthes, Roland. *The Mourning Diary*. London: Notting Hill Editions, 2010.

———. *Sade, Fourier, Loyola*. Paris: Éditions du Seuil, 1971.

Bastide, Mario. "Les actes de parole dans *Aliscans*." *L'Information littéraire: Revue paraissant cinq fois par an* 45, no. 5 (1993): 5–13.

Baswell, Christopher. "Marvels of Translation and Crises of Transition in the Romances of Antiquity." In *The Cambridge Companion to Medieval Romance*, edited by Roberta L. Krueger, 29–44. Cambridge: Cambridge University Press, 2000.

———. "Men in the *Roman d'Enéas*: The Construction of Empire." In *Medieval Masculinities: Regarding Men in the Middle Ages*, edited by Clare E. Lees, Thelma Fenster, and Jo Ann McNamara, 149–68. Minneapolis: University of Minnesota Press, 1994.

Bataille, Georges. *Erotism: Death and Sensuality*. Translated by Mary Dalwood. San Francisco: City Lights Books, 1962.

———. *L'érotisme*. Paris: Éditions de Minuit, 1957.

Beaton, Roderick. *The Medieval Greek Romance*. 2nd ed. London: Routlege, 1996.

Beer, Jeanette M. A., and Kenneth Lloyd-Jones, eds. *Translation and the Transmission of Culture between 1300 and 1600*. Kalamazoo: Medieval Institute Publications, Western Michigan University, 1995.

Bercé, Yves-Marie. "Bataille et l'histoire des mentalités." In *L'histoire-Bataille: Actes de la journée d'études consacrée à Georges Bataille, Paris, École Nationale des Chartes, 7 Décembre 2002*, edited by Christophe Gauthier and Laurent Ferri, 21–26. Geneva: Droz, 1996.

Binski, Paul. *Medieval Death: Ritual and Representation*. Ithaca, NY: Cornell University Press, 1996.

Blaise, Marie. *Terres gastes. Fictions d'autorité et mélancolie*. Montpellier: Presses Universitaires de la Méditerranée, 2005.

Blanchfield, Lyn A. "The Sincere Body: The Performance of Weeping and Emotion in Late Medieval Italian Sermons." *Quidditas* 20 (1999): 117–35.

Blessing, Patricia, and Rachel Goshgarian, eds. *Architecture and Landscape in Medieval Anatolia, 1100–1500*. Edinburgh: Edinburgh University Press, 2017.

Bloch, R. Howard. *Etymologies and Genealogies: A Literary Anthropology of the French Middle Ages*. Chicago: University of Chicago Press, 1983.

———. "From Grail Quest to Inquest: The Death of King Arthur and the Birth of France." *Modern Language Review* 69, no. 1 (1974): 40–55.

Blumenfeld-Kosinski, Renate. "Chrétien de Troyes as a Reader of the Romans Antiques." *Philological Quarterly* 64, no. 3 (Summer 1985): 398–405.

Boer, Cornelis de. "Chrétien de Troyes, auteur de *Philomena*." *Romania* 41, no. 161 (1912): 94–100.

Bonte, Pierre. *Épouser au plus proche: Inceste, prohibitions et stratégies matrimoniales autour de la Méditerranée*. Paris: Éditions de l'École des Hautes Études en Sciences Sociales, 1994.

Bouchard, Constance Brittain. *Those of My Blood: Constructing Noble Families in Medieval Francia*. Philadelphia: University of Pennsylvania Press, 2001.

Bousquet-Labouérie, Christine. "Un espace révélé: Les miniatures du livre de Jean de Mandeville MS Fr 2810." *Cahiers de recherches médiévales (XIIIe–XVe siècles)* 3 (1997): 71–78.

Boutet, Dominique. "La pusillanimité de Louis dans *Aliscans*: Idéologie ou topos de cycle? Topique, structure et historicité." *Moyen Âge: Revue d'histoire et de philologie* 103, no. 2 (1997): 275–92.

Brault, Pascale-Anne, ed. Introduction to *The Work of Mourning*, by Jacques Derrida. Chicago: University of Chicago Press, 2001.

Brophy, Christina S. *Keening Community: Mná Caointe, Women, Death, and Power in Ireland*. Boston: Boston College, 2010.

Bruckner, Matilda Tomaryn. "The Shape of Romance in Medieval France." In *The Cambridge Companion to Medieval Romance*, edited by Roberta L. Krueger, 13–28. Cambridge: Cambridge University Press, 2000.

Brundage, James A. *Sex, Law, and Marriage in the Middle Ages*. Aldershot, UK: Variorum, 1993.

Burger, Glenn. *Conduct Becoming: Good Wives and Husbands in the Later Middle Ages*. Philadelphia: University of Pennsylvania Press, 2018.

Burns, E. Jane. *Bodytalk: When Women Speak in Old French Literature*. Philadelphia: University of Pennsylvania Press, 1993.

——. "Courtly Love: Who Needs It? Recent Feminist Work in the Medieval French Tradition." *Signs: Journal of Women in Culture and Society* 27, no. 1 (Fall 2001): 23–57.

——. "Raping Men: What's Motherhood Got to Do with It?" In *Representing Rape in Medieval and Early Modern Literature*, edited by Elizabeth Robertson and Christine M. Rose, 127–60. New York: Palgrave, 2001.

Busby, Keith. "L'intertextualité du *Livre d'Artus*." In *Arturs Rex, II: Acta Conventa Louvanensis 1987*, edited by W. van Hoecke, G. Tournoy, and W. Verbeke, 306–19. Leuven: Leuven University Press, 1991.

Busby, Keith, et al. *Les manuscrits de Chrétien de Troyes*. Amsterdam: Rodopi, 1993.

Butler, Judith P. *Excitable Speech: A Politics of the Performative*. New York: Routledge, 1997.

——. *Gender Trouble: Feminism and the Subversion of Identity*. New York: Routledge, 1999.

——. "Melancholy Gender—Refused Identification." *Psychoanalytic Dialogues* 5, no. 2 (1995): 165–80.

——. *Precarious Life: The Powers of Mourning and Violence*. New York: Verso, 2006.

Bynum, Caroline Walker. "Death and Resurrection in the Middle Ages: Some Modern Implications." *Proceedings of the American Philosophical Society* 142, no. 4 (December 1, 1998): 589–96.

———. *Fragmentation and Redemption: Essays on Gender and the Human Body in Medieval Religion.* New York: Zone Books, 1991.

———. *Jesus as Mother: Studies in the Spirituality of the High Middle Ages.* Berkeley: University of California Press, 1982.

Callahan, Leslie Abend. "The Widow's Tears: The Pedagogy of Grief in Medieval France and the Image of the Grieving Widow." In *Constructions of Widowhood and Virginity in the Middle Ages,* edited by Cindy L. Carlson and Angela Jane Weisl, 245–63. New York: St. Martin's, 1999.

Camille, Michael. *Master of Death.* New Haven, CT: Yale University Press, 1996.

Carlson, Cindy L., and Angela Jane Weisl, eds. *Constructions of Widowhood and Virginity in the Middle Ages.* New York: St. Martin's, 1999.

Carruthers, Mary. *The Book of Memory: A Study of Memory in Medieval Culture.* 2nd ed. Cambridge: Cambridge University Press, 2008.

———. "On Affliction and Reading, Weeping and Argument: Chaucer's Lachrymose Troilus in Context." *Representations* 93, no. 1 (2006): 1–21.

Cartlidge, Neil. "Masters in the Art of Lying? The Literary Relationship between Hugh of Rhuddlan and Walter Map." *Modern Language Review* 106, no. 1 (January 1, 2011): 1–16.

Casebier, Karen. "Order, Anarchy, and Emotion in the Old French *Philomena*." In *The Inner Life of Women in Medieval Romance Literature,* edited by Jeff Rider and Jamie Friedman, 27–51. New York: St. Martin's, 2011.

———. "Ovid's Medieval Metamorphosis: Techniques of Persuasion in Chrétien de Troyes's *Philomena*." *Philological Quarterly* 80, no. 4 (Fall 2001): 441–62.

Chelte, Judith Segzdowicz. "Philomela's Tapestry: Empowering Voice through Text, Texture, and Silence." *Dissertation Abstracts International* 55, no. 11 (May 5, 1995).

Ciggaar, Krijna Nelly. "Encore une fois Chrétien de Troyes et la 'Matière Byzantine': La révolution des femmes au palais de Constantinople." *Cahiers de Civilisation Médiévale* 38, no. 3 (1995): 267–74.

Classen, Albrecht. "Death Rituals and Manhood in the Middle High German Poems *The Lament,* Johannes Von Tepl's *The Plowman,* and Heinrich Wittenwiler's *Ring*." In *Grief and Gender, 700–1700,* edited by Jennifer Vaught and Lynne Dickson Bruckner, 33–47. New York: Palgrave, 2003.

———. "Marco Polo and John Mandeville: The Traveler as Authority Figure, the Real and the Imaginary." In *Authorities in the Middle Ages: Influence, Legitimacy, and Power in Medieval Society,* edited by Sini Kangas, Mia Korpiola, and Tuija Ainonen, 229–48. Berlin: De Gruyter, 2013.

Coelho, Paulo. *Eleven Minutes.* New York: HarperCollins, 2009.

Cohen, Jeffrey Jerome. "Pilgrimages, Travel Writing, and the Medieval Exotic." In *The Oxford Handbook of Medieval Literature in English,* edited by Elaine Treharne and Greg Walker, 611–28. Oxford: Oxford University Press, 2010.

Cormier, Raymond. "Virgil Re-purposed in the Old French *Roman d'Eneas*." *Carte Romanze* 3, no. 1 (2015): 87–105.

Danforth, Loring M. *The Death Rituals of Rural Greece.* Princeton, NJ: Princeton University Press, 1982.

Daniel, Christopher. *Death and Burial in Medieval England, 1066–1550.* New York: Routledge, 1998.

Dean, Carolyn J. *The Self and Its Pleasures: Bataille, Lacan, and the History of the Decentered Subject*. Ithaca, NY: Cornell University Press, 2016.

Deluz, Christiane. *Le livre de Jehan de Mandeville: Une "géographie" au XIVe siècle*. Louvain: Institut d'Études Médiévales de l'Université Catholique de Louvain, 1988.

Derrida, Jacques. *The Work of Mourning*. Edited by Pascale-Anne Brault. Chicago: University of Chicago Press, 2001.

Deschellette, Émilie. "L'identité à l'épreuve du mythe: La fabrique des origines, d'Énéas à Brutus." *Questes: Revue pluridisciplinaire d'études médiévales* 24 (2012): 66–84.

Duby, Georges, and Jacques Le Goff. "Famille et parenté dans l'occident médiéval : Actes du colloque de Paris (6–8 juin 1974): Organisé par l'École Pratique des Hautes Études (VIe Section) en collaboration avec le Collège de France et l'École Française de Rome: Communication et débats." Rome: L'École Française de Rome, 1977.

———. *Love and Marriage in the Middle Ages*. Translated by Jane Dunnett. Chicago: University of Chicago Press, 1994.

Duch, Anna Maria. "The Royal Funerary and Burial Ceremonies of Medieval English Kings, 1216–1509." PhD diss., University of York, 2016.

Dufallo, Basil, and Peggy McCracken. *Dead Lovers: Erotic Bonds and the Study of Premodern Europe*. Ann Arbor: University of Michigan Press, 2006.

Felman, Shoshana. *Le scandale du corps parlant: Don Juan avec Austin, ou, la séduction en deux langues*. Paris: Seuil, 1980.

Foehr-Janssens, Yasmina. *La veuve en majesté: Deuil et savoir au féminin dans la littérature médievale*. Geneva: Droz, 2000.

Frappier-Mazur, Lucienne. "Marginal Canons: Rewriting the Erotic." *Yale French Studies*, no. 75 (1988): 112–28.

Freud, Sigmund. *Dora: An Analysis of a Case of Hysteria*. Edited by Philip Rieff. New York: Touchstone, 1997.

———. *The Standard Edition of the Complete Psychological Works*. Edited by Anna Freud. Translated by James Strachey. Vol. 14. London: Hogarth Press and the Institute of Psycho-Analysis, 1974.

Frijda, Nico H. *The Emotions*. Cambridge: Cambridge University Press, 1986.

Gadrat-Ouerfelli, Christine. "La diffusion et la circulation manuscrite d'un texte médiéval: L'exemple du *Devisement du Monde* de Marco Polo." In *Les échanges en Méditerranée médiévale. Marqueurs, réseaux, circulations, contacts*, edited by Elisabeth Malamut and Mohamed Ouerfelli, 273–88. Aix-en-Provence: Presses Universitaires de Provence, 2012.

Gallop, Jane. *The Daughter's Seduction: Feminism and Psychoanalysis*. New York: Palgrave, 1982.

Gaunt, Simon. *Love and Death in Medieval French and Occitan Courtly Literature: Martyrs to Love*. Oxford: Oxford University Press, 2006.

Gay, Lucy M. "Hue de Rotelande's *Ipomédon* and Chrétien de Troyes." *PMLA* 32, no. 3 (1917): 468–91.

Geary, Patrick. *The Myth of Nations: The Medieval Origins of Europe*. Princeton, NJ: Princeton University Press, 2002.

Gély, Véronique, Jean-Louis Haquette, and Anne Tomiche, eds. *Philomèle: Figures du rossignol dans la tradition littéraire et artistique*. Clermont-Ferrand: Presses Universitaires Blaise Pascal, 2006.

Gérard-Zai, Marie-Claire. "L'auteur de *Philomena*." *Revista de Istorie și Teorie Literară* 25 (1976): 361–68.

Gingras, Francis. "La chevelure de Méduse au miroir du roman d'après une interpolation du *Roman de la Rose*." In *La chevelure dans la littérature et l'art du Moyen Âge*, edited by Chantal Connochie-Bourgne, 167–79. Aix-en-Provence: Presses Universitaires de Provence, 2014.

Given-Wilson, Chris. "The Exequies of Edward III and the Royal Funeral Ceremony in Late Medieval England." *English Historical Review* 124, no. 507 (2009): 257–82.

Goldwyn, Adam J. *Byzantine Ecocriticism: Women, Nature, and Power in the Medieval Greek Romance*. New York: Palgrave Macmillan, 2018.

Goodland, Katharine. "'Us for to Wepe No Man May Lett': Accommodating Female Grief in the Medieval English Lazarus Plays." In *The Representation of Women's Emotions in Medieval and Early Modern Culture*, edited by Lisa Perfetti, 91–118. Gainesville: University Press of Florida, 2005.

Gravdal, Kathryn. "Chrétien de Troyes, Gratian, and the Medieval Romance of Sexual Violence." *Signs: Journal of Women in Culture and Society* 17, no. 3 (April 1, 1992): 558–85.

———. "Confessing Incests: Legal Erasures and Literary Celebration in Medieval France." *Comparative Literature Studies* 32, no. 2 (1995): 280–95.

———. *Ravishing Maidens: Writing Rape in Medieval French Literature and Law*. Philadelphia: University of Pennsylvania Press, 1991.

Green, Jeff. "Covid-19 Is Becoming the Disease That Divides Us: By Race, Class and Age." Bloomberg. https://www.bloomberg.com/news/articles/2020-03-21/covid-19-divides-u-s-society-by-race-class-and-age?utm_campaign=news&utm_medium=bd&utm_source=applenews.

Greene, Thomas M. "The Natural Tears of Epic." In *Epic Traditions in the Contemporary World: The Poetics of Community*, edited by Margaret Beissinger, Jane Tylus, and Susanne Lindgren Wofford, 189–202. Berkeley: University of California Press, 1999.

Greene, Virginie. "Le deuil, mode d'emploi, dans deux romans de Chrétien de Troyes." *French Studies: A Quarterly Review* 52, no. 3 (1998): 257–78.

Guerreau-Jalabert, Anita. *Index des motifs narratifs dans les romans arthuriens français en vers (XIIe–XIIIe siècles)*. Geneva: Droz, 1992.

Guest, Gerald B. "Illuminated Manuscripts as Machines." *Manuscripta* 55, no. 2 (2011): 139–69.

Guidot, Bernard. "*Aliscans*: Structures parentales ou filiation spirituelle?" In *Les relations de parenté dans le monde médiéval*, edited by Centre Universitaire d'Études et de Recherches Médiévales d'Aix, 25–45. Aix-en-Provence: Université de Provence, 1989.

Habermas, Jürgen, and Frederick Lawrence. "The French Path to Postmodernity: Bataille between Eroticism and General Economics." *New German Critique* 33 (1984): 79–102.

BIBLIOGRAPHY

Hanning, Robert W. "Engin in Twelfth Century Romance: An Examination of the *Roman d'Enéas* and Hue de Rotelande's *Ipomédon*." *Yale French Studies* 51 (1974): 82–101.

Harré, Rom, ed. *The Social Construction of Emotions*. Oxford: Blackwell, 1986.

Hartman, Geoffrey. "The Voice of the Shuttle: Language from the Point of View of Literature." *Review of Metaphysics* 23, no. 2 (1969): 240–58.

Herlihy, David. "Making Sense of Incest: Women and the Marriage Rule of the Early Middle Ages." In *Women, Family, and Society in Medieval Europe: Historical Essays, 1978–1991*, 96–109. Providence, RI: Berghahn Books, 1995.

Herzman, Ronald B. "Cannibalism and Communion in Inferno XXXIII." *Dante Studies, with the Annual Report of the Dante Society*, no. 98 (1980): 53–78.

Hoepffner, Ernst. "La *Philomena* de Chrétien de Troyes." *Romania* 57, no. 225–26 (1931): 13–74.

Hollo, Kaarina. "Laments and Lamenting in Early Medieval Ireland." In *Medieval Celtic Literature and Society*, edited by Helen Fulton, 83–94. Dublin: Four Courts, 2005.

Holsinger, Bruce W. *Music, Body, and Desire in Medieval Culture: Hildegard of Bingen to Chaucer*. Stanford, CA: Stanford University Press, 2001.

Holst-Warhaft, Gail. *Dangerous Voices: Women's Laments and Greek Literature*. New York: Routledge, 2002.

Horowitz, Jason, and Emma Bubola. "Italy's Coronavirus Victims Face Death Alone, with Funerals Postponed." *New York Times*," March 16, 2020. https://www.nytimes.com/2020/03/16/world/europe/italy-coronavirus-funerals.html.

Hult, David F. "The *Roman de la Rose*, Christine de Pizan, and the Querelle des femmes." In *The Cambridge Companion to Medieval Women's Writing*, edited by Carolyn Dinshaw and David Wallace, 184–94. Cambridge: Cambridge University Press, 2003.

Ingham, Patricia Clare, and Michelle R. Warren. "From Kinship to Kingship: Mourning, Gender, and Anglo-Saxon Community." In *Grief and Gender: 700–1700*, edited by Jennifer C. Vaught and Lynne Dickson Bruckner, 17–31. New York: Palgrave Macmillan, 2003.

———. *Postcolonial Moves: Medieval through Modern*. New York: Palgrave Macmillan, 2003.

Izard, Carroll E., ed. *Human Emotions*. New York: Plenum, 1977.

Jackson, William T. H. "The *De Amore* of Andreas Capellanus and the Practice of Love at Court." *Romanic Review* 49 (1958): 243–51.

Jaeger, C. Stephen. *Ennobling Love: In Search of a Lost Sensibility*. Philadelphia: University of Pennsylvania Press, 1999.

Jeay, Madeleine. "Consuming Passions: Variations on the Eaten Heart Theme." In *Violence against Women in Medieval Texts*, edited by Anna Roberts, 75–96. Gainesville: University Press of Florida, 1998.

Jones, Nancy A. "The Daughter's Text and the Thread of Lineage in the Old French *Philomena*." In *Representing Rape in Medieval and Early Modern Literature*, edited by Elizabeth Roberston and Christine Rose, 161–87. New York: St. Martin's, 2001.

Karras, Ruth Mazo. *Sexuality in Medieval Europe: Doing unto Others*. New York: Routledge, 2005.

Katja Altpeter-Jones. "Love Me, Hurt Me, Heal Me: Isolde Healer and Isolde Lover in Gottfried's *Tristan*." *German Quarterly* 82, no. 1 (2009): 5–23.

Kaufhold, Shelley D. "Ovid's Tereus: Fire, Birds, and the Reification of Figurative Language." *Classical Philology* 92, no. 1 (1997): 66–71.

Kay, Sarah. *Parrots and Nightingales: Troubadour Quotations and the Development of European Poetry*. Philadelphia: University of Pennsylvania Press, 2013.

———. "Women's Body of Knowledge: Epistemology and Misogyny in the *Romance of the Rose*." In *Framing Medieval Bodies*, edited by Sarah Kay and Miri Rubin, 211–35. Manchester: Manchester University Press, 1994.

Kay, Sarah, and Miri Rubin. *Framing Medieval Bodies*. Manchester: Manchester University Press, 1994.

Kelly, Douglas. *The Art of Medieval French Romance*. Madison: University of Wisconsin Press, 1992.

———. "Courtly Love in Perspective: The Hierarchy of Love in Andreas Capellanus." *Traditio* 24 (1968): 119–47.

Kim, Margaret. "The Material Culture of Princely Power and the Art of the Exotic East: The Miniatures of MS Français 2810 of the Bibliothèque Nationale de France." *Sun Yat-Sen Journal of Humanities* 43 (July 7, 2017): 25–43.

Kinoshita, Sharon. "Pagans Are Wrong and Christians Are Right: Alterity, Gender, and Nation in the *Chanson de Roland*." *Journal of Medieval and Early Modern Studies* 31, no. 1 (2001): 79–112.

Kleiman, Irit Ruth. "A Sorrowful Song: On Tears in Chrétien de Troyes's *Philomena*." In *Crying in the Middle Ages: Tears of History*, edited by Elina Gertsman, 208–29. New York: Routledge, 2012.

Klinck, Anne L. *Anthology of Ancient and Medieval Woman's Song*. New York: Palgrave Macmillan, 2004.

———. "Singing a Song of Sorrow: Tropes of Lament." In *Laments for the Lost in Medieval Literature*, edited by Jane Tolmie and M. Jane Toswell, 1–20. Turnhout, Belgium: Brepols, 2010.

Klossowski, Pierre. *Sade My Neighbor*. Translated by Alphonso Lingis. Evanston, IL: Northwestern University Press, 1991.

Kristeva, Julia. *Powers of Horror: An Essay on Abjection*. New York: Columbia University Press, 1982.

———. "Stabat Mater." Translated by Arthur Goldhammer. *Poetics Today* 6, no. 1/2 (January 1, 1985): 133–52.

Krueger, Roberta L. "*Philomena*: Brutal Transitions and Courtly Transformations in Chrétien's Old French Translation." In *A Companion to Chrétien de Troyes*, edited by Norris Lacy and Joan Tasker Grimbert, 87–102. Cambridge: D. S. Brewer, 2005.

———. *Women Readers and the Ideology of Gender in Old French Verse Romance*. Cambridge: Cambridge University Press, 1993.

Lacy, Norris J., and Joan Tasker Grimbert, eds. *A Companion to Chrétien de Troyes*. Cambridge: D. S. Brewer, 2005.

Laqueur, Thomas W. *The Work of the Dead: A Cultural History of Mortal Remains*. Princeton, NJ: Princeton University Press, 2015.

Le Blanc, Julie. "Lamentations of the Past: An Echo of the Medieval Irish Keening Women." PhD thesis, Trinity College Dublin, 2001.

Leach, Elizabeth Eva. *Sung Birds: Music, Nature, and Poetry in the Later Middle Ages*. Ithaca, NY: Cornell University Press, 2007.

Lefay-Toury, Marie-Noëlle. *Mort et fin'Amor dans la poésie d'oc et d'oeil aux XIIe et XIIIe siècles*. Nouvelle bibliothèque du Moyen Âge. Paris: Champion, 2001.

Levy, Allison. "Augustine's Concessions and Other Failures: Mourning and Masculinity in Fifteenth-Century Tuscany." In *Grief and Gender, 700–1700*, edited by Jennifer C. Vaught and Lynne Dickson Bruckner, 81–93. New York: Palgrave, 2003.

Levy, Raphael. "État présent des études sur l'attribution de *Philomena*." *Les Lettres Romanes* 5 (1951): 46–52.

———. "The Motivation of Perceval and the Authorship of *Philomena*." *PMLA: Publications of the Modern Language Association of America* 71, no. 4 (1956): 853–62.

Leys, Ruth. "The Turn to Affect: A Critique." *Critical Inquiry* 37, no. 3 (Spring 2011): 434–72.

Llambas Pombo, Elena. "Beauté, amour et mort dans les *Ovidiana* français du XII siècle." In *Le beau et le laid au moyen âge*, 337–50. Aix-en-Provence: Presses Universitaires de Provence, 2000.

Lochrie, Karma. "Provincializing Medieval Europe: Mandeville's Cosmopolitan Utopia." *PMLA* 124, no. 2 (2009): 592–99.

MacKinnon, Catharine A. *Toward a Feminist Theory of the State*. Cambridge, MA: Harvard University Press, 1989.

Marder, Elissa. "Disarticulated Voices: Feminism and *Philomela*." *Hypatia* 7, no. 2 (1992): 148–66.

Margolis, Nadia. "Christine de Pizan's Life in Lament: Love, Death, and Politics." In *Laments for the Lost in Medieval Literature*, edited by Jane Tolmie and M. Jane Toswell, 265–81. Turnhout, Belgium: Brepols, 2010.

Marinis, Vasileios. "Tombs and Burials in the Monastery Tou Libos in Constantinople." *Dumbarton Oaks Papers* 63 (2009): 147–66.

Matzke, John E. "The Legend of the Eaten Heart." *Modern Language Notes* 26, no. 1 (1911): 1–8.

McCash, June Hall. "Philomena's Window: Issues of Intertextuality and Influence in the Works of Marie de France and Chrétien de Troyes." In *De Sens Rassis: Essays in Honor of Rupert T. Pickens*, edited by Keith Busby et al., 415–30. Amsterdam: Rodopi, 2005.

McCracken, Peggy. "The Body Politic and the Queen's Adulterous Body in French Romance." In *Feminist Approaches to the Body in Medieval Literature*, edited by Linda Lomperis and Sarah Stanbury, 38–64. Philadelphia: University of Pennsylvania Press, 1993.

———. *The Curse of Eve, the Wound of the Hero: Blood, Gender, and Medieval Literature*. Philadelphia: University of Pennsylvania Press, 2003.

———. "Engendering Sacrifice: Blood, Lineage, and Infanticide in Old French Literature." *Speculum* 77, no. 1 (2002): 55–75.

———. *The Romance of Adultery: Queenship and Sexual Transgression in Old French Literature*. Philadelphia: University of Pennsylvania Press, 1998.

McDevitt, Arthur S. "The Nightingale and the Olive." In *Antidosis, Festschrift für Walther Kraus zum 70. Geburtstag*, edited by Rudolf Hanslick et al., 227–37. Vienna: Böhlau, 1972.

McLaughlin, Megan. "'Abominable Mingling': Father-Daughter Incest and the Law." *Medieval Feminist Newsletter* 24 (1997): 26–30.

Meale, Carol M. "The Middle English Romance of *Ipomédon*: A Late Medieval 'Mirror' for Princes and Merchants." *Reading Medieval Studies* 10 (1984): 136–91.

Ménard, Philippe. "L'illustration du 'Devisement du Monde' de Marco Polo." *Bulletin de la Société Nationale des Antiquaires de France* (1987): 85–91.

Metzler, Irina. "Perceptions of Hot Climate in Medieval Cosmography and Travel Literature." In *Medieval Ethnographies: European Perceptions of the World Beyond*, edited by Joan-Pau Rubiés, 379–415. Farnham, UK: Ashgate, 2009.

Miller, William Ian. "Threat." In *Feud, Violence and Practice: Essays in Medieval Studies in Honor of Stephen D. White*, edited by Belle S. Tuten, Stephen D. White, and Tracey L. Billado, 9–28. Farnham, UK: Ashgate, 2010.

Millinger, Susan P. "Epic Values: *The Song of Roland*." In *The Middle Ages in Texts and Texture: Reflections on Medieval Sources*, edited by Jason Glenn, 141–52. Toronto: University of Toronto Press, 2011.

Mills, Kristen. "Grief, Gender and Mourning in Medieval North Atlantic Literature." PhD diss., University of Toronto, 2013.

Mirrer, Louise. *Upon My Husband's Death: Widows in the Literature and Histories of Medieval Europe*. Ann Arbor: University of Michigan Press, 1992.

Mitchell, Juliet. *Psychoanalysis and Feminism: A Radical Reassessment of Freudian Psychoanalysis*. New York: Penguin Books, 2000.

Mitter, Partha. *Much Maligned Monsters: A History of European Reactions to Indian Art*. Chicago: University of Chicago Press, 1977.

Moore, Alison M. *Sexual Myths of Modernity: Sadism, Masochism, and Historical Teleology*. Lanham, MD: Lexington Books, 2016.

Moore, Megan. "Chrétien's Romance of Grief: Widows and Their Erotic Bodies in *Yvain*." In *Masculinities and Femininities in the Middle Ages*, edited by Fred Kiefer, 101–16. Turnhout, Belgium: Brepols, 2010.

———. *Exchanges in Exoticism: Cross-Cultural Marriage and the Making of the Mediterranean in Old French Romance*. Toronto: University of Toronto Press, 2014.

———. "Romance and the Love of Death in the Medieval Mediterranean." In *A Handbook to the Late Byzantine Romances*, edited by Ingela Nilsson and Adam Goldwyn, 299–320. Cambridge: Cambridge University Press, 2017.

———. "Romancing Death: The Erotics of Grief in the Old French *Philomena*." *Literature Compass* 13, no. 6 (2016): 400–411.

Nickolaus, Keith. *Marriage Fictions in Old French Secular Narratives, 1170–1250: A Critical Re-evaluation of the Courtly Love Debate*. New York: Routledge, 2002.

Nussbaum, Martha. *Upheavals of Thought: The Intelligence of Emotions*. Cambridge: Cambridge University Press, 2001.

Ortony, Andrew, Gerald L. Clore, and Allan Collins. *The Cognitive Structure of Emotions*. Cambridge: Cambridge University Press, 1988.

Oswald, Dana. *Monsters, Gender and Sexuality in Medieval English Literature*. Suffolk, UK: D. S. Brewer, 2010.

Pancaroğlu, Oya. "Devotion, Hospitality and Architecture in Medieval Anatolia." *Studia Islamica* 108, no. 1 (2013): 48–81.

Perfetti, Lisa, ed. *The Representation of Women's Emotions in Medieval and Early Modern Culture*. Gainesville: University Press of Florida, 2005.

Pfeffer, Wendy. *The Change of Philomel: The Nightingale in Medieval Literature.* New York: Peter Lang, 1985.
———. "Constant Sorrow: Emotions of the Women Trouvères." In *The Representation of Women's Emotions in Medieval and Early Modern Culture*, edited by Lisa Perfetti, 119–32. Gainesville: University Press of Florida, 2005.
Phillips, Kim M. "Oriental Sexualities in European Representation, c. 1245–c. 1500." In *Old Worlds, New Worlds: European Cultural Encounters, c. 1000–c. 1750*, edited by Lisa Bailey, Lindsay Diggelmann, and Kim M. Phillips, 53–74. Turnhout, Belgium: Brepols, 2009.
Plamper, Jan. *Geschichte und Gefühl. Grundlagen der Emotionsgeschichte.* Munich: Siedler Verlag, 2012.
———. "The History of Emotions: An Interview with William Reddy, Barbara Rosenwein, and Peter Stearns." *History and Theory: Studies in the Philosophy of History* 49, no. 2 (2010): 237–65.
Poole, Gordon. "Andreas Capellanus's *De Amore*." *Explicator* 49, no. 4 (1991): 198.
Ramey, Lynn Tarte. *Christian, Saracen and Genre in Medieval French Literature: Imagination and Cultural Interaction in the French Middle Ages.* New York: Routledge, 2001.
Raskolnikov, Masha. "Between Men, Mourning: Authorship, Love, and the Gift in the *Roman de la Rose*." *GLQ* 10, no. 1 (2003): 47–55.
Reddy, William M. "Against Constructionism: The Historical Ethnography of Emotions." *Current Anthropology* 38, no. 3 (June 1997): 327–51.
———. *The Making of Romantic Love: Longing and Sexuality in Europe, South Asia, and Japan, 900–1200 CE.* Chicago: University of Chicago Press, 2012.
———. *The Navigation of Feeling: A Framework for the History of Emotions.* Cambridge: Cambridge University Press, 2001.
Rehm, Rush. *Marriage to Death: The Conflation of Wedding and Funeral Rituals in Greek Tragedy.* Princeton, NJ: Princeton University Press, 1994.
Reinach, Salomon. "La tête magique des Templiers." *Revue de l'histoire des religions* 63 (January 1, 1911): 25–39.
Reinhard, Kenneth. "Kant with Sade, Lacan with Levinas." *MLN* 110, no. 4 (1995): 785–808.
Reuter, Timothy. "Nobles and Others: The Social and Cultural Expression of Power Relations in the Middle Ages." In *Nobles and Nobility in Medieval Europe: Concepts, Origins, Transformations*, edited by Anne J. Duggan, 85–98. Woodbridge, UK: Boydell & Brewer, 2000.
Richards, Earl Jeffrey. "Christine de Pizan and the Freedom of Medieval French Lyric: Authority, Experience, and Women in the Republic of Letters." In *Christine de Pizan and Medieval French Lyric*, edited by Earl Jeffrey Richards, 1–24. Gainesville: University Press of Florida, 1998.
———. "'Seulette a part'—the 'Little Woman on the Sidelines' Takes Up Her Pen: The Letters of Christine de Pizan." In *Dear Sister: Medieval Women and the Epistolary Genre*, edited by Karen Cherewatuk and Ulrike Wiethaus, 138–70. Philadelphia: University of Pennsylvania Press, 1993.
Richman, Michele. "Eroticism in the Patriarchal Order." *Diacritics* 6, no. 1 (Spring 1976): 46–53.

Rider, Jeff. "The Inner Life of Women in Medieval Romance Literature: Grief, Guilt and Hypocrisy." In *The Inner Life of Women in Medieval Romance Literature*, edited by Jeff Rider and Jaimie Friedman, 1–25. New York: Palgrave, 2011.

Rigby, S. H. "The Wife of Bath, Christine de Pizan, and the Medieval Case for Women." *Chaucer Review* 35, no. 2 (2000): 133–65.

Riha, Ortrun. "Emotionen in Mittelalterlicher Anthropologie, Naturkunde und Medizin." *Das Mittelalter: Perspektiven Mediävistischer Forschung* 14, no. 1 (2009): 12–27.

Rinoldi, Paolo. "Boccaccio e il 'gouffre de Satalie.'" *Studi sul Boccaccio* 36 (2008): 89–110.

Robertson, Elizabeth Ann, and Christine M. Rose, eds. *Representing Rape in Medieval and Early Modern Literature*. New York: Palgrave, 2001.

Rosenstreich, Susan L. "Reappearing Objects in *La chanson de Roland*." *French Review* 79, no. 2 (December 1, 2005): 358–69.

Rosenwein, Barbara H. *Emotional Communities in the Early Middle Ages*. Ithaca, NY: Cornell University Press, 2006.

Scarpini, Paola. "Locating the Audience(s) in Hue de Rotelande's *Ipomédon*." In *In Search of the Medieval Voice: Expressions of Identity in the Middle Ages*, edited by Lorna Bleach et al., 90–108. Newcastle upon Tyne: Cambridge Scholars, 2009.

——. "Quand les topoi ne sont plus les mêmes: *D'Ipomédon* de Hue de Rotelande." In *Stealing the Fire: Adaptation, Appropriation, Plagiarism, Hoax in French and Francophone Literature and Film*, edited by James Day, 113–27. Amsterdam: Rodopi, 2010.

Scarry, Elaine. *The Body in Pain: The Making and Unmaking of the World*. Oxford: Oxford University Press, 1987.

Scheer, Monique. "Are Emotions a Kind of Practice (And Is That What Makes Them Have a History)? A Bourdieuian Approach to Understanding Emotion." *History and Theory* 51, no. 2 (May 1, 2012): 193–220.

Schulze-Busacker, Elisabeth. "*Philomena*: Une révision de l'attribution de l'oeuvre." *Romania* 107, no. 4 (1986): 459–85.

Shapiro, Michael J. "Eighteenth Century Intimations of Modernity: Adam Smith and the Marquis de Sade." *Political Theory* 21, no. 2 (1993): 273–93.

Siraisi, Nancy G. *Medieval and Early Renaissance Medicine: An Introduction to Knowledge and Practice*. Chicago: University of Chicago Press, 1990.

Small, Neil. "Theories of Grief: A Critical Review." In *Grief, Mourning, and Death Ritual*, edited by Neil Small, Jenny Hockey, and Jeanne Katz, 153–58. Oxford: Oxford University Press, 2001.

Small, Susan. "The Language of Philomena's Lament." In *Laments for the Lost in Medieval Literature*, edited by Jane Tolmie and M. J. Toswell, 109–27. Turnhout, Belgium: Brepols, 2010.

Sobecki, Sebastian I. "Mandeville's Thought of the Limit: The Discourse of Similarity and Difference in *The Travels of Sir John Mandeville*." *Review of English Studies* 53, no. 211 (2002): 329–43.

Sprengnether, Madelon. *The Spectral Mother: Freud, Feminism, and Psychoanalysis*. Ithaca, NY: Cornell University Press, 1992.

Stahuljak, Zrinka. *Bloodless Genealogies of the French Middle Ages: Translatio, Kinship, and Metaphor*. Gainesville: University Press of Florida, 2005.

Stanford, Charlotte A. "The Body at the Funeral: Imagery and Commemoration at Notre-Dame, Paris, about 1304–18." *Art Bulletin* 89, no. 4 (2007): 657–73.

Stets, Jan E., and Jonathan H. Turner, eds. *Handbook of the Sociology of Emotions*. New York: Springer, 2006.

Strossen, Nadine. "A Feminist Critique of 'the' Feminist Critique of Pornography." *Virginia Law Review* 79 no. 5 (1993): 1099–1190.

Suard, François. "L'espace épique dans *Aliscans*." *Op. Cit.: Revue de littératures française et comparée* 2 (November 11, 1993): 5–13.

Suksi, Aara. "The Poet at Colonus: Nightingales in Sophocles." *Mnemosyne* 54, no. 6 (December 1, 2001): 646–58.

Tolmie, Jane, and M. J. Toswell, eds. *Laments for the Lost in Medieval Literature*. Turnhout, Belgium: Brepols, 2010.

Trigg, Stephanie. "Introduction: Emotional Histories—beyond the Personalization of the Past and the Abstraction of Affect Theory." *Exemplaria* 26, no. 1 (2014): 3–15.

Tulk, John. *Marco Polo and the Encounter of East and West*. Toronto: University of Toronto Press, 2008.

Van Wees, Hans. "A Brief History of Tears: Gender Differentiation in Archaic Greece." In *When Men Were Men: Masculinity, Power and Identity in Classical Antiquity*, edited by Lin Foxhall and J. B. Salmon, 10–53. New York: Routledge, 1998.

Vàrvaro, Alberto. *Apparizioni fantastiche: Tradizioni folcloriche e letteratura nel medioevo—Walter Map*. Bologna: Il Mulino, 1994.

Vaught, Jennifer C., and Lynne Dickson Bruckner, eds. *Grief and Gender, 700–1700*. New York: Palgrave Macmillan, 2003.

Veyssière, Gérard. "Les illustrations du *Livre des merveilles* sont-elles exotiques?" In *L'exotisme*, edited by Alain Buisine and Norbert Dodille, 163–77. Paris: Didier-Érudition, 1988.

Vilmer, Jean-Baptiste Jeangène. *Sade moraliste: Le dévoilement de la pensée Sadienne à la lumière de la réforme pénale au XVIIIe siècle*. Geneva: Droz, 2005.

Wack, Mary Frances. *Lovesickness in the Middle Ages: The Vatican and Its Commentaries*. Philadelphia: University of Pennsylvania Press, 1990.

Walecka, Anna. "The Concept of Incest: Medieval French and Normative Writings in Latin." *Romance Languages Annual* 5 (1993): 117–23.

———. "Incest and Death as Indices of the Female Hero in Romance." *Romance Languages Annual* 4 (1992): 159–65.

Wallis, Faith, ed. *Medieval Medicine: A Reader*. Toronto: University of Toronto Press, 2010.

Wang, Oliver. "Music Review: 'You're Dead!' by Flying Lotus." NPR.org. October 22, 2014. http://www.npr.org/2014/10/22/358120457/music-review-youre-dead-by-flying-lotus.

Weisl, Angela Jane, and Cindy L. Carlson, eds. *Constructions of Widowhood and Virginity in the Middle Ages*. New York: St. Martin's, 1999.

Weiss, Judith. "Ineffectual Monarchs: Portrayals of Regal and Imperial Power in *Ipomédon*, *Robert le Diable* and *Octavian*." In *Cultural Encounters in the Romance of*

Medieval England, edited by Corinne Saunders, 55–68. Woodbridge, UK: D. S. Brewer, 2005.

Weisser, Olivia. "Grieved and Disordered: Gender and Emotion in Early Modern Patient Narratives." *Journal of Medieval and Early Modern Studies* 43, no. 2 (Spring 2013): 247–73.

Wheaton College (Massachusetts). "Tools—Lexomics." July 15, 2014. http://wheatoncollege.edu/lexomics/tools/.

Wheeler, Bonnie. "Grief in Avalon: Sir Palomydes' Psychic Pain." In *Grief and Gender: 700–1700*, edited by Lynne Dickson Bruckner and Jennifer Vaught, 65–77. New York: Palgrave, 2003.

White, Sarah Melhaldo. "Sexual Language and Human Conflict in Old French Fabliaux." *Comparative Studies in Society and History* 24, no. 2 (1982): 185–210.

Williams, John D. "Notes on the Legend of the Eaten Heart in Spain." *Hispanic Review* 26, no. 2 (1958): 91–98.

Wolf-Bonvin, Romaine. "À la cour de Laon: Le *furor* sarrasin de Guillaume (*Aliscans*, laisses LXI–LXX)." In *Chanter de geste: L'art épique et son rayonnement. Hommage à Jean-Claude Vallecalle*, edited by Marylène Possamaï-Perez and Jean-René Valette, 473–89. Paris: H. Champion, 2013.

Woodward, Kathleen. "Freud and Barthes: Theorizing Mourning, Sustaining Grief." *Discourse* 13, no. 1 (1990): 93–110.

Yavuz, N. Kıvılcım. "'Seulette suy et Seulette veuil estre': The Allegory of Emplacement in Christine de Pizan's *Cité des dames*." In *Selves at Home, Selves in Exile: Stories of Emplacement and Displacement; Proceedings of the Seventh Cultural Studies Symposium, Ege University, Izmir, May 2002*, edited by Ayşe Lahur Kirtunç et al. 101–6. Izmir: Ege University, 2003.

Zago, Esther. "Women, Medicine, and the Law in Boccaccio's *Decameron*." In *Women Healers and Physicians: Climbing a Long Hill*, edited by Lilian R. Furst, 64–78. Lexington: University Press of Kentucky, 1997.

Žižek, Slavoj. "Courtly Love, or, Woman as Thing." In *Metastases of Enjoyment: Six Essays on Women and Causality*, edited by Slavoj Žižek, 89–112. London: Verso, 1994.

Zumthor, Paul. "The Medieval Travel Narrative." Translated by Catherine Peebles. *New Literary History* 25, no. 4 (1994): 809–24.

Index

abject, 37, 39, 56–67, 75, 97, 121
Aeneid, 134
affect, 4–6, 33, 48, 65, 88, 109, 120, 130, 137, 140, 162
   manuscripts and, 14
   See also emotions
affective travel, 120–125, 146, 155
Alexander the Great, 124–127, 129
Aliscans, 105–107, 111
ancient Greece, 28–31, 63–64
anger, 9, 46, 67, 74, 91, 92
   See also emotions; rage
Aquinas, 18, 31, 32
Arthur, 22, 109–112, 129, 152, 153–154
audience, 12–13, 35, 45, 65, 73, 92, 106, 111, 124–125, 131, 134, 162
Augustine, 6, 11
authority, 63, 125, 127, 130, 131, 134
authors, 12, 17, 27, 54, 73, 77, 81, 124, 139, 146
   metaphors of fatherhood and, 73, 134
   See also individual authors

Barthes, Roland, 40n37, 44, 62–64, 96–99, 103, 118, 132, 134
Bataille, Georges, 19–20, 41–44, 52, 53, 117, 162–163
Battuta, Ibn, 148, 149
Bel inconnu, 60n2, 70, 77n41, 83–84
Belthandros and Chysandza, 88, 142, 159
Boccaccio, 20, 121
body, 7, 40, 71, 107, 115–116, 133
   dead bodies, 150–151
   fainting, 7, 58, 71, 87–88, 101, 117, 132
   narrative, 70–75, 107
   palimpsest, 45, 58, 63, 73–75, 78, 99, 117n34

plaie d'amour, 83–85, 87
torture, 45–52, 75, 81–82
wounds, 46, 70–71, 75–79, 84–87, 90, 98, 115, 157, 159
   See also hair
boundaries, 13, 23, 28, 29, 32, 33, 36, 37, 40–42, 49, 57–58, 63, 92, 116, 122–23, 139, 144, 146, 150, 155, 159
burial practices, 147–150
Butler, Judith, 7, 13, 66, 82–83, 89, 99, 127–128, 134, 163
Byzantium, 122n7, 141–144, 149n53, 150, 169

cannibalism, 36, 37, 49–53, 54, 57, 158
Chanson de Roland, 90, 91, 100, 103, 108
Charlemagne, 22, 91, 100–104, 108, 129, 158
Chaucer, 50, 60n2
children, 27, 49, 57, 64, 68, 95
chivalric renown, 70, 72, 79, 81
   See also feudalism
Chrétien de Troyes, 30–34, 36, 42, 45, 47–49, 54–56, 73n32, 137
   Chevalier de la charrette, 85
   Erec et Enide, 18, 22, 34, 63, 88, 94, 142, 153
   Yvain, 22, 71–72, 81–82
Christianity, 10–11, 56
Christine de Pizan, 24, 65–69, 157–158
circuitry, 11–12, 77, 131, 146–147, 151, 155, 158
class, 9, 11, 12, 14, 39, 75, 83, 100, 106, 116–117, 128, 135, 143, 162, 175
   See also power; privilege
codicology, 12–13, 140, 144, 149–151, 154–155
   illuminators' choices in, 151
   political uses of the book, 146
   See also manuscripts

INDEX

commemoration, 3–4, 11, 14, 21, 71, 74–75, 80–82, 97–99, 100–103, 110, 111–112, 134, 137–138
community, 4–7, 9–10, 16, 22, 29–30, 32–34, 36–37, 42–44, 56–57, 65–68, 110, 112, 115, 118, 124–125, 127–128, 133–134, 148, 161–162
    class and, 11–12, 82–83, 87, 94–96, 117–118, 128, 140, 146
    constituting the mourned, 126, 128, 133
    Mediterranean and, 123, 125, 142–143, 155
    reading, 70, 77, 83, 117, 122, 123, 131, 146–147, 161
    See also class; codicology: community and; nobles; peasants
courtly, 30, 32–35, 40, 43, 61, 64, 82, 83, 84, 87, 88, 89, 110, 111, 118
crying, 21, 49, 54, 77, 94–95, 107
    See also tears

Dante, 52
death, 3, 4, 6, 9, 10, 17–20, 22, 23, 25, 26–28, 34, 38, 40–41, 43, 46, 48, 49–51, 57, 58, 62–63, 73–75, 78, 80, 83–86, 89, 90, 97–99, 103–107, 110–111, 114–118, 125, 127, 133, 134, 139, 141, 143, 148, 154, 156, 157, 161–163
    cemeteries, 150
    Christian attitudes towards, 10–11
    immortality, 11, 57, 78, 82, 115, 117–118, 162
    See also burial practices; dying
Derrida, Jacques, 97–99, 103, 107, 118, 128, 133–134, 161n4, 163
desire, 1, 3, 4, 9, 11, 15–20, 22, 23, 24, 26, 28, 29–32, 34, 36, 37, 39–45, 50–53, 60–61, 70, 73, 78, 81–82, 84, 103–104, 94, 104, 112, 114–118, 121–124, 134–135, 147, 154, 162, 163
    nobility and, 15, 135–136
    See also emotions; love
Dido, 64, 134–139
digital humanities analysis, 15–17, 33–35, 86–87, 115–116
Drosilla and Charikles, 141–142
dying, 10, 46, 64, 105, 106, 111, 117, 141
    See also death

economies, 69, 44–45, 49, 52, 71–72, 77, 79, 82, 92, 114, 116–117, 135, 140n27
    homosocial, 78, 87, 89, 91, 94–95, 112, 118
emotional exceptionalism, 13, 18, 37, 117, 122, 135, 139–141, 147, 150, 152–153, 158–159

emotions
    as community, 8, 57, 103, 118
    economics of, 68
    education, 142, 159
    as a language, 41–42, 70, 98, 139–140, 142
    as performatives, 7–8, 32, 45, 137
    as a political practice, 5, 8–9, 14, 94, 112–117, 143–144, 151–152
    precognitive, 29, 32
    See also entries for individual emotions; affect; feelings; intertextuality: emotions and
Enide, 18, 59–60, 70–72
Ephesian Tale, 141–142
epic, 91–93, 96, 99–105, 114–118
    See also genre
Eros, 10, 142–143
eroticism, 13, 18, 19–22, 30, 40–48, 49, 53, 69, 72, 74–75, 79, 83, 107, 111–112, 139–141, 145, 150, 152–153, 154–155, 162–163
    education and, 142
    homoerotics and, 82, 162
    See also Eros
etymology, 9, 26, 33, 36

fabliaux, 1–2, 8, 18, 81, 158
    See also genre
fainting, 7, 585, 71, 87, 101, 103, 117, 132
fatherhood, 29, 37, 38, 49, 50, 53, 57, 73, 94, 99, 127, 134, 140, 142
feelings, 4–5, 7–8, 19, 22, 32, 41, 57, 68, 70, 96, 98, 138, 143
    feeling rules, 8–9, 67, 123–124, 129, 139, 141, 146, 151, 154–155
    See also emotions
femininity, 2, 28, 62, 67–70, 80, 95
feminist theory, 8, 35n27, 53, 60, 62, 68
feudalism, 79, 89, 103–108, 110–112, 117–118, 136–138, 162
Floire et Blancheflor, 87–88, 140
foreign, 104, 120, 145, 151, 154
Freud, Sigmund, 44, 61–63, 83–89, 132, 133, 134

gaze, 18, 60
    erotics of, 88
    gendering of, 72, 75, 81
    onlookers and, 15, 78, 82, 102, 128, 158
    See also eroticism; mourning
gender, 2–4, 6–7, 18, 22, 34, 46–47, 49, 53–54, 60, 62, 70, 79–81, 83, 86–89, 94–95, 106, 16
    See also femininity; gaze; masculinity

INDEX

genealogy, 14, 43, 53, 104, 106, 123, 124, 129, 134
genre, 34n26, 35, 48, 91–92, 105, 144, 154, 155, 158
  See also entries for individual genres
gods, 38, 44–45, 58, 159
Gratian, 31, 32, 150
grief, 38, 60–64, 79–83, 103–107
  erotics of, 3–4, 18, 20, 107–108
  gendering of, 7, 94–95, 112–115, 133, 162
  grievable lives, 10, 13, 18, 22, 82, 88, 91, 99, 109, 117, 127, 132–133
  as narrative, 3–4, 60–63, 66–67, 72–76, 79–80, 88, 100
  poetics of, 65–69
  terminology for, 9–10, 66
  See also melancholia; mourning; hair: tearing out; rending of garments; wails and wailing
Guillaume d'Orange, 104–107, 154

hair, 46, 74, 81, 101–102
  beards, 6, 101–102
  tearing out, 18, 21, 59, 70–71, 74–75, 99, 101, 102, 114, 132
hate, 54
Homer, 28
Hue de Rotelande, 131–132
human, 36, 40, 54–56, 66, 89, 162
humoral theory, 5–7

Iliad, 63–64, 99–100, 103, 114–115
incest, 31, 42–43, 55–57, 139
infanticide, 36–37, 49–53
intertextuality, 34n27
  emotions and, 123, 144, 151, 155
Ipomédon, 129–131, 138, 144
iterability, 40n37, 97–99, 106, 110, 117, 118, 121, 127, 128, 133
Itys, 50–53, 57, 142

joy, 56, 142–143, 152–153
justice, 8, 55, 56, 92, 109, 148
  See also law
Justine (character in Sade), 18, 39, 40, 41

kingship, 95, 100, 108–110, 126–129, 142, 147

La mort le roi Artu, 109–112, 118, 154
laide semblance episode, 151–155
lament. *See* mourning

Latin, 9, 13, 33, 36, 38, 46, 130, 135, 137, 140, 142, 143
law, 22, 56, 107, 109–110, 109, 137
  Canon law, 31–32
  See also justice
Le mesnagier de Paris, 67
liberty, 32, 38, 39
literacy, 12–13, 69
Livistros and Rhodamni, 142–143
Livre d'Artus, 151, 154, 158
longing, 15, 20, 28, 88, 116, 143
love, 2–4, 10–13, 15–17, 18, 20, 22–25, 31, 33–37, 38, 41, 42, 44, 48, 60, 61, 63, 64–66, 67, 73, 80, 83, 84, 85–88, 95, 115, 120, 125, 129, 131, 135–138, 140–144, 155, 156, 157, 159, 160, 161
  parental, 37, 48, 49, 52, 53, 57
  platonic, 17–18, 33, 36
  sororal, 29, 37, 49, 50
  terminology for, 15–16, 33, 52
  transgression and, 39–47, 52–53, 95, 151–154
  unrequited, 81, 84, 142
  See also desire
lovesickness, 61, 83–88

Mandeville's *Travels*, 120–122, 144–147, 149–150, 155, 158
manuscripts, 9, 12, 13, 14, 20, 30, 105, 120, 145–146, 160
  BNF Fr. 2810, 144–148, 150–151, 154, 155, 158
  community and, 144–146, 161
  illuminated, 24, 145–146, 150
  See also codicology
Marie de France, 26
  Chaitivel, 79
  Chevrefeuille, 86
Marquis de Sade, 18, 19, 22, 38–44, 162–163
marriage, 71, 119–120, 140n27
masculinity, 22, 80–83, 86–89, 95, 98, 115
  See also gender
Mediterranean, 10–13, 22, 114–115, 120–125, 128, 130, 139, 140, 142, 144, 161
  affective economy of, 121, 129, 142–143, 161
  feeling rules and, 121, 123–124, 129, 130–132, 146, 151, 154, 155
  mourning in, 63–64
  origin stories and, 129, 134, 154
  See also sea
Medusa, 121, 153,n57, 158
melancholia, 61–63, 133
  See also stasis

INDEX

memory. *See* commemoration
metamorphosis, 28, 54–58
modern, 2, 19, 20, 37–39, 41–44, 53, 162, 163
monsters, 121, 147, 151–155, 158
motherhood, 27–28, 37, 49, 51–53, 55, 57, 68
mourning, 4, 6–14, 18–28, 60–64, 66, 68, 78–80, 82–83, 85–89, 97–98, 102–103, 104, 114–115, 124–130, 132–134, 138–139, 161n4
   gendering of, 62–69
   melancholy vs., 61–64
   men's, 83–86
   promise of, 78, 107, 111, 115, 133–134, 138
   time of, 62–63, 133–134, 138
   See also grief: grievable lives; melancholia

narrative, 42, 72–74, 102–103, 110–112
   community and, 111, 124
   Mediterranean and, 125–126
   gender and, 69
   storytelling and, 45, 47, 60, 63–67, 80–82, 97–100, 106, 110, 115–116, 151–153
   promise of, 103, 115, 134, 137
   time, 78, 133
   witnessing and, 114–115
Narratology, 13, 21–23, 45, 124
nature, 29, 38–43, 97
necrophilia, 120–121, 141, 147–148, 151–154, 155
nightingale, 24–28, 50, 53–54, 57, 159–161
   Mediterranean use of, 26–28, 142
nobles, 11, 13, 18, 26, 32–37, 41, 43, 49, 50, 52, 54, 57, 60, 71, 75–77, 83, 87–88, 94, 95, 98, 106, 108, 117, 118, 121, 124, 126, 127–128, 130, 131–134, 138–140, 143, 146, 147, 150–152, 154, 158
   See also power; privilege; class

Ovid, 28–29, 32–35, 46–48

peasants, 126–127
performatives, 7, 32, 37, 45
   misperformances of emotion, 8, 37, 44, 46, 134–136, 138, 142, 152
   See also Speech Act theory
Philip II, 125–127
Philippe Mousket, 124–128
Philomela, 28, 35, 142, 159

Philomena, 22, 35, 137, 159
pity, 2, 45, 55, 113, 143
polysemy, 33, 44, 66
pornography, 53
power, 3, 4, 7–9, 11, 12–15, 18–20, 22, 24, 26, 32, 33, 37, 38, 39–42, 43, 45–49, 50, 53, 54–57, 60, 94, 95, 96, 97, 102, 104, 106, 107–108, 114, 115, 120, 121, 123, 124, 125, 126, 128–130, 135, 136–137, 138, 139, 140, 141, 145, 146, 147, 151, 154, 158, 161, 162
   See also privilege
practices, 5, 7, 8, 9, 10, 11, 12–14, 18, 19, 22, 30, 31, 49, 50, 57, 60, 64, 65, 66, 68, 94, 119, 120–122, 123–125, 128, 130, 139, 143, 144, 146, 147, 149, 150, 155, 158, 161
   See also emotions: as a political practice
privilege, 12–13, 106, 132–134, 140–141, 145–146, 161–162
   See also class; power

rage, 8, 92, 98, 101, 114–115
   See also anger
Raoul de Cambrai, 95–97
rape, 43–52, 55–58, 60, 81–82, 140–141, 158–159
readers, 12, 13, 14, 20, 29, 37, 50, 54, 56, 68, 70, 77, 78, 82, 83, 96, 103, 124, 144–146, 151, 156
rending of garments, 70, 75, 89
revenge. *See* vengeance.
ritual, 9–11, 14, 64, 115, 132–133, 149
Roman de Brut, 21–22
Roman d'Eneas, 134–142
Roman de la Rose, 24, 37, 68, 73, 156–158
Roman de Rou, 93–95
romance (genre), 33–35, 42, 48, 59–62, 69, 88–89, 91, 94, 112, 154–155

Satalia, 120–121, 147–151, 153–156
sea, 86, 122, 125, 130, 143, 154
   See also Mediterranean
self, 16, 32, 36, 42, 66, 82, 97, 121, 123, 142, 147, 155
shame, 25, 45, 47, 56
sisterhood, 29, 33, 35, 36, 44, 48, 49, 51, 52, 111
Sophocles, 28, 63
sorrow. See grief.
soul, 10, 11, 18, 30, 74, 107, 108, 143

INDEX 189

Speech Act theory, 7, 45, 133–134
　oaths, 135–137, 143
　See also performatives
stasis, 61–63, 87, 96, 103, 128, 132–133
　See also melancholia
subjectivity, 32, 39, 66–68, 97, 100, 128, 132
supplement, 98, 107, 151, 152

taboo, 19–20, 30, 37, 39, 43–44, 53, 56, 135, 145, 154, 158, 159
tapestry, 10, 22, 29, 48–49, 102
tears, 3, 18, 70, 74, 89, 90–91, 96, 103, 108, 110–111, 116, 127
　See also crying
time, 4, 8, 10, 12, 13, 22, 24, 27, 34, 35, 38, 52, 62–63, 75, 78, 80, 93, 98–99, 103, 110, 131, 133, 134, 138, 141, 151
translatio, 123–126, 129, 130–132, 134, 139

travel, 3, 13, 18, 22, 23, 120–123, 139, 142–145, 147–151, 154, 155
　See also affective travel
Tristan et Yseut, 15–17, 85–87

vengeance, 8, 29, 36, 43–45, 49, 50, 51, 52, 54, 57, 77, 84, 101–102, 115
Virgil, 27, 64, 134, 135, 137
voice, 44, 48, 76
　silence and, 45–48, 73

wails and wailing, 8, 18, 27, 56, 60, 75, 76, 78, 88, 90, 95, 99, 104, 106, 114, 127
weaving. *See* tapestry.
wedding, 16, 38, 42
widows, 1, 2, 58, 60, 63–69, 74, 81–82, 102, 112, 158
　sexuality of, 2–3
　finances and, 68–69